*Interactive 3D*
*Computer Graphics*

# Interactive 3D
# Computer Graphics

**Leendert Ammeraal**

*Hogeschool Utrecht*
*The Netherlands*

JOHN WILEY & SONS
Chichester · New York · Brisbane · Toronto · Singapore

*Library of Congress Cataloging in Publication Data*
Ammeraal, L. (Leendert)
    Interactive 3D computer graphics / Leendert Ammeraal.
        p.        cm.
    Bibliography: p.
    Includes index.
    ISBN 0 471 92014 2 (pbk.) ISBN 0 471 92018 5
(software)
        1. IBM microcomputers—Programming.    2. C (Computer program
language)    3. Computer graphics.    I. Title.
QA76.8.I1015A46 1988
006.6'765–dc 19                                                                88-10047
                                                                               CIP

*British Library Cataloguing in Publication Data*
Ammeraal, L.    (Leendert)
    Interactive 3D computer graphics.
    1. IBM PC microcomputer systems. Graphic
    displays    Programs—Manuals
    I. Title.
    006.6'865

    ISBN 0 471 92014 2


Printed and bound in Great Britain by Anchor Brendon Ltd., Tiptree, Essex

# Contents

Preface . . . . . . . . . . . . . . . . . . . . . . . . . . .   vii

### Part A: User Information

**1  Designing in Three Dimensions** . . . . . . . . . . . . . . . .   **3**
   1.1   Three-dimensional Coordinates . . . . . . . . . . . . .   3
   1.2   Object, Viewpoint, and Perspective Image . . . . . . .   5
   1.3   Point Manipulation and Cursor Control . . . . . . . .   12
   1.4   Line Segments, Faces, and Objects . . . . . . . . . .   16
   1.5   Entire Screen, Hidden Lines, Printing . . . . . . . . .   22
   1.6   Object Files . . . . . . . . . . . . . . . . . . . .   30
   1.7   Concave Vertices, Holes . . . . . . . . . . . . . . .   33
   1.8   Transformations . . . . . . . . . . . . . . . . . . .   40

**2  Applications and Utility Programs** . . . . . . . . . . . . . .   **51**
   2.1   Objects Composed of Right Prisms . . . . . . . . . . .   51
   2.2   Some Other Standard Components . . . . . . . . . . .   56
   2.3   Solids of Revolution and Cutaway Views . . . . . . . .   62
   2.4   Smooth 3D Curves . . . . . . . . . . . . . . . . .   65
   2.5   Cables and Knots . . . . . . . . . . . . . . . . . .   69
   2.6   Square Screw Thread . . . . . . . . . . . . . . . .   76
   2.7   Exploded Views . . . . . . . . . . . . . . . . . . .   79

### Part B: Writing Application Programs

**3  C Programs to Generate Input Files for Program D3D** . . . . . . . .   **83**
   3.1   Function Prototypes in Turbo C . . . . . . . . . . .   83
   3.2   Cylinders and Prisms . . . . . . . . . . . . . . . .   89
   3.3   Cones and Pyramids . . . . . . . . . . . . . . . .   92
   3.4   Traditional Approximation of a Sphere . . . . . . . .   94
   3.5   Regular Polyhedra . . . . . . . . . . . . . . . . .   97
   3.6   Sphere Approximation with 80 Triangles . . . . . . . .   112
   3.7   Three-dimensional Rotations . . . . . . . . . . . . .   117
   3.8   B-spline Space Curves . . . . . . . . . . . . . . .   123
   3.9   Cables . . . . . . . . . . . . . . . . . . . . . .   127

3.10  B-spline Surfaces  . . . . . . . . . . . . . . . . . . . . 134
3.11  Intersecting Cylinders  . . . . . . . . . . . . . . . . . . 144
3.12  A Program for Square Screw Thread  . . . . . . . . . . . . 149

*Part C: Graphics Programming Details*

**4  Programs D3D and PLOTHP** . . . . . . . . . . . . . . . **159**
   4.1  Introduction  . . . . . . . . . . . . . . . . . . . . . 159
   4.2  D3D Main Module  . . . . . . . . . . . . . . . . . . . 160
   4.3  Low-level Graphics Functions  . . . . . . . . . . . . . 163
   4.4  Hidden-line Elimination  . . . . . . . . . . . . . . . 189
   4.5  A Utility Program for HP Plotters  . . . . . . . . . . 194


**Appendix A: Source Text of Module D3D**  . . . . . . . . . . . **205**

**Appendix B: Source Text of Module HLPFUN**  . . . . . . . . . **237**

**Bibliography**  . . . . . . . . . . . . . . . . . . . . . . . **251**

**Index**  . . . . . . . . . . . . . . . . . . . . . . . . . . **253**

# *Preface*

Like computers themselves, *Computer Graphics* and *CAD* can be viewed from two distinct angles. There are *users*, who are interested in the external aspects of graphics software, and there are those who want to know more about the internals because they intend to write similar software themselves. Let us briefly call the latter group *programmers*, being aware that they include people who, although having considerable programming skills, normally call themselves otherwise. In contrast to my previous four Wiley books, which are about programming, the present book has been written for both groups of readers: Chapters 1 and 2 are intended primarily for users, Chapters 3 and 4 for programmers. Actually, if you want to concentrate on the algorithms and program text in this book, you had better read Chapters 1 and 2 as well, since you should know what a program is supposed to do before you bother about how it works. On the other hand, if you are a user, possibly not interested in programming at all, you may appreciate the fact that the complete source text of all software under discussion is included. It frequently occurs that users are enthusiastic about their software except for one or two minor points, which they want to be changed. If this should happen with the software in this book, you are not dependent on the author (although I would appreciate it if you could let me know of any problems) but you can also ask any C programmer in whom you have enough confidence. Complex software is much like a chain, which is as strong as its weakest link, and the more means you have to replace any weak link, the better. The latter remark is not to imply that I expect any trouble. I have been using the interactive program D3D, which is the main subject of this book, to design a great many three-dimensional objects without encountering any problems. For a quick impression of what you can do with D3D, please refer to some illustrations near the end of each of Chapters 1, 2, and 3.

In contrast to some authors of more general books on interactive computer graphics, I have been very specific about the hardware and the basic software. What you need is an IBM PC (XT or AT), an IBM PS/2, or a machine that is compatible with these; obviously, there must also be a graphics adapter (CGA, EGA, VGA, or HGA). As for the basic software, all programs have been written in the C language; among the many good C compilers available for the IBM PC, I have this time been using Turbo C of Borland, which I think is extremely good value for money. Note that if you are only a CAD user, not familiar with compilers and the like, you can simply purchase the accompanying software disk from the publisher. Besides source program text (which has been included to save programmers a lot of typing work), there are also executable versions (xxx.EXE files) of the programs so that you as a user can work with the programs straight away. Not only does it save you the work of compiling and linking, but you don't even need to bother about an 'installation procedure':

the software itself finds out which graphics adapter is in use.

In classrooms where the graphics output of an IBM PC can be directly shown to all students (by using, for example, an overhead projector), program D3D could be useful in teaching technical mathematics and many other subjects. For most students and lecturers, transformations of the objects under consideration and changing the user's viewpoint by simple commands offer good opportunities for discussing three-dimensional situations that are difficult to imagine otherwise.

Although I have just been trying to convince IBM PC users that this book is precisely what they need, I also want to emphasize that much in it is machine-independent. For example, it discusses such mathematical subjects as three-dimensional rotations, space curves, Platonic solids, several ways of approximating a sphere, B-spline surface fitting, and hidden-line elimination. You may therefore regard the IBM PC as just an example of a tool that makes mathematical concepts useful in practice.

The C language is famous for its portability, and Turbo C supports both the classic Kernighan & Ritchie style and the modern proposed ANSI standard; the main differences between these two styles are discussed in detail in Section 3.1, that is, in the first section that is intended for programmers.

The present book is related to my previous graphics books *Programming Principles in Computer Graphics* (*PPCG*) and *Computer Graphics for the IBM PC* (*CGIP*). Perspective representations of 3D objects and hidden-line elimination are dealt with in *PPCG*, and low-level graphics functions were the subject of *CGIP*. Here these important subjects are presented primarily as tools, used in the D3D program. The hidden-line algorithm is briefly explained in this book as well, and it has now been implemented in a more general and more efficient way, but *PPCG* may be more suitable to study the essentials of this algorithm. Similarly, the low-level graphics routines, the source text of which is listed in Section 4.3, are explained in *CGIP* in greater detail. However, unlike *CGIP*, the present book also pays some attention to the new Turbo C graphics facilities, available only in Version 1.5 and higher, and it even uses these in an alternative low-level graphics package (also included in Section 4.3). Besides, it is now possible to obtain graphics output on a plotter, as discussed in Section 4.5. Many illustrations in the book have been made in this way, thanks to the fact that I could use a Hewlett-Packard 7475A plotter, connected to an IBM PC/AT, at Hogeschool Utrecht, Department of Mechanical Engineering, Hilversum.

*L. Ammeraal*

*PART A*

# User Information

# CHAPTER 1

# *Designing in Three Dimensions*

## 1.1  THREE-DIMENSIONAL COORDINATES

This book is about a D3D, a program to design objects in three dimensions. The source code of this program, written in Turbo C, is discussed and listed near the end of this book. Fortunately, you need not do the tedious work of typing this program yourself on the keyboard of your computer, but, instead, you can obtain a copy of both the source text and the executable code on disk from the publisher. Thanks to the executable version on the disk, you can use the program without being familiar with the C programming language and without using a C compiler. If you want to understand how the programs in this book work you may find interesting material in Chapters 3 and 4, which presume some familiarity with both C programming and mathematics. No programming knowledge is required for Chapters 1 and 2, which have been written for D3D *users*. Some elementary mathematics will be needed though, as the rest of this section will show.

In science and engineering it is customary to use a three-dimensional coordinate system with an $x$-axis, a $y$-axis, and a $z$-axis, as shown in Fig. 1.1. We call this a rectangular (or Cartesian) coordinate system: any two of these three axes are mutually perpendicular. The three axes pass through the *origin* O and are infinitely long. Only small portions of three half axes have been drawn in Fig. 1.1, and we call these halves the *positive* axes. Coordinates are real numbers. Point P has the (rectangular) coordinates $x_P$, $y_P$, $z_P$, which means that, starting in the origin O, we can reach P by traveling first a distance $x_P$ in the direction of the positive $x$-axis, then a distance $y_P$ in the direction of the positive $y$-axis, and, finally, a distance $z_P$ in the direction of the positive $z$-axis.

We say that the coordinate system in Fig. 1.1 is *right-handed*. This means the following. Imagine a rotation of the positive $x$-axis through an angle of 90° about the $z$-axis, in such a way that after this rotation the $x$-axis would coincide with the $y$-axis, and compare this rotation to turning a right-handed (that is, a normal) screw. Then the screw will slowly move a little in the direction of the $z$-axis. There are, of course, various ways of placing a right-handed 3D coordinate system in space. As Fig. 1.1 shows, we choose its position such that the positive $z$-axis point upwards, which implies that the $x$- and the $y$-axis lie in a horizontal plane, the so-called *xy-plane*.

Besides rectangular coordinates, *spherical coordinates* will be useful for our purposes. Again, we use three real numbers for the position of a point P. Instead of $x_P$, $y_P$, $z_P$ (or simply $x$, $y$, $z$), we use the Greek letters $\rho$, $\theta$, $\varphi$ (rho, theta, phi) for them. As Fig. 1.2 shows, $\rho$ is the distance between P and O, or, in other words, it is the radius of the sphere whose center is O and which passes through P.

The symbols $\theta$ and $\varphi$ denote angles, which are also shown in Fig. 1.2. We measure $\theta$ in the $xy$-plane, using point P', the projection of P in this plane; we find P' by dropping

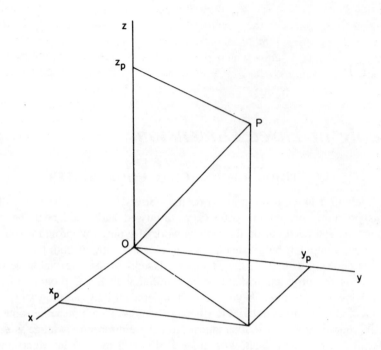

Fig. 1.1 Rectangular coordinates

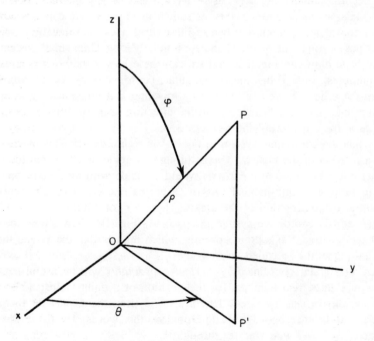

Fig. 1.2 Spherical coordinates

a perpendicular from P. Then $\theta$ is the angle through which the positive $x$-axis would have to rotate (about the $z$-axis) in the positive sense until it passes through P$'$. (In a right-handed coordinate system a rotation about the $z$-axis is said to be in the *positive sense* if it corresponds to turning a screw which at the same time advances in the direction of the positive $z$-axis.) For example, $\theta$ lies between 0 and 90° if P$'$ lies in the first quadrant, that is, in the area between the positive $x$-axis and the positive $y$-axis.

The meaning of $\varphi$ can be expressed in few words: it is the angle, measured in a vertical plane, between the $z$-axis and the line OP. The value of $\varphi$ lies between 0 and 180°. If you are familiar with the trigonometric functions *sine* and *cosine*, you will be able to verify the following relationship between the spherical coordinates $\rho$, $\theta$, $\varphi$ on the one hand and the rectangular coordinates $x$, $y$, $z$ on the other:

$$x = \rho \sin \varphi \cos \theta$$
$$y = \rho \sin \varphi \sin \theta$$
$$z = \rho \cos \varphi$$

## 1.2   OBJECT, VIEWPOINT, AND PERSPECTIVE IMAGE

When using D3D, we will be dealing with points, line segments, and, more interestingly, finite *solid objects* that are essentially bounded by flat faces. Curved surfaces can be approximated by a set of flat faces, which is similar to approximating a curve by a sequence of straight line segments. Such a bounding face can be any polygon, possibly with holes in it. As we want the computer to produce a perspective image, it is obvious that we have to specify the position of the vertices of those polygons in some way or other. For this purpose we use rectangular coordinates in a right-handed coordinate system, as discussed in Section 1.1. We need not worry about whether or not the desired perspective image of the object will fit on the screen of our computer. As all scaling and positioning is done automatically, we may use any unit of length, such as, for example, an inch, a millimeter, or a meter. However, we should be consistent in our choice in that we use the same unit in all directions. This also applies to the way we specify the position of our eye, briefly called the *viewpoint*. Let us use the letter E (after the word *Eye*) to denote this viewpoint. Point E is important in connection with a *central object point* O, which is some point lying more or less central in the object. Then the line EO is called the *line of sight* and the direction from E to O is the *viewing direction*. As shown in Fig. 1.3, we can see everything in a certain cone whose axis is the line of sight EO.

To specify the viewpoint E relative to the object, we imagine a new coordinate system with the central object point O as its origin and with each axis parallel to the corresponding original axis. Then we have to give the spherical coordinates $\rho$, $\theta$, and $\varphi$ of viewpoint E relative to this new coordinate system. Thus, $\rho$ is the length of line segment EO, as Fig. 1.3 shows; in other words, it is the *viewing distance*. Figure 1.3 also shows the *viewing surface*, which is a plane perpendicular to the line of sight. All visible points of the object send rays of light to the eye E. The intersections of these rays with the viewing surface is the perspective image that we are interested in. This way of projecting an object on to a plane is called *central projection*, because all projection lines pass through viewpoint E, the center of projection.

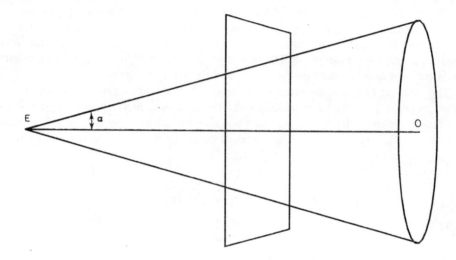

*Fig. 1.3 Cone and line of sight*

It will be clear that the distance between the viewing surface and the viewpoint E deter-mines the size of the image. Program D3D will automatically choose this distance in such a way that the image of the entire object nicely fits into the screen of our visual display, so we need not bother about the position of the viewing surface.

The angle $\alpha$ between the axis of the cone and a line on it should be rather small in order that the perspective image may be what most people will appreciate. This is accomplished by taking the viewing distance $\rho$ much larger than the size of the object. For example, if we want to display a cube with sides of length 1, then a value $\rho \geq 5$ is to be recommended. With some very large value, say $\rho = 100\,000$, the image will be no smaller than with a rather small value for $\rho$, so why not always take such a very large viewing distance? The answer is that if $\rho$ is large we will not obtain a truly perspective image, but lines that are parallel in the object will also appear parallel in the image. To understand this, we should realize that in the latter case the angle $\alpha$ in Fig. 1.3 is so small that all rays of light emanating from various points of the object and passing through the viewpoint E are practically parallel lines. Thus, with a large distance $\rho$ we approximate *parallel projection*, which is often used in drafting practice because it is easier to use than real perspective. In Fig. 1.4 we see three representations of a cube with edges of length 1, where we have chosen various values of $\rho$.

Most people will prefer Fig. 1.4(a), with $\rho = 5$. It shows that line segments are foreshort-ened if they are far away, which may be helpful in interpreting a complex image (especially if the object is a wire-frame model). There is nothing essentially wrong with Fig. 1.4(b), where $\rho = 100\,000$, but that picture might be considered somewhat dull because it does not display any perspective effect. Parallel cube edges are parallel in Fig. 1.4(b), and line segments are not foreshortened if they are far away. (It is true that there are still foreshort-ened line segments, but this is only because of their directions, not because of their distance to the viewpoint.) Strictly speaking, there still remains some perspective effect, because $\rho$, though very large, is not infinite, so theoretically there is a small difference in the lengths of the images of parallel cube edges. However, such differences are too small to be noticed,

(a)

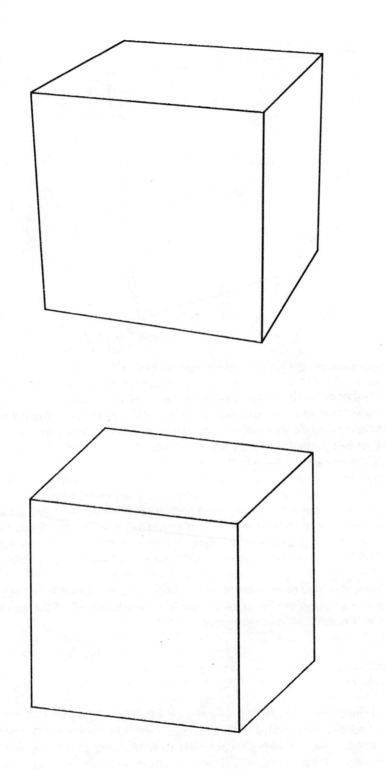

(b)

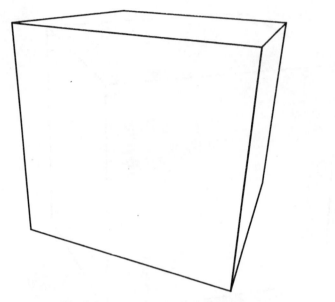

(c)

*Fig. 1.4 (a) ρ = 5, (b) ρ = 100 000, (c) ρ = 2*

so we will ignore them and say that in the image any two parallel cube edges have the same length and are parallel. In this way we can regard parallel projection as a special case of perspective projection rather than as a fundamentally different subject. Thus, our program D3D can be used not only for perspective images but also for images of parallel projection, as Fig. 1.4(b) demonstrates. The cube in Fig. 1.4(c), with $\rho = 2$, looks unnatural. Here we have an exaggerated perspective effect because $\rho$ was chosen too small. So it may not be superfluous to warn against choosing the viewing distance $\rho$ too small. As for the angles $\theta$ and $\varphi$, any values can be chosen. If we keep $\rho$ and $\varphi$ constant and let $\theta$ grow from 0 to 360°, it is as if our eye rotates about the object in a horizontal plane through one full revolution. If we choose $\varphi = 0$, the viewpoint lies vertically above the object, whereas with $\varphi = 90°$ the line of sight is horizontal. In most practical cases we use some value of $\varphi$ between 45° and 90°, so that our eye is somewhat higher than the object. This was also the case in Fig. 1.4, where I used the angles $\theta = 20°$ and $\varphi = 70°$ for all three representations of the cube.

   If the software disk that belongs to this book (and can be purchased from the publisher) is in your possession, you can immediately use the file EXAMPLE1.DAT to experiment with various viewpoints. We start the program by typing

   D3D

or, equivalently,

   d3d

In the rest of this book we shall normally use capital letters for commands. In this way commands are clearly distinguished from normal text mainly consisting of lower-case letters. However, if you like, any command written here in capital letters may be entered in lower-case.

The message area displays:

```
D3D
Available commands:
X/Y/Z: Cursor control
?: Show coordinates
Mode (Axes etc.)
F1 (Help)   | Quit
Step        | Clear
Insert      | Delete
Faces       | List
Read        | Write
Entire      | Hidden
Viewpoint   | Transform
Command:
```

*Fig. 1.5 Initial screen*

After starting program *D3D*, some general information will appear on the screen. After reading this information, just press the Enter key. Then the screen shown in Fig. 1.5 appears. As you see, the screen is divided into two portions: one for the three-dimensional image we are interested in and the other for a command menu, messages, and data entered on the keyboard. Let us call the latter portion the *message area*.

For a quick result, we can now type

    R

which is the *Read* command. It will display the message

    Input file:

which means that we are asked to enter the name of a file that contains input data. If we now enter the name

    EXAMPLE1.DAT

(followed by pressing the Enter key), we obtain Fig. 1.6(a) on the screen.

(a)

(b)

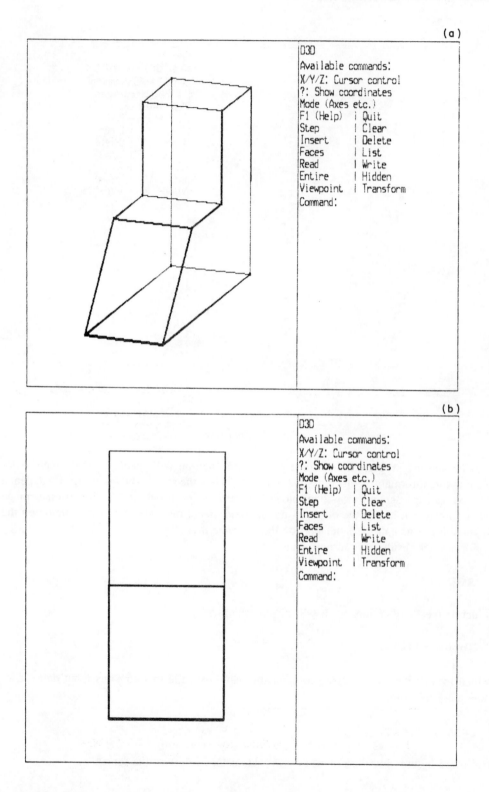

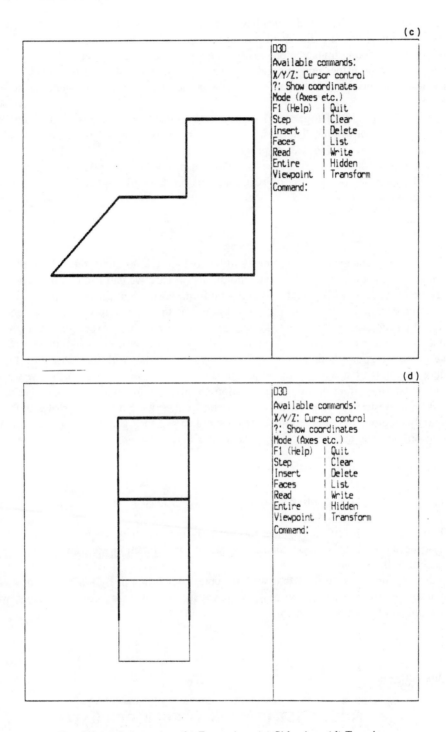

*Fig. 1.6 (a) Perspective, (b) Front view, (c) Side view, (d) Top view*

You may wonder why not all lines have the same thickness. Well, lines of the object that are near the viewpoint are displayed thicker than those that are far away. This may help us to interpret wire-frame images more easily than with all lines of the same thickness. I admit that sometimes the effect may be odd, but, fortunately, if we like, we can display all lines of a wire-frame model with the same thickness in the final result, as we shall see in Section 1.5.

After having produced Fig. 1.6(a) we can now obtain other images of the same object by changing the viewpoint. The position of this point is specified by means of spherical coordinates, as shown in Fig. 1.2. At program start, the viewpoint has the ('default') spherical coordinates $\rho = 1000$, $\theta = 20°$, $\varphi = 75°$. We can place this viewpoint anywhere in space (provided that it lies outside the object), and thus produce all kinds of images. To change the viewpoint we use command

V

The screen then changes and becomes similar to Fig. 1.2, to show the meaning of these spherical coordinates $\rho$, $\theta$, $\varphi$ of the viewpoint, just in case we can't remember. The current values are then successively displayed in digital form. For each of them we are now expected either to enter a new value or to press the Enter key, the latter implying that we accept its displayed current value. Note that the angles $\theta$ and $\varphi$ are to be expressed in degrees. As soon as $\rho$, $\theta$, and $\varphi$ have been dealt with in this way, the perspective image that corresponds to the given viewpoint is displayed. It is a good idea to play with the program a little and produce all kinds of images of the object in this example. We have seen that, if we insist, we can obtain the effect of parallel projection simply by choosing a very large value of $\rho$, say 100 000. Besides, we can easily produce the front, side, and top views of the object, as commonly employed in engineering drawings and shown in Fig. 1.6(b), (c), and (d). All we have to do is to use again a very large value of $\rho$ and to choose $\theta$ and $\varphi$ as follows:

Front view (view from positive $x$-axis):     $\theta = 0°$,     $\varphi = 90°$
Side view (view from positive $y$-axis):     $\theta = 90°$,     $\varphi = 90°$
Top view (view from positive $z$-axis):     $\theta = 0°$,     $\varphi = 0°$

These views are useful in engineering, not only because they are easy to draw by hand but also because all lines perpendicular to the viewing direction are true length (not fore-shortened) in the image.

In this section we have seen that we can 'enter' our program by typing its name, *D3D*. Of course, we also need to know how to 'leave' it. As with many other programs, we use the command *Quit*, abbreviated to

Q

for this purpose.

## 1.3   POINT MANIPULATION AND CURSOR CONTROL

We will now see how we can design and draw new objects, rather than reading an existing object from a file as we did in the previous section. As before, images of three-dimensional objects will be represented by straight line segments. Drawing these is possible only if both endpoints of each line segment are known, so we first have to deal with *points*. When we are defining a point, we shall say that we *insert* that point in 3D space, and we can use command *I* for that purpose. Actually, this command is listed as *Insert* in the message area on the screen, but as soon as we have pressed the first letter

```
I
```

of this word we are asked to enter four numbers

```
n    x    y    z
```

Here is an example of what we may actually enter:

```
5    1.49    0.8    3
```

After typing 3 on this line, the computer must know that it is the final digit of the line, so we have to press the Enter key. From now on, we shall not explicitly mention this in situations like this. Remember, if you have to wait a very long time, and nothing seems to happen, you can always try pressing the Enter key. (If it is done superfluously, the message *Invalid command* may appear, but then you can simply ignore this message.) The numbers $x$, $y$, and $z$ just entered are the rectangular coordinates of the new point. Number $n$ is simply a positive integer by which we can identify this point later. After all, it is much more convenient for us to use a single integer (such as 5 in our example) than three coordinates $x$, $y$, $z$ (such as 1.49, 0.8, 3). The inserted new point (point 5) is then displayed, as Fig. 1.7 shows. Besides the point itself, we also see a perpendicular dropped from it to the $xy$-plane. To see clearly where point $(x, y, z)$ lies in 3D space, it has been connected to the auxiliary point $(x, y, 0)$. Also, point number 5 is shown on the screen.

During the process of constructing a new object, we normally want point numbers and coordinate axes to be displayed, whereas we don't want them to appear in the final result. We can always display or remove them by means of command

```
M
```

as we will be discussing at the end of Section 1.4.

If we are inserting many points, we need not use command *I* for each of them. Program D3D remembers that we are inserting points as long as we do not use any other command. If, after inserting some points, we do use another command, then we can resume entering points only if we first enter command *I* again; if we forget to do this, the first digit entered will cause the message

```
Don't begin with digit
```

to appear. (This might seem intolerant, but it is the best way to avoid confusion with command *F*, as we will see in Section 1.4.)

Points can be deleted by means of command *Delete*, abbreviated

```
D
```

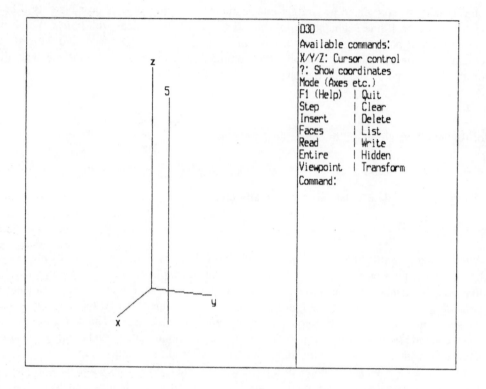

*Fig. 1.7 Point inserted by command I*

After typing this letter, we can delete all points whose numbers lie between two bounds: we have to enter a lower and a upper bound, and all points with numbers that are neither less than the lower nor greater than the upper bound are deleted. If only one point is to be deleted we enter its number in reply to

```
Lower bound:
```

and simply press the Enter key when, after this, the line

```
Upper bound:
```

is displayed. If the given range includes at least one defined point, then a new image will appear on the screen, in which such points no longer occur.

It would be awful if a complete object were destroyed as a result of our pressing D by mistake and not knowing what to do next. Therefore command D is made very safe: as a suggested lower bound a number is displayed which is one higher than the highest point number used so far, so that an empty set of points (that is, nothing at all) is deleted if after D we press the Enter key twice. (In complex situations, where not all point numbers can be displayed in the drawing in readable form, we can use command D in a tricky way, namely just to know what our highest point number is: after pressing D, we read the displayed suggested lower bound and decrease it by one; then we press the Enter key twice.)

If we have been inserting many points, we may want to know the coordinates of one of them. We then enter the question mark

    ?

which causes the message

    Point number?

to be displayed. After entering the number of the point in question the desired coordinate values are displayed in the message area.

There is another way of inserting points, which in most cases is more attractive than explicitly entering their coordinates. We can use a *cursor*, displayed on the screen as a little square. In two-dimensional graphics it is customary to use the four arrow keys (left, right, up, down) to move the cursor in the four corresponding directions. In three-dimensional graphics, we want the cursor to move in six directions instead of four, for we have three axes and we must be able to move the cursor on each axis in both the positive and the negative directions. In *D3D* this problem is solved by using the keys $X$, $Y$, $Z$, in combination with the keys $+$ and $-$. On most keyboards we find two plus and minus keys. We had better use those which are near the arrow keys, since they do not require us to press the Shift key (which would be needed if we used the plus sign that shares a key with the equal sign). As soon as we press one of the keys $X$, $Y$, $Z$, the cursor appears on the screen in the origin of the coordinate system. As long as we want the cursor to move along the corresponding axis, we can use the keys $+$ and $-$. To change the direction (other than switching from $+$ to $-$ and vice versa), we again type the name of the chosen axis, and so on.

By default, the step size for the cursor is 0.2; if desired, we can change it by pressing $S$. For example, suppose that we want to define point (0.6, 0.4, −0.2). This can be done by pressing

    X + + + Y + + Z - I

The following table shows all successive cursor positions:

| Key pressed | Cursor position | | |
|---|---|---|---|
| | x | y | z |
| X | 0.0 | 0.0 | 0.0 |
| + | 0.2 | 0.0 | 0.0 |
| + | 0.4 | 0.0 | 0.0 |
| + | 0.6 | 0.0 | 0.0 |
| Y | 0.6 | 0.0 | 0.0 |
| + | 0.6 | 0.2 | 0.0 |
| + | 0.6 | 0.4 | 0.0 |
| Z | 0.6 | 0.4 | 0.0 |
| − | 0.6 | 0.4 | −0.2 |
| I | 0.6 | 0.4 | −0.2 |

By pressing *I* the current position is used to insert a new point in that position. The new point will automatically be given a point number, which is displayed on the screen. The program simply uses the smallest positive integer that is not used yet. Note that the cursor position does not change by our pressing $I$, nor does the current direction ($Z$), so if, for example, the next desired cursor position is $(0.6, 0.4, -0.4)$ then we only have to press the minus key once more.

The above example looks more complicated than it really is. First, the current position of the cursor is displayed in digital form in the message area of the screen, so instead of carefully counting the cursor steps we can simply read its coordinates and change them as we like. Second, and more importantly, in many applications we do not begin with given coordinates to determine a point in space; it is the other way round. We normally want to place some points (and other geometrical objects) somewhere in three-dimensional space in such a way that their positions please the eye, and the coordinates of these points are used afterwards merely as a means to describe the position of these points verbally and analytically.

In some situations it may be desired to place the cursor in a point that we have inserted previously. The quickest way to do this is moving the cursor until it is closer to the chosen point than to all other defined points and pressing

J

This causes the cursor to *jump* to the nearest defined point, which saves us the trouble of moving the cursor very accurately to that point ourselves.

We have seen that there are in fact two commands $I$, namely one at the level of the main menu displayed on the screen, and the other in cursor-control mode (that is, when the cursor is visible on the screen). This also applies to command

D

to delete a point. However, in cursor-control mode we can use command $D$ only immediately after command $J$, which ensures that the cursor is exactly in the position of the point we want to delete. Also, we can now delete only one point at a time.

Incidentally, if we want to delete all inserted points we need not do this one by one, but we can clear the entire screen by command

C

This command is useful, for example, when we have been playing around a bit to see how D3D works, and all defined points have to be deleted now in order to start again with a fresh screen for more serious work. We also need it if we have been using command $R$ to read an object from a file and if, after contemplating it for some time, we want to create something ourselves, which, after all, will give us more satisfaction.

## 1.4   LINE SEGMENTS, FACES, AND OBJECTS

Three-dimensional solid objects can be displayed in two ways, namely as wire-frame models and as (opaque) solid models. As Fig. 1.8 shows, this means that with a cube as the chosen object, viewed from some random viewpoint, we see either all six or only three bounding faces. In terms of edges, we see either all twelve or only nine of them. We shall be displaying

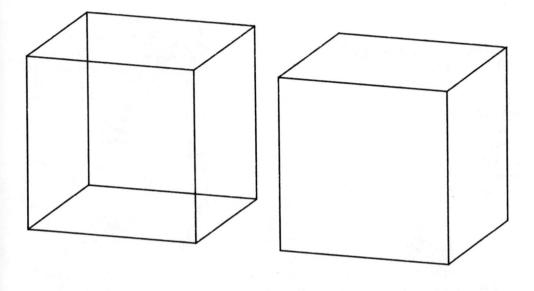

*Fig. 1.8 Wire-frame model and solid object*

both kinds of images, and although we begin with displaying wire-frame models we shall build the objects in such a way that our program will be able to remove hidden line segments when we require this.

Let us assume that we have defined the eight vertices of a cube by inserting them in one of the two ways discussed in Section 1.3, that is, either by entering their point numbers and coordinates explicitly or by means of cursor control. In the former case we might have entered the following eight lines of text, preceded by command $I$:

| | | | |
|---|---|---|---|
| 1 | 1 | 1 | 1 |
| 2 | 0 | 1 | 1 |
| 3 | 0 | 0 | 1 |
| 4 | 1 | 0 | 1 |
| 5 | 1 | 1 | 0 |
| 6 | 0 | 1 | 0 |
| 7 | 0 | 0 | 0 |
| 8 | 1 | 0 | 0 |

but in practice cursor control will provide a more convenient means of doing this. In either case, the points will be visible on the screen as shown in Fig. 1.9. (Of course, what actually appears on the screen also depends on the viewpoint. In Fig. 1.9, the default values $\rho = 1000$, $\theta = 20°$, $\varphi = 75°$ have been used.)

We define line segments and faces by typing command

F

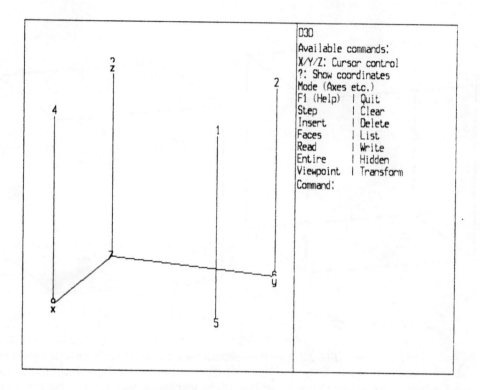

*Fig. 1.9 Vertices of a cube*

which displays the following message:

```
Nrs. closed by period:
```

If we were interested only in wire-frame models, we could now specify first the two horizontal faces (by their four vertices) and then the four vertical edges (by their two endpoints),
as follows:

```
1 2 3 4.
5 6 7 8.
1 5.
2 6.
3 7.
4 8.
```

This rather simple set of input data is sufficient to draw the wire-frame model of the cube.
However, a somewhat different approach is required if we want the input data to be stored
in such a way that the program will be able to draw a solid model of the cube. We then
have to specify all six faces of the cube. Moreover, we have to give the four vertices of each

face in counter-clockwise order when viewed from outside the cube. Therefore, instead of the above six lines of input data, we prefer to enter:

```
1  2  3  4.
8  7  6  5.
8  5  1  4.
5  6  2  1.
6  7  3  2.
7  8  4  3.
```

To understand the second of these six input lines, we note that if we view the bottom face not from the outside (with our eye beneath the cube) as required but, instead, from a more comfortable position somewhat higher than the cube, so that we see it as shown in Figs. 1.8 and 1.9, then the given number sequence

```
8  7  6  5
```

corresponds to the clockwise orientation. We can say that we have done things wrong twice. First, we have been viewing the bottom face through the (transparent) material of the cube instead of from the outside and, second, we have traversed the vertices clockwise instead of counter-clockwise. We then use the fact that these two 'errors' cancel each other. Thus, whenever we find it difficult to imagine viewing a face from the outside to find out what 'counter-clockwise' means, we may instead view the face from the 'wrong' side, provided that at the same time we choose the 'wrong', that is, the clockwise, orientation. You may wonder why the program should require the point sequence to be given in counter-clockwise order. It is used only in the algorithm for hidden-line elimination, for which we shall use command $H$, to be discussed in the next section. As we just have seen, the notion of counter-clockwise orientation depends on the way we view the face in question: if viewed from the wrong side, 'counter-clockwise' becomes 'clockwise' and vice versa. This fact is used by the program to find out quickly if a given face, viewed from the given viewpoint, is a so-called *backface*. If it is, it is simply ignored in the rather time-consuming process of hidden-line elimination, and this speeds up this process considerably. In our example of the cube, with the viewpoint as used in Figs. 1.8 and 1.9, there are three backfaces. (Actually, D3D uses only the first three vertices of a face to decide if it is a backface. This implies that the second vertex number must denote a *convex* vertex, as will be discussed in Section 1.7.)

There is one case in which the order of the point numbers is absolutely irrelevant, namely if there are only two of them, as, for example, in

```
F
2  8.
```

which, in our example, corresponds to a diagonal connecting two opposite vertices of the cube. Thus, an input line with the numbers of precisely two points denotes the *line segment* between these two points. If precisely three are given they denote a triangle, provided that these three points do not lie on the same line. With four or more points, all kinds of problems may arise if these points are not really the vertices of a polygon. It should be clear that the points must lie in the same plane. If not, the error message

```
   Not in the same plane
```

will be displayed.

As with command *I*, discussed in the previous section, command *F* has to be given only once; as long as we are entering faces program D3D remembers this. After some other command, we have to type *F* once again to resume the process of entering faces. In this way the meaning of an input line beginning with a vertex number, if valid, will always be clear: it belongs either to command *I* or to command *F*. If invalid, the first digit entered will produce the message

```
   Don't begin with a digit
```

Note that a period (.) must be entered after the final vertex number of each face. The reason for this is that a bounding face may be any polygon (instead of a square in our example), and such a polygon may have so many vertices that their numbers would not fit into a single line on the portion of the screen used for this purpose. In that case we may write the vertex numbers on several lines. There must then be a signal to end the number sequence, and as we cannot use a newline character for this purpose we use the period.

When we are entering faces, we may make a mistake, which usually results in the insertion of a face that we do not want to enter. We then obviously want to delete the face just entered. Besides, it would be nice if we could delete a face in a way similar to point deletion by means of commands *D*. We may wonder what happens if a point is deleted which has been used to insert a face. If this means that such a face is then deleted as well, then we could (mis)use point deletion for the deletion of a face. In fact, this is indeed possible, but we should be aware that the deletion of a point implies the deletion of *all* faces (and line segments) of which that point is a vertex, so in most cases this method is too rigorous: it may delete faces that we want to keep. Therefore there is another means to delete faces. We can type

```
   L
```

which means *List*; it lists all faces one by one in the form of their vertex number sequence and inquires if it is OK, as, for example, in:

```
1  2  3  4.
OK?  (Y/N):
```

If we type *N*, the face with vertices 1 2 3 4 will be deleted; by pressing *Y* the picture will remain the same. In either case, the next face will be listed, and so on. If we want this process to stop, we simply press some key other than *Y* or *N*.

After having entered all data for an object, such as a cube in our example, that object will be visible on the screen. We can now remove both the vertex numbers and the axes (along with the vertical projection lines) by using the *mode* command

```
   M
```

and typing *N* in reply to the questions:

```
Point numbers? (Y/N):
Axes? (Y/N):
```

(Actually, any answer different from *Y* and *y* is interpreted as *N*). If *Y* is answered in reply to the latter question, then the following question will appear:

```
Aux. lines? (Y/N):
```

It is about the vertical auxiliary lines, dropped from each defined point perpendicular to the *xy*-plane. They are useful to see where 'loose' points lie in 3D space, but undesirable in most cases where the points are connected by line segments. The following two questions will now be displayed:

```
Bold lines? (Y/N):
Entire screen? (Y/N):
```

If our answers are *Y* and *N*, respectively, the object will be redrawn as shown in Fig. 1.10. There are now no vertex numbers, nor are there axes or auxiliary lines. As mentioned in Section 1.2, object edges that lie in the foreground are displayed as thicker lines than those which lie in the background. This enables us to interpret wire-frame models more easily than with all lines equally thin, as Fig. 1.10 clearly demonstrates. In some other cases the effect of various line thicknesses may not be so good. If we want all lines to be displayed

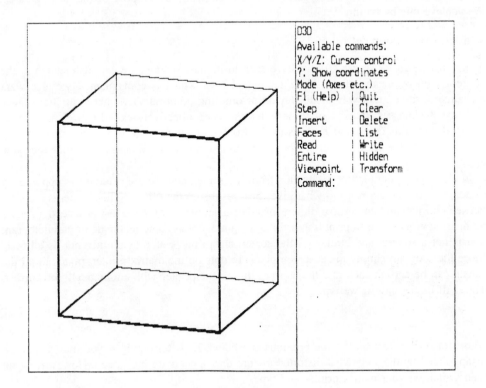

*Fig. 1.10 Cube*

equally thin we can type $N$ in answer to the above question about bold lines. Finally, we can use the entire screen (instead of only its left-hand part) for the perspective image by typing $Y$ in answer to the last question shown above. This is similar to using command $E$, to be discussed in the next section.

It may be worthwhile to note that the 'default mode', that is, the situation immediately after we have started the program by typing

D3D

corresponds to answering $Y, Y, Y, Y, N$, in that order, in reply to the five above questions. As soon as a complete object is on the screen, we normally use command $M$ to remove vertex numbers, axes and auxiliary lines. In accordance with this, the default mode is different from the one just mentioned if a complete object is read from a file by means of command $R$, as we have been discussing in Section 1.2. Unless only a set of points (without any faces or line segments) is read from a file, point numbers and axes are invisible by default, so command $R$ alters the default mode. However, we can use command $M$ to make them visible.

## 1.5   ENTIRE SCREEN, HIDDEN LINES, PRINTING

We now want to print our graphics results on a matrix printer. Before we do this, we will use the entire screen for an enlarged perspective drawing and dispose of the message area. We achieve this by typing

E

which means *Entire screen*. As we have seen in the last section, we can also switch to the entire screen by means of the *Mode*-command ($M$), which is convenient if we also want a change in the current way of displaying or omitting point numbers, axes, auxiliary lines, and line thicknesses. If none of these latter aspects (collectively called *mode*) need to be changed, then this command $E$ saves us the trouble of typing $Y$ or $N$ several times. As far as switching to the entire screen is concerned, both commands, $M$ and $E$, produce the same effect.

In either case, the picture disappears from the screen and we are offered the opportunity of adapting the *aspect ratio* to what gives best results on the printer. This concerns the ratio between horizontal and vertical dimensions. For example, if we have just produced a square on the screen, we want to print it exactly as a square, not as some rectangle or parallelogram that is not a square, and circles on the screen are to be printed as circles, not as ellipses. Since the program simply maps screen pixels to dots on the matrix printer, pixels lit on the screen can be chosen such that the aspect ratio on the printer will automatically be correct. This will be the case if we type

A

(short for *Aspect ratio*) after the previous command, $E$. After typing $A$ you may at first be disappointed by the somewhat distorted picture that appears on the screen. However, if you then switch on your matrix printer and type

P

the picture will appear with the correct dimensions on the printer. If you prefer a correct aspect ratio on the screen (for example, because you do not want to print anything at all), then, instead of A, you should press any other key. Remember, you cannot have it both ways at the same time: either the aspect ratio is correct on the screen but incorrect on the printer or it is correct on the printer but incorrect on the screen.

Instead of A, we can type O, which causes the image to be written to an *output file*, primarily intended as input data for another program, PLOTHP, in order to produce a drawing on a Hewlett-Packard plotter. This will be discussed in detail in Section 4.6. It is a very interesting option if such a plotter or another graphics device for 'deferred output' is available. You may have observed that this book has two kinds of illustrations; the drawings that contain somewhat ragged lines of moderate quality have been produced on a matrix printer, whereas those which have well-drawn straight lines have been produced on an HP plotter in the way just mentioned. At this stage, the most important thing to remember is that input files for D3D and the output files obtained by command O have different format (although they are both ASCII files). To avoid any confusion, we will call the former *object files* and give them names ending in *.DAT*, whereas the latter will be called *plotfiles*, with name extension *.PLT*.

After the picture has been printed as a consequence of your typing P, or after you have pressed the Enter key if you do not want it to be printed, the large perspective image will disappear, and the screen will be as it was before you gave command E.

Basically, command E magnifies the picture that is already visible on the screen. As we have seen, this may not be true for the aspect ratio, but it does apply to vertex numbers and axes. Thus, if these are included in the picture and you don't want them in your final result then you should use command M instead of E, as discussed in Section 1.4. Besides changing the 'mode', it may also be desired to change the viewpoint, for which you can use command V, as discussed in Section 1.2. Until further notice, the viewpoint last specified will remain in use.

Figure 1.11(a) and (b) shows the screen before and after command E is applied to a simple object, which is a solid letter L, displayed as a wire-frame model.

In most applications we prefer *solid models* to wire-frame models; in other words, we want *hidden lines* to be eliminated.Program D3D is capable of doing this. When the object in question is visible as a wire-frame model, we can type

    H

as an abbreviation for *hidden-line removal*. Then the following question appears on the screen:

    Do you want the object faces to approximate curved surfaces? (Y/N):

For the time being, let us answer in the negative by typing

    N

We can then choose one of the following two options, discussed above in connection with command E:

A to be recommended in combination with command *P* for output on a matrix printer or
O to obtain a plotfile.

If neither is desired then we have to press any other key. After this, we can enter command *P*
to obtain output on a matrix printer. Apart from the question about curved surfaces, command
*H* is similar to command *E*, as far as their options are concerned. Again, by typing *A* we say
that we want the aspect ratio to be correct when the picture will be printed, at the cost of an
incorrect aspect ratio in the picture on the screen, and by using *O* there will be a plotfile as
a by-product, which can be used later if a plotter is available. Anyway, the computation for
hidden-line elimination will now take place. For a complicated object (and using a low-cost
PC with an 8088 processor) it may take some time before the desired picture is displayed,
so we must have some patience. Using our previous example again, we obtain Fig. 1.11(c).
Note that besides edges that are completely visible and those that are completely invisible,
there is one edge that is more interesting in that it is partly visible and partly invisible. The
mode command, *M*, does not apply to command *H*, and the hidden-line result always uses
the entire screen. The drawing thus produced does not display point numbers, axes, and
auxiliary lines, and all lines are equally thin. After returning to the normal work screen, the
message area reappears, and the old mode (as regards point numbers, axes, auxiliary lines,
and bold lines) is restored.

(a)

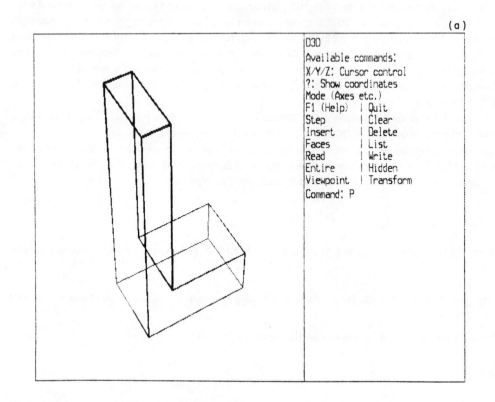

**( b )**

**( c )**

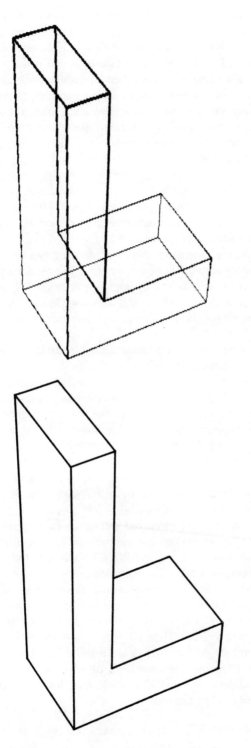

*Fig. 1.11 Sample object (a) on the working screen, (b) after command E, (c) after command H*

Actually, Fig. 1.11(c) has been produced on an HP plotter by means of both option $O$ and program PLOTHP (see Section 4.5), whereas Fig. 1.11(a) and (b) has simply been printed on a (Star NL10) matrix printer. We can use command $P$ not only after $E$ or $H$, but also directly from the work screen, as Fig. 1.11(a) demonstrates; as this is not a very interesting option, it is not mentioned in the command menu. Output on the plotter through program PLOTHP will neither include vertex numbers, nor display various line thicknesses. This may explain an apparent inconsistency in the way I have made most illustrations. On the one hand, I wanted them to be of good quality, which led to my using the plotter wherever possible, but, on the other, I sometimes wanted to show various line thicknesses or point numbers. I therefore decided to use the plotter in cases such as Fig. 1.11(c) (where, even on the video screen, all lines are equally thin and there are no vertex numbers) and to use the printer otherwise. Remember that, depending on your applications, you may not really need a plotter, because you can obtain drawings such as Fig. 1.11(c) also by means of a matrix printer. If you take care that there is a new ribbon in the printer, the quality of the result will be quite acceptable for most purposes.

Returning to our real subject, the commands $E$ and $H$, let us consider another example, shown in Fig. 1.12(a) and (b), produced by them, respectively. The object is a dodecahedron, which nicely fits in a cube. It can be obtained by applying command $R$, briefly discussed in Section 1.1, to the file EXAMPLE2.DAT on the software disk. A dodecahedron has twelve bounding faces that are all regular pentagons, as will be discussed in greater detail in Section 3.5.4.

Figure 1.12(a) shows the object as a wire-frame model, whereas in Fig. 1.12(b) the dodecahedron is a solid object. The edges of the cube are 'loose' line segments. As discussed in Section 1.4, we can enter such line segments one by one with command $F$, as faces with only two vertices, so to speak. In this way, the cube is essentially a wire-frame model, without any faces that can hide line segments. On the other hand, the edges of the cube can be hidden by faces of the dodecahedron, as Fig. 1.12(b) shows. Again, the edges that are partly visible and partly invisible are the most interesting; they clearly suggest that we are dealing with a three-dimensional object, so the computations to accomplish this result are worth their price. The wire-frame representation of the dodecahedron in Fig. 1.12(a) may be considered less aesthetic than Fig. 1.12(b), but it is nonetheless reasonably clear, thanks to the distinction between various line thicknesses.

We return now to the above question about curved surfaces, which appears on the screen immediately after command $H$. To explain this in a simple way, let us consider Fig. 1.13(a), (b), and (c), which can be produced by using the file EXAMPLE3.DAT on the software disk. Section 3.11 will show how such a file can be generated.

This object, in the form of the letter T, suggests that it is composed of two cylinders. Actually, our program accepts portions of only flat planes as bounding faces, but by using a good many of them, we can approximate curved surfaces. In Fig. 1.13(a) we see all flat bounding faces (as far as they are visible). Here all visible lines of intersection have been represented by drawn line segments. Most of them are lines on a cylinder, parallel to the cylinder axis. They arise only from our approximation process, and they do not exist as lines of intersection on real cylinders. In Fig. 1.13(c) those lines have been omitted. We can achieve this by typing $Y$ in reply to the question

```
Do you want the object faces to approximate curved surfaces? (Y/N):
```

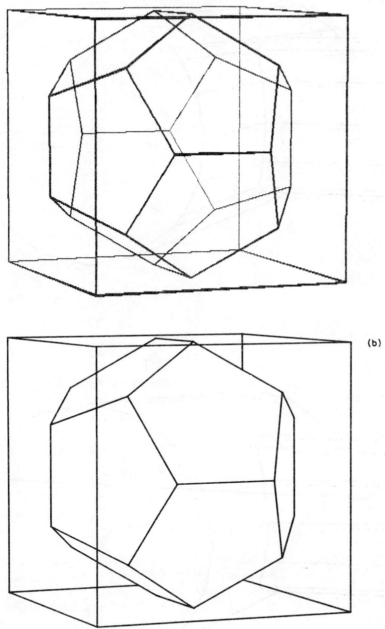

Fig. 1.12 *Dodecahedron in cubic frame (a) Wire-frame model, (b) Solid object*

(a)

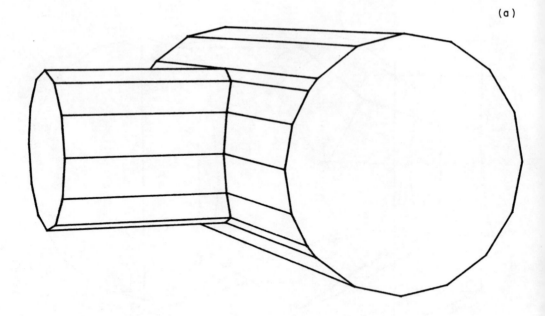

(b)

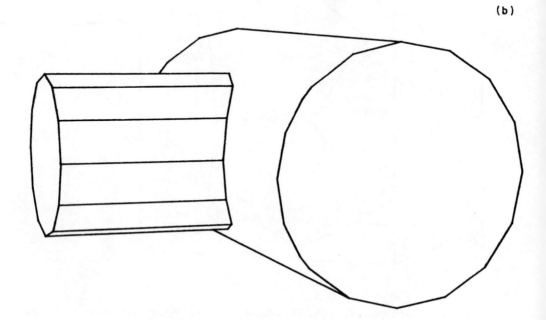

(c)

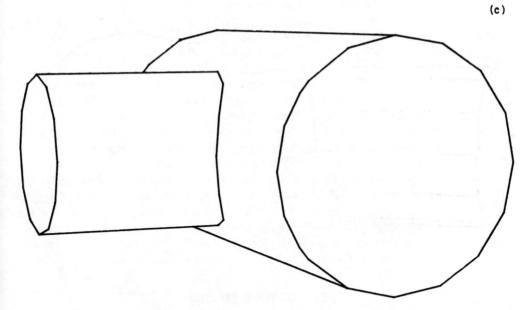

Fig. 1.13 Intersecting cylinders (a) α = 0°, (b) α = 25°, (c) α = 35°

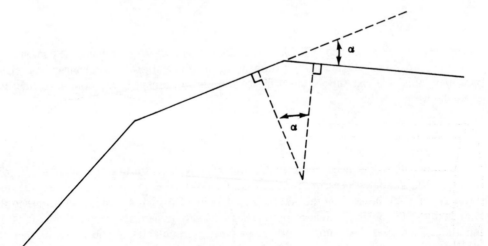

Fig. 1.14 Threshold angle α

and by entering an appropriate 'threshold' angle $\alpha$, which is now requested. Figure 1.14 shows its meaning. The angle $\alpha$ will be used to compare other angles with, namely, those between any two adjacent faces, or rather between the normal vectors of two such faces. If that angle is less than or equal to $\alpha$ the edge between the two faces will not be drawn; if it exceeds $\alpha$, the edge (as far as it is visible) will be drawn. Thus, $\alpha$ is used to decide which (visible) edges are to be drawn and which are not. Increasing $\alpha$ may reduce the number of edges to be drawn. If $\alpha = 0°$, all edges will be drawn, in the same way as when we answer $N$ in reply to the above question about curved surfaces. Note that the threshold value $\alpha$ applies only to visible lines, so it has nothing to do with hidden-line elimination: hidden lines will never be drawn, regardless of the value of $\alpha$. Of course, a non-zero value of $\alpha$ may influence computation time favorably because it may reduce the number of edges that are candidates to be drawn, and this would in turn reduce the amount of work in hidden-line computation. You can use EXAMPLE3.DAT to experiment with the value of $\alpha$. Using $\alpha = 25°$ will cause the parallel edges on the smaller cylinder to be drawn while those on the larger one are omitted, as shown in Fig. 1.13(b). With $\alpha = 35°$ the parallel edges on both cylinders are omitted, as shown in Fig. 1.13(c). Incidentally, the latter threshold value is used as a default if, instead of entering a number, you press just the Enter key.

### 1.6   OBJECT FILES

In Section 1.1 we have seen that command

    R

can be used to read a file such as EXAMPLE1.DAT. Since we very often use the combination of starting program D3D and using command $R$, there is a slightly more convenient means to achieve this. We can supply the name of the file to be read in the command line. For example, we can write

    D3D EXAMPLE1.DAT

In this way, we do not need command $R$ immediately after starting the program. If your computer has an 8088 processor (as mine has), then differences in line thicknesses will slow down the drawing process on the screen considerably. This may be annoying if, due to the complexity of the object, a great many line segments are to be displayed on the basis of the input file. Therefore, if we supply a file name when starting D3D, as shown above, then we are given the opportunity of requiring all lines on the screen to be equally thin. We then have to type $N$ in reply to the following question, which now appears on the screen:

    Do you want difference in line thicknesses? (Y/N):

This is similar to the question about 'bold lines', which appears after command $M$, as discussed near the end of Section 1.4.

The new way of supplying an input file does not make command $R$ superfluous, for we can use it if there is already a picture on the screen. In that case, the following question is displayed:

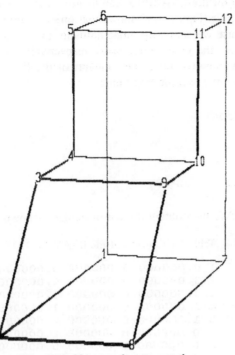

*Fig. 1.15 Object and vertex numbers*

```
Clear screen? (Y/N)
```

To understand what this means, we should realize that we may desire either of two possibilities:

1 We want the screen to be cleared so that the new object, to be read from a file, will replace the old one. If this is the case, we have to answer $Y$.
2 We wish to keep the current object visible on the screen, and we want it to be supplemented with what is read from the file. Any conflict between point numbers must be resolved by renaming the points to be read in a systematic way, so that in fact a compound object is constructed. For this option we have to respond with $N$ to the above question.

The latter option provides a means to use a library with certain objects that we often want to use in combination with others, but it will not be really useful until we are familiar with transformations, to be discussed in Section 1.8.

If we have been constructing a perspective image of an object, we can store the object by writing it to an object file, which has the same structure as those used as input. Thus, files written in this way can be read by command $R$. We write our current object (visible on the screen) to an object file by means of command

W

Let us use the object of file EXAMPLE1.DAT once again to discuss the structure of what we are calling *object files*. Figure 1.15 shows that object with its point numbers. The axes are not included because we can easily imagine them: point 1 is the origin, and the points 2, 7, and 6 lie on the *x*-, the *y*-, and the *z*-axes, respectively.

When program D3D is not running, the contents of file EXAMPLE1.DAT can be made visible in various ways, for example by typing

    TYPE EXAMPLE1.DAT

or

    TYPE EXAMPLE1.DAT >LPT1

if we want a printout. We then obtain the list of numbers shown in Table 1.1.

Table 1.1 Contents of file EXAMPLE1.DAT

```
 1  0.000000  0.000000  0.000000
 2  3.000000  0.000000  0.000000
 3  2.000000  0.000000  1.000000
 4  1.000000  0.000000  1.000000
 5  1.000000  0.000000  2.000000
 6  0.000000  0.000000  2.000000
 7  0.000000  1.000000  0.000000
 8  3.000000  1.000000  0.000000
 9  2.000000  1.000000  1.000000
10  1.000000  1.000000  1.000000
11  1.000000  1.000000  2.000000
12  0.000000  1.000000  2.000000
Faces:
 1  2  3  4  5  6.
 7 12 11 10  9  8.
 2  8  9  3.
 3  9 10  4.
 4 10 11  5.
 5 11 12  6.
 1  6 12  7.
 2  1  7  8.
```

If you have read my earlier book *Programming Principles in Computer Graphics*, you may notice that this file has the same structure as similar files in that book, except for its beginning: in my earlier book object files begin with the three coordinates of a more or less central object point. These are no longer needed (and must in fact not occur) because the program itself will compute them. (The characters # in input files in that book may be used in input files for D3D as well, if preferred to the periods shown above.) Let us now see how an object file describes an object. Table 1.1 begins with twelve rows each consisting of four numbers: a positive integer which is a vertex number as displayed in Fig. 1.15 and its three coordinates *x*, *y*, *z*. After this description of all points, we come to the second part of the file, which begins with the line

    Faces:

Each bounding face is now specified by its vertices, given in counter-clockwise order when viewed from outside the object; the final vertex number of each face is immediately followed by a period. A bounding face can be a polygon with so many vertices that they do not fit into one line of text. That is why we cannot use the end of the line as a signal that we have had the final vertex number. The reason for using some special character (a period) will now be clear. If this character is preceded by only two vertex numbers then these denote a line segment instead of a polygon.

## 1.7   CONCAVE VERTICES, HOLES

In most cases the interior angle at a vertex of a polygon is less than 180°. We call such vertices *convex*; if all vertices of a polygon are convex the polygon itself is said to be convex. A vertex is called *concave* if its interior angle is greater than 180°. This is the case with vertex 2 in Fig. 1.16(a), which is the front face of the solid letter V shown in Fig. 1.16(b). As we know, a bounding face of objects is given as a sequence of vertex numbers, corresponding to a counter-clockwise traversal of all vertices. Program D3D (or, more specifically, command $H$) uses the orientation of the first three vertices of such sequences to tell (potentially) visible faces from backfaces. For example, we may specify the polygon of Fig. 1.16(a) as

    3  1  6  5  2  4.

As the first three vertex numbers (3, 1, 6) are traversed counter-clockwise, this polygon is potentially visible. However, it would be confusing if we gave the sequence

    5  2  4  3  1  6.

Now the first three vertex numbers (5, 2, 4) correspond to a clockwise orientation, and this would cause program D3D to mistake this polygon for a backface. The source of the trouble lies in the unfortunate choice of a concave vertex (with number 2) in the second position of the sequence. Thus we must forbid this situation, and demand the second vertex number to correspond to a convex vertex.

So far, we have been dealing with proper polygons, that is, we have assumed that the entire inner area of each polygon forms a bounding face of an object. We now turn to polygons with holes, for which we will employ a special technique. Consider, for example, the rectangle with two holes shown in Fig. 1.17. Since this is not a proper polygon, we transform it into one by imagining two new edges, namely 3-11 and 4-8, as indicated by dashed lines in Fig. 1.17. We can now defend the standpoint that the number sequence

    1  2  3  11  10  9  12  11  3  4  8  7  6  5  8  4

denotes a polygon, in which the two edges 3-11 and 11-3 coincide (as do the edges 4-8 and 8-4). However, these dashed lines must be prevented from being drawn, so in some way or other we must indicate that the two pairs of coinciding edges in our example are purely artificial. We do this by adopting the convention that instead of the vertex-number pair

P Q

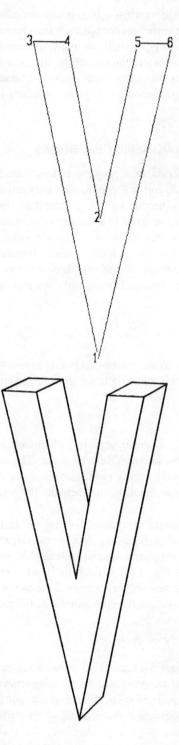

*Fig. 1.16 (a) Polygon with a concave vertex, (b) Result of command H*

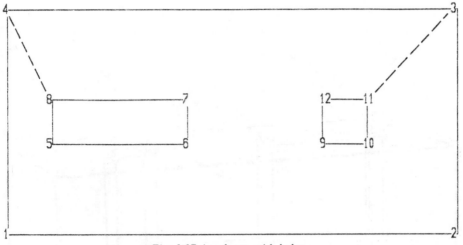

*Fig. 1.17 A polygon with holes*

we use the pair

P  −Q              .

if PQ is such an artificial edge. The minus sign will prevent line segment PQ from being drawn. Therefore, in our example of Fig. 1.17, the object file may contain the line

1  2  3  −11  10  9  12  11  −3  4  −8  7  6  5  8  −4.

instead of the above sequence of positive numbers. Note that if we traverse all vertices in Fig. 1.17 in this order, always facing the next vertex, then during this entire traversal the 'material' of the polygon we are describing is on our left-hand side. For a simple convex polygon, such as a rectangle, this means that we traverse it counter-clockwise, but inside a hole we follow the vertices in clockwise order. This explains, for example, the above subsequence

10  9  12  11

which must not be replaced with

12  9  10  11

We have been paying much attention to the structure of object files for two reasons. First, object files can be generated by other programs, as we shall see in Chapters 2 and 3, and besides using some ready-to-run programs discussed there, you may also want to write such programs yourself. Second, now that we understand how polygons with holes are represented by number sequences, we can complement our discussion about entering faces in Section 1.4. After command *F*, we can use the same technique with negative point

(a)

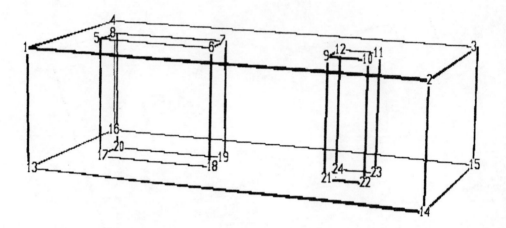

(b)

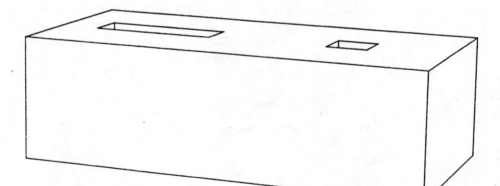

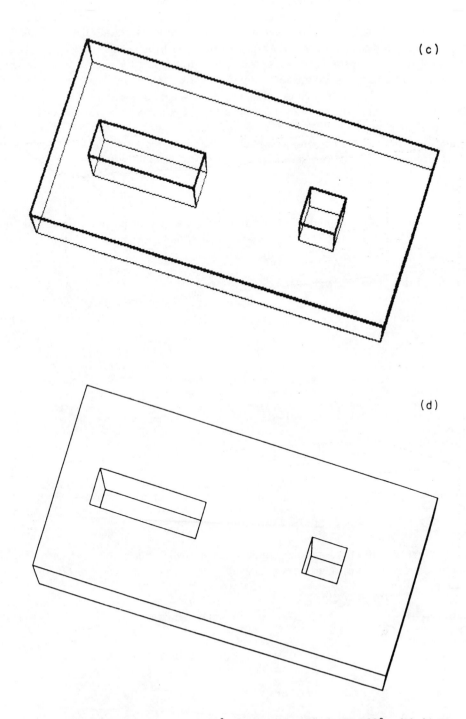

*Fig. 1.18 Prism with holes (a) $\varphi = 80°$, wire-frame model; (b) $\varphi = 80°$, solid object; (c) $\varphi = 10°$, wire-frame model; (d) $\varphi = 10°$, solid object*

numbers. For example, let us assume that Fig. 1.17 shows the top view of an object, which is a prism with two prismatic holes in it. The bottom face of the object is similar to the top face. We shall assume that its vertex numbers are obtained by increasing the corresponding vertex numbers in the top face by 12. Figure 1.18(a) to (d) shows this object.

We shall now give a list of all keys to be pressed and data to be entered to construct this object and to display these images. All points will be entered by using the cursor keys. Pressing the Enter key is indicated by <Enter>; blank spaces between numbers are actually to be entered; any other spaces shown below are not. Comments, not actually entered, are given within braces {}. Recall that we may use lower case instead of capital letters. In fact, the following list looks much more complicated than it really is because it does not show what is displayed on the screen during this process. For example, the line

```
HNAP
```

which occurs twice below, might look awful, but the program helps you to find these four letters as follows. The letter $H$ is the first letter of *Hidden*, which is visible in the main command menu. If we type it, the question

```
Do you want the object faces to approximate curved surfaces? (Y/N):
```

appears, which accounts for $N$, the second letter of *HNAP*. Then the following piece of text appears on the screen:

```
After displaying the picture on the screen, you can print
it on a matrix printer by giving command P. (If, instead,
you press any other key, the previous graphics screen will
be restored.) As for printing, please note the following:
We say that we are using a 'correct aspect ratio' if a
circle is displayed as a real circle, not as an ellipse.
Normally, the aspect ratio will be correct on the screen.
If you want a correct aspect ratio on the printer (accepting
an incorrect aspect ratio on the screen), then please
enter A. Instead, you can enter the letter O if you want
an output file (xxx.PLT), which, for example, can be read
by program PLOTHP to produce output on an HP plotter. If
neither is desired, press any other key ...
```

This fully explains the third and the fourth letter of *HNAP*. Once you have entered *D3D* to start the program, most other lines below are just as easy to use because of explanatory text on the screen.

```
D3D<Enter>              {Start program execution}
<Enter>
V 10000<Enter>   0<Enter>   0<Enter>
                        {Top view:  ρ = 10000, θ = 0°, φ = 0°}
Z+++                    {Go to top face}
X+++++I                 {Point 1}
Y++++++++++I            {Point 2}
X-----I                 {Point 3}
Y----------I            {Point 4}
```

```
X+++Y+I                    {Point 5}
+++I                       {Point 6}
X-I                        {Point 7}
Y---I                      {Point 8}
++++++X+I                  {Point 9}
Y+I                        {Point 10}
X-I                        {Point 11}
Y-I                        {Point 12}
F                          {Define top face:}
1 2 3 -11 10 9 12<Enter>
11 -3 4 -8 7 6<Enter>
5 8 -4.<Enter>
V <Enter> <Enter> 180<Enter>
                           {Bottom view:
```
$$\rho = 10000, \ \theta = 0°, \ \varphi = 180°\}$$

{We will now perform exactly the same typing
as shown above, starting with X+++++I and
ending with F; each point number j above
corresponds to a point number j + 12 below:}

```
X+++++I                    {Point 13}
Y++++++++++I               {Point 14}
X-----I                    {Point 15}
Y----------I               {Point 16}
X+++Y+I                    {Point 17}
+++I                       {Point 18}
X-I                        {Point 19}
Y---I                      {Point 20}
++++++X+I                  {Point 21}
Y+I                        {Point 22}
X-I                        {Point 23}
Y-I                        {Point 24}
F                          {Define bottom face:}
16 15 14 -22 23 24<Enter>
21 22 -14 13 -17<Enter>
18 19 20 17 -13.<Enter>
V 8<Enter> 20<Enter> 80<Enter>
```
{Perspective, $\rho = 8$, $\theta = 20°$, $\varphi = 80°$}
```
F                          {Define all vertical faces}
13 14 2 1.<Enter>          {Outer faces}
14 15 3 2.<Enter>
15 16 4 3.<Enter>
16 13 1 4.<Enter>
18 17 5 6.<Enter>          {Faces in left-hand hole}
17 20 8 5.<Enter>
20 19 7 8.<Enter>
19 18 6 7.<Enter>
22 21 9 10.<Enter>         {Faces in right-hand hole}
21 24 12 9.<Enter>
24 23 11 12.<Enter>
23 22 10 11.<Enter>
MYNYY                      {Mode; Point numbers? Yes.
                           Axes? No. Bold lines? Yes.
                           Entire screen? Yes.}
AP                         {Aspect ratio, Print Fig. 1.18(a)}
HNAP                       {Hidden lines, No curved surfaces,
```

```
                         Aspect, Print Fig. 1.18(b)}
     MNNYN               {Mode, No point numbers, No axes,
                         Bold lines, No entire screen}
     V 20<Enter> 20<Enter> 10<Enter>
                         {Perspective, ρ = 20, θ = 20°, φ = 10°}
     EAP                 {Print Fig. 1.18(c)}
     HNAP                {Print Fig. 1.18(d)}
     W                   {Save the object}
     HOLES.DAT<Enter>    {Name of file to be written}
     Q                   {Quit}
```

Undoubtedly, the most difficult part of this is entering the faces, where we have to use the correct orientation. There are several 'tips and tricks' to make this task easier, and since knowing them can make program D3D much more useful to you, we shall discuss them in detail:

1  For complex polygons, especially if they have holes, such as the top and the bottom face of our sample object, it may be worthwhile to change the viewpoint, in such a way that we view the face from outside the object. For example, when describing the bottom face of our object, we can place the viewpoint below the object by using $\varphi = 180°$.

2  It is strongly recommended to choose a systematic order, both for the faces themselves and for the vertices in each face. In our example, we have three sets of four rectangles, and for each of them we begin with the nearest edge in the bottom plane.

3  Sometimes the vertex numbers become illegible because they overlap. In such situations command $E$ may be useful; by using the entire screen the picture is enlarged, which may reveal point numbers. It may also be a good idea to make a printout or, if you don't mind using pencil and paper, to make a rough sketch of the picture produced so far, including the point numbers. Recall that after command $E$, pressing any key will cause the smaller picture on the work screen to reappear. If the key pressed happens to be the letter $P$ then the enlarged picture is printed before it disappears.

4  If we want to check or to correct the faces we have entered, we can use command $L$, as discussed in Section 1.4. This is particularly important if we have made a typing error which may seem to destroy all our work due to the appearance of some face that was not intended. Command $L$ then lists all faces and offers us the possibility to remove the wrong one, simply by typing $N$ in response to the question *O.K.? (Y/N)*.

5  Instead of manually defining several faces that are similar, we can define only one, and derive the others from it by means of transformations, to be discussed in the next section.

## 1.8   TRANSFORMATIONS

This section deals with the rather advanced subject of transformations in three-dimensional space. With D3D, we can perform rotations, translations, scaling, and reflections. With each of these four types of transformations we can either move or copy the three-dimensional object that is visible on the screen. (Besides moving or copying the entire object, we can also apply our transformations to some part of it; let us ignore this at the moment for the sake of simplicity.) If we *move* the object, a new version of it appears but at the same time the old one is deleted; in this case the vertex numbers that are in use do not change, because the vertices of the new object will have exactly the same numbers as those of the original one. On the other hand, if we are copying an object, the old one remains, so in that case we do not replace but rather duplicate it, and, after this operation, there will be about twice as many vertex numbers as before. For any transformation, we type

> T

The following question is then displayed:

> Move/Copy? (M/C)

This question should be read as follows:

> Do you want the result of the transformation to replace the
> present object or do you want the object to be duplicated?

Obviously, you should answer *M* if you want replacement and *C* if you want duplication. (The distinction between these two options is similar to what you may be familiar with in connection with a text processor or text editor, where you can either move or copy portions of text.) In either case, the following line appears:

> Lower bound: 1

where the digit 1 is blinking. As usual, the latter means that you can simply press the Enter key to accept that value 1. Instead, you can enter some different lower bound, say *L*. Then the line

> Upper bound: ...

appears, where ... denotes the largest vertex number in use. Again, you can accept that value by pressing the Enter key, or enter a different upper bound, say *U*. The transformation to be specified will then apply to all vertices with vertex numbers *i* satisfying

$$L \leq i \leq U.$$

Thus, if we have been pressing the Enter key twice to accept the proposed values of *L* and *U*, then the entire object will be transformed. If a transformation has *duplicated* the object, or some part of it, the range of the newly assigned vertex numbers is displayed. For example, if the vertices of the original object had the numbers 1, 2, ..., 10, and all vertices have taken part in the duplicating (or 'copying') process, then the following three lines will appear in the message area:

> Range of new points:
> 11-20
> Press any key...

This range provides useful information, because we often want to perform not just one transformation but rather apply, for example, a translation, a rotation, and a scaling transformation to some part of the object. It is therefore a good idea to make a note of this range if we may need it later to enter a lower and an upper bound ($L$ and $U$) for another transformation. Of course, the vertex numbers can also be displayed in the picture itself by means of command $M$, but in complex objects they will soon overlap so that we cannot clearly read them. In such cases we had better use command $M$ to *remove* the vertex numbers from the picture rather than display them, and use the number range as displayed in the message area instead. To prevent the displayed range from being overwritten by another message, we now have to press some key to proceed.

We have discussed the message about the newly created vertices at this stage, because it is an aspect that the four types of transformations have in common. Actually, this message will appear only after the vertices in question have been transformed, so it is about time to discuss the transformations themselves. After we have supplied a lower and an upper bound of vertex numbers, one or more of the following questions will successively be displayed:

```
Rotation? (Y/N)
Translation? (Y/N)
Scaling? (Y/N)
Reflection? (Y/N)
```

We can select one of these four transformations by answering $Y$. Only if we do not answer $Y$ will the next question appear; if even our reply to the final one, *Reflections? (Y/N)*, is $N$, no transformation is performed at all, and we return to the main D3D command level. We will discuss these four transformations in detail in Sections 1.8.1 to 1.8.4.

In each of the four types of transformations to be discussed, you will be asked to enter one or more vertex numbers to give detailed information about the transformation that is to be performed. It will then be allowed to use the integer 0 to denote the origin O of the coordinate system. This possibility is not explicitly mentioned in the following sections. For example, if Section 1.8.1 warns you that you should define two points P and Q before you give command $T$, then you actually need define only one if you can use O for the other. Note that using integer 0 will not cause any confusion because all user-defined points have numbers greater than 0.

For the sake of completeness, we have to discuss yet another facility, which, sooner or later, may be useful, and which applies to all four types of transformations. Again, it concerns the vertex numbers that we will be entering when giving detailed information about some transformation. If we enter these numbers in the normal way, that is, as positive integers, they will take part in the transformation process. If, instead, we want to exclude them from being transformed (although they may lie in the given range $L$, $U$, discussed above), then we can simply enter them preceded by a minus sign, for example, as $-25$ instead of 25. Although the absolute value of the number entered is used as a vertex number, the minus sign will be remembered at the time the transformation takes place, and the point in question will then be skipped as if its number was outside the range $L$, $U$. Note that this facility applies only to some special points such as the two given points that determine the axis of a rotation, as we will discuss in Section 1.8.1.

### 1.8.1  Rotation

A rotation in three-dimensional space is performed about an axis, two points of which must be given; let us call these points P and Q. To be able to define the orientation of the rotation, we regard PQ as a directed line segment; P and Q can be chosen anywhere in three-dimensional space, so the axis of rotation need not be horizontal or vertical. We also have to give an angle, $\alpha$. Then a rotation will take place about the axis PQ and through the angle $\alpha$ in such a way that moving from P to Q corresponds to the forward movement of a right-handed screw when turned in the sense of this rotation.

The points P and Q may be vertices of the object itself, but in most applications this is not what we want. So usually we have to define the two points P and Q *before* **we give command T**. We are not really in trouble if we have forgotten to do this, for then we can simply answer N to all questions or, if we have already said that we want to rotate, we can perform a rotation about any axis through an angle of 0°. In case of such a 'false start', we automatically return to the main menu. We then define P and Q, either immediately through command *I* or through cursor control, and give command *T* once again.

Starting with the object shown in Fig. 1.19, we can obtain the situation of Fig. 1.20 by 'copying' the object in a rotation, which takes place through an angle of 90° and about the vertical line through the points 15 and 16, shown in Fig. 1.19.

Let us assume that we have given command *T* (for *Transform*) and that our answer to the question *Move/Copy? (M/C)* has been *C*. After we have pressed the Enter key twice to indicate that all vertices are to be included in the transformation, and after we have selected a rotation, as discussed above, the following two lines are displayed:

```
Rotate about PQ.
Point nrs. P and Q:
```

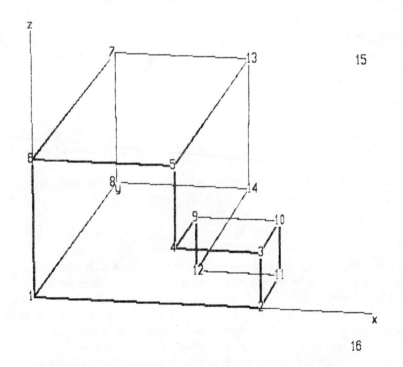

*Fig. 1.19 Object to be rotated and axis of rotation*

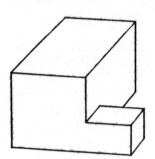

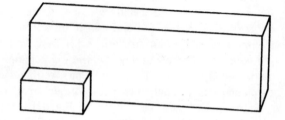

*Fig. 1.20 Result of rotation*

In our example, we type

    15 16

and press the Enter key. Then we are asked to enter an angle:

    Angle in degrees:

If we then enter

    90

a copy of the original object, rotated through 90° given axis, is created; after subsequent elimination of hidden lines (by means of command *H*), we obtain the result shown in Fig. 1.20.

Note that the points P and Q are transformed into themselves, so we may write

$$P' \equiv P$$
$$Q' \equiv Q$$

We say that P and Q (and in fact all points on the line PQ) are *fixed points*. Now suppose that we have typed *C* as an answer to the question *Move/Copy? (M/C)*. Since point P′ coincides with point P, it is not strictly necessary to assign a new vertex number to it, and the same applies to Q and Q′. We normally want new vertex numbers to be assigned to these two points if these are vertices of the object. Then we want the original object and the new copy to have a set of point numbers of their own, so that we can use the new range of vertex numbers in a subsequent transformation which is to be applied to the new copy only. In Fig. 1.19, however, the points 15 and 16 do not belong to the object, and in cases like this we normally do not want new vertex numbers to be assigned to these fixed points. Therefore, when assigning new vertex numbers during a copying process, program D3D will make an exception for the vertices P and Q if these two point numbers are preceded by a minus sign when they are entered. In our example, we could have entered

```
-15   -16
```

to achieve this. (Note that in this example there is another way of doing this, namely by entering 14 as the upper bound of all vertex numbers involved in the transformation, instead of simply pressing the Enter key, as suggested above.)

## 1.8.2   Translation

We say that we are performing a *translation* when we move an object by a simple shift, without altering its orientation. Expressed more precisely, we use three constants *delta x*, *delta y*, *delta z*, to compute

$$x' = x + delta\ x$$
$$y' = y + delta\ y$$
$$z' = z + delta\ z$$

for any point $P(x, y, z)$ of the object, in order to find the corresponding new point $P'(x', y', z')$.

In D3D we can either enter the three values *delta x*, *delta y*, *delta z* explicitly as three numeric constants or use a *shift vector* AB. Any directed line segment AB can be used as a shift vector. After our answer Y to the question *Translation? (Y/N)*, the following line is displayed:

```
Shift vector?  (Y/N)
```

We type N if we want to enter the three values *delta x*, *delta y*, *delta z*, and Y if some shift vector AB is to be used. In the former case we are asked to enter those three values and in the latter the following two lines appear:

```
AB is shift vector
Point nrs. A and B:
```

We then have to enter the numbers of two points defined previously. (Recall that this is similar to rotation, where we had to define the points P and Q beforehand.) Although we enter the numbers of the points A and B, their coordinates $x_A$ etc. are known, and these coordinates define *delta x*, *delta y*, *delta z* as follows:

$$delta\ x = x_B - x_A$$
$$delta\ y = y_B - y_A$$
$$delta\ z = z_B - z_A$$

Figure 1.21 shows an example of a translation. This result is again based on Fig. 1.19; the vertices 16 and 15, in that order, have been used as the shift vector PQ.

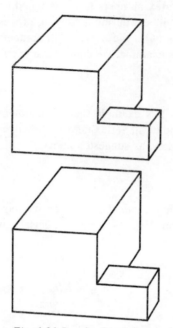

*Fig. 1.21 Result of translation*

If we are *copying* an object (rather than 'moving' it) the points A and B themselves, though possibly lying within the range of vertices to be transformed, are not copied if their numbers have been entered with a minus sign.

### 1.8.3   Scaling

Scaling an object means altering its size. Very often we want the new object to be similar to the old one, that is, although we want the dimensions to change, their proportions are to remain unchanged. In that case we are using *uniform* scaling. The real number $S$ by which all dimensions are multiplied is called the *scaling factor*. A generalization of this is to apply different scaling factors $S_x$, $S_y$, $S_z$ to the three directions X, Y, Z of the coordinate system. Obviously, uniform scaling is a special case of this, with

$$S_x = S_y = S_z = S$$

Before we can perform the scaling operation we also have to know the *fixed point*, which remains unchanged after the scaling transformation. If we use the origin O of the coordinate system for this purpose, then any point $P(x, y, z)$ is assigned a new point $P'(x', y', z')$ as follows:

$$x' = S_x \cdot x$$
$$y' = S_y \cdot y$$
$$z' = S_z \cdot z$$

Again, we want to generalize this, so that we can use points other than O as the fixed point. With a given fixed point $F(x_F, y_F, z_F)$ instead of O, we use $x - x_F$ instead of $x$, $x' - x_F$ instead of $x'$, and so on, which leads to the following scaling formulae:

$$x' - x_F = S_x \cdot (x - x_F)$$
$$y' - y_F = S_y \cdot (y - y_F)$$
$$z' - z_F = S_z \cdot (z - z_F)$$

This can easily be written in the following form, which is more suitable for efficient computation:

$$x' = S_x \cdot x + C_1$$
$$y' = S_y \cdot y + C_2$$
$$z' = S_z \cdot z + C_3$$

where $C_1, C_2, C_3$ are constants, not depending on $x, y, z$, and therefore computed only once before the actual scaling process:

$$C_1 = x_F - S_x \cdot x_F$$
$$C_2 = y_F - S_y \cdot y_F$$
$$C_3 = z_F - S_z \cdot z_F$$

In D3D we perform scaling as follows. After command $T$, we answer $Y$ to the question *Scaling? (Y/N)*. Then the following line is displayed:

```
Uniform? (Y/N)
```

If we answer $Y$ the line

```
Sx=Sy=Sz=
```

is displayed and we enter the required uniform scaling factor. If our answer is $N$, the three lines

```
Sx =
Sy =
Sz =
```

successively appear, each of them asking us to enter the scale factor for the direction indicated. Then the following three lines are displayed:

```
Fixed point:
Center (C), Origin (O)
or a Vertex (V):
```

We now have to type one of the three letters $C, O,$ or $V$. After our above discussion it will be clear what it means to have O or a vertex as the fixed point of the scaling operation. If we type

```
V
```

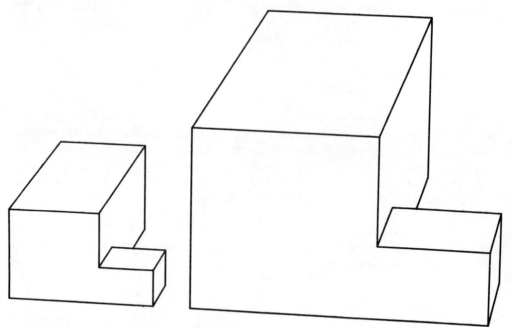

*Fig. 1.22 Result of scaling*

we are asked a point number as follows:

```
Point number:
```

The third option, *C* for *Center*, simply means that the center of the object is used as the fixed point. (This center is known anyhow because of the perspective transformation used to display the object on the screen.) If axes are visible on the screen, their endpoints also contribute to the computation of the center of the entire object, so the computed center might be slightly different from what you expect. If the choice of the fixed point is critical you had better take one of the options *O* or *V*. With option *V*, you may type a minus sign in front of the number of the fixed point; in case of 'copying', this will prevent the point from being assigned a new number.

Figure 1.22 shows an example of scaling with a uniform scaling factor 2. By choosing the fixed point far to the left of the original object (visible on the left), the new object, twice as large as the original one, is displayed on the right.

### 1.8.4   Reflection

A reflection is a transformation that produces a mirror image of an object. An object is reflected about a plane, the *plane of reflection*, or, simply, *mirror*. In Fig. 1.23 the object on the right has been obtained by reflecting the one on the left about a vertical plane of reflection between the two objects. With program D3D reflection is done quite easily. If, after command *T*, our answer to the question

```
Reflection? (Y/N)
```

is $Y$, the following two lines are displayed:

```
PQR is plane of refl.
Point nrs. P, Q, R:
```

We then enter the numbers of the points P, Q, R, which should not lie on the same line, so that they uniquely determine the plane of reflection. Again, we must have defined these points before giving command $T$. They may or may not be vertices of the object. Like the points P and Q used in Section 1.8.1 for the axis of rotation, the points P, Q, and R in the plane of reflections are fixed points. We can enter them as negative numbers if we do not want them to be assigned new point numbers.

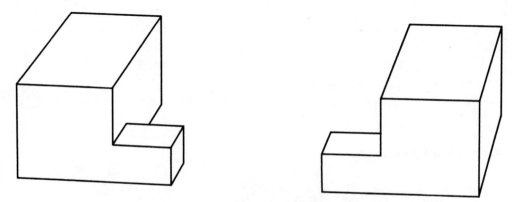

*Fig. 1.23 Result of reflection*

As with the other three types of transformations, we can either 'move' or 'copy' the object to be reflected. In Fig. 1.23 the original object is still present in the result, so it has been 'copied', not 'moved'. (Reflecting creates a mirror image, the shape of which will normally not be identical to the original, so the terms *move* and *copy* should not be taken too literally here!)

# CHAPTER 2

# Applications and Utility Programs

## 2.1 OBJECTS COMPOSED OF RIGHT PRISMS

The D3D commands *Read* and *Transform* (abbreviated *R* and *T*) enable us to build complex objects in a simple way, provided that these objects consist of components for which object files are available. Thanks to the possibility of non-uniform scaling, we can even go a step further and deform one single basic element into others of different shapes. Consider, for example, the cube with edges of length 1, shown in Fig. 2.1. After drawing this cube in the way discussed in Chapter 1 we can use the *Write* command to produce the file CUBE.DAT with the following contents:

```
1 0.000000 0.000000 0.000000
2 1.000000 0.000000 0.000000
3 1.000000 1.000000 0.000000
4 0.000000 1.000000 0.000000
5 0.000000 0.000000 1.000000
6 1.000000 0.000000 1.000000
7 1.000000 1.000000 1.000000
8 0.000000 1.000000 1.000000
Faces:
  2 3 7 6.
  4 1 5 8.
  3 4 8 7.
  1 2 6 5.
  6 7 8 5.
  3 2 1 4.
```

You may consider this to be a rather unpractical thing to do because cubes do not occur very frequently in everyday life. However, all kinds of right prisms do occur frequently, and with program D3D we can very easily transform a cube into any right prism (with only rectangular faces), using non-uniform scaling. Consider, for example, the table shown in Fig. 2.2. This table consists of nine right prisms with dimensions in inches as shown below:

| Part # | Quantity | x-dim. | y-dim. | z-dim. |
|--------|----------|--------|--------|--------|
| 1 | 1 | 35 | 50 | 2 |
| 2 | 4 | 3 | 3 | 29 |
| 3 | 2 | 1 | 40 | 3 |
| 4 | 2 | 25 | 1 | 3 |

51

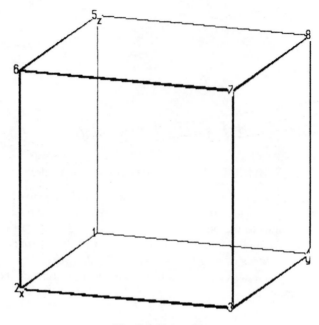

*Fig. 2.1 Unit cube*

Instead of *length*, *width*, and *height*, we prefer the terms '$x$-dimension', '$y$-dimension', and '$z$-dimension' here, because these give us some information about how each part will be used to construct the table. In terms of D3D-commands, these three dimensions tell us how to apply non-uniform scaling to the unit cube of Fig. 2.1. For example, we obtain part 1, the table top, by using the scale factors $Sx = 35$, $Sy = 50$, $Sz = 2$, when, after command $T$, we have selected non-uniform scaling. As usual, there are various ways that lead to the same result, but let us discuss just one way to construct the (imaginary) table in question. We will use the origin O of the coordinate system as the fixed point of the scaling transformations that transform the unit cube into the desired table parts. After scaling part 1 in this way, we save it in the file PART1.DAT, so that we can load it later. In a similar way we obtain the files PART2.DAT, PART3.DAT, and PART4.DAT for the parts 2, 3, and 4.

We now have to choose the position of the coordinate system relative to the table, but before doing this we will pay some attention to the position of the table itself. If we had to construct a real table of this type, we would probably place the table top upside down on the floor, and then place the legs on top of it, and so on. In any technical drawing, the most complex details should be made as clearly visible as possible, and, in our case, this means that Fig. 2.2(a) is not suitable for the construction process. In perspective drawings, we are used to a viewpoint that lies somewhat higher than the object we are viewing, which means that Fig. 2.2(b) is not attractive either for our purpose. Fortunately, program D3D enables us to turn a table whose legs point upwards into the right position, either by a rotation (through 180°, about a horizontal axis) or by a reflection (about a horizontal plane of reflection), so why not begin with a table that is upside down? Now consider the table as shown in Fig. 2.3(a).

(a)

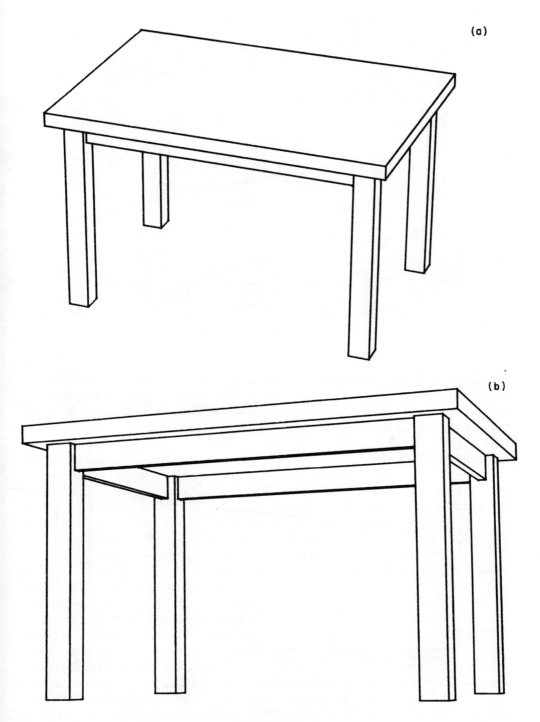

(b)

*Fig. 2.2 Table*

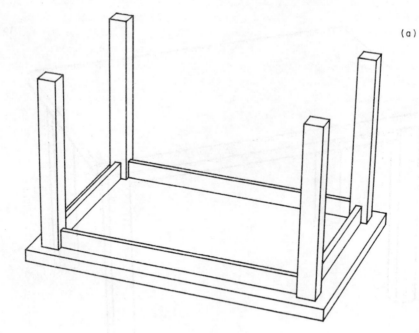

(a)

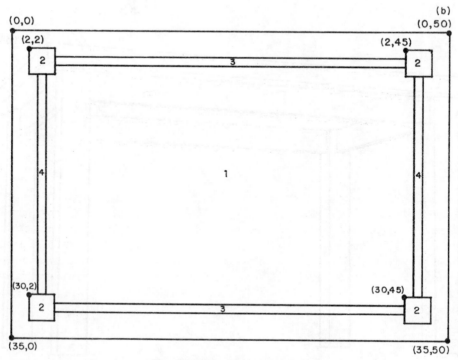

(b)

Fig. 2.3 Table during construction

Based on this position of the table, we may call Fig. 2.3(b) a *top view*. Technical drawings similar to this picture are quite popular, because they are much easier to produce than a correct perspective image and because all lines parallel to the plane of the drawing are true length. Note that Fig. 2.3(b) also shows the part numbers that we are using.

Now that the table is in a convenient position for our work, we can define the coordinate system that we shall be using. Let us choose the plane where the legs meet the table top as the *xy*-plane, as the incomplete table in Fig. 2.4 shows. The positions of some important points (with zero *z*-coordinates) indicated in Fig. 2.3(b) are based on this coordinate system. We actually have to sketch this top view to avoid any confusion in the actual construction process.

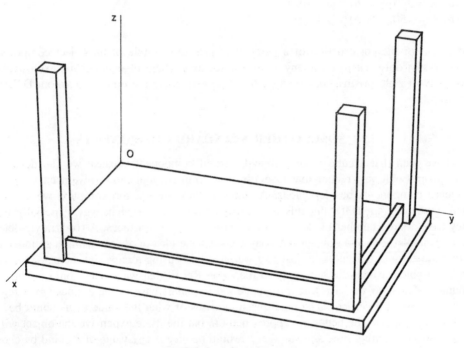

*Fig. 2.4 Coordinate system*

After all these preparations, we will combine the various parts, stored in the files PART1.DAT through PART4.DAT, to construct the table. We successively load part 1, part 2, part 3, and part 4 (using command *R*) and shift each of them to their correct position (using command *T*). Each time, we apply a translation to a carefully selected range of points which we have either read from a file or obtained as the result of a previous transformation. We begin by loading the file PART1.DAT (using command *R*), and perform a translation with *delta x = delta y = 0, delta z = −2*. Then we load the file PART2.DAT: when using command *R*, we answer *N* in reply to the question

```
Clear screen? (Y/N)
```

so that both part 1 and part 2 appear on the screen at the same time. The vertices of the newly loaded part 2 are automatically renumbered, and the range of the new numbers (9–16) is displayed. This enables us to move part 2 to its correct position (while part 1 remains unaltered) by means of a translation with *delta x* = 2, *delta y* = 2, *delta z* = 0. For the second leg, we can simply use the option *Copy* and apply a translation with *delta x* = 0, *delta y* = 43, *delta z* = 0 to the point range (9–16) of the first leg, and so on. When the table, in upside-down position, is completed, we can reflect it about any horizontal plane, say the one through the points 1, 2, and 3, to turn it into its normal position. Then command *H* will produce an image of the table as a solid object. Of course, this should be preceded by command *V* to choose a suitable viewpoint. Figures 2.2(a),(b) have been obtained in this way, with the following spherical coordinates for the eye:

(a) $R = 300$, $\theta = 20°$, $\varphi = 65°$;
(b) $R = 150$, $\theta = 20°$, $\varphi = 95°$.

So much for the construction of a table. It is just an example of an object composed of right prisms only. There are many other applications where objects consist exclusively or primarily of right prisms, so, besides table designers, there are others for whom D3D may be useful.

## 2.2  SOME OTHER STANDARD COMPONENTS

We have seen that a cube is an extremely useful component because we can derive any right prism (with only rectangular faces) from it. In many applications, we need some more standard components besides cubes. As long as they are not too complex, we can build them with program D3D, but this is not always the most efficient way, especially not if they have a large number of faces that approximate curved surfaces. A (right) cylinder is a good example of such an object. We may consider the idea of always using a cylinder with unit diameter and unit altitude, just like we have been using a cube, but here we are faced with a problem which did not apply to the cube. Recall that we can use only polygons as bounding faces, so we have to approximate the (circular) base of the cylinder by a regular polygon, say, of $n$ vertices. Then the question arises of what the value of $n$ should be. The larger we choose $n$, the better the approximation, but the more expensive the object will be in terms of computing time and storage. It would be nice if any value of $n$ could be chosen. As program D3D is already rather complex, the possibility of generating any approximation of a cylinder (and similar solids) has not been incorporated in this program, but we will instead use a separate program for this. As you may already have seen in the directory of the software disk, there are several other programs than D3D. One of them is CYLINDER. If you have not (yet) bought this software disk, this program is listed in this book in Section 3.2. We start the program by typing its name:

```
CYLINDER
```

Successively, the following questions will appear on the screen:

```
Direction of axis? (X/Y/Z)
Diameter?
Altitude?
Number of polygon edges?
Name of output file?
```

If the cylinder axis is to be parallel to one of the three axes of the coordinate system, then the first three questions enable us to obtain a cylinder with the correct orientation and the correct dimensions immediately, so that we need not obtain these by means of any rotation or scaling operations. We will normally need a translation, however, since the center of the cylinder will coincide with the origin of the coordinate system, which in most cases is not what we want. Our answer to the fourth question will determine the actual shape of the object. Let us denote this number of polygon edges by $n$. Actually, the solid in question is a prism, not a cylinder; if we choose $n = 4$, we obtain a right prism whose base is a square. Normally, some larger value of $n$ will be chosen, say 30. The resulting approximated cylinder will be written to a file, the name of which we enter in reply to the fifth question. This file will have the format required by program D3D and discussed in Section 1.6. Thus after running program CYLINDER, we can run program D3D with the file just produced as its input file, as Fig. 2.5 illustrates. If we execute program CYLINDER with the following answers to the above five questions:

```
Z
5
2
30
CYL.DAT
```

and we then execute program D3D by typing

```
D3D CYL.DAT
```

then commands $H$ (with the default threshold value of 35°) will produce the image shown in Fig. 2.6. Although not shown in this picture, the origin of the coordinate system lies exactly in the center of the cylinder.

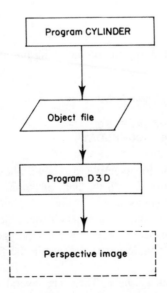

Fig. 2.5 Object file, produced by CYLINDER and used by D3D

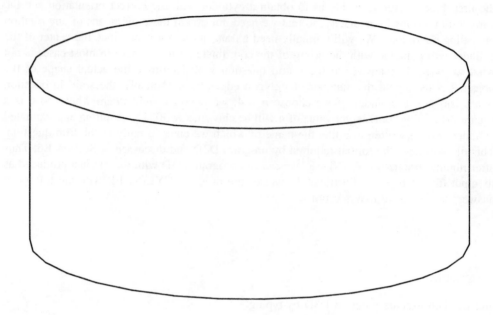

*Fig. 2.6 Cylinder*

We can approximate a *cone* by a pyramid, which is similar to approximating a cylinder by a prism. We will use program CONE, listed in Section 3.3, to achieve this. This program generates a (right) cone with its base circle in the *xy*-plane and its vertex on the positive *z*-axis. If we start its execution by typing

    CONE

then the questions shown below (up to and including the question mark) will appear on the screen:

```
Diameter of base circle? 5
Altitude? 3
Number of polygon edges? 30
Name of output file? CONE.DAT
```

If we answer these questions, for example, as shown above, then program D3D with file CONE.DAT as its input data (and with the help of commands *H* and a threshold value 0) will produce an image of a cone as shown in Fig. 2.7. Note that our cone is a solid object. In Fig. 2.7 the viewpoint lies somewhat beneath this object so that we view it from the bottom. As this is a non-transparent face (a regular polygon with 30 edges) we can only see the sloping sides of the triangle edges that are in the foreground, not those that are in the background.

Another standard element is a *sphere*. There are several ways of approximating a sphere by an object bounded by flat faces, and we will use two essentially different methods. Our

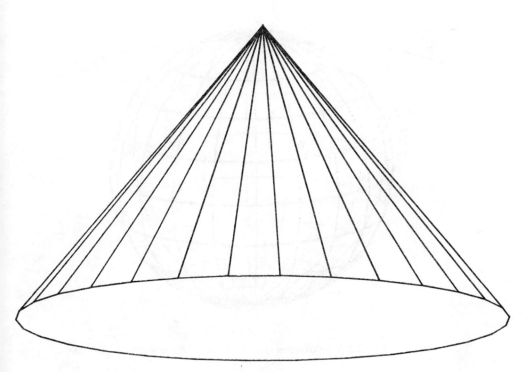

*Fig. 2.7 A cone*

first method is based on circles that are usually found on a globe, as shown in Fig. 2.8. We have two poles, a north pole at the top and a south pole at the bottom, and $n$ vertical circles, the *lines of longitude*, that pass through them. All these vertical circles have the same radius, $r$, which is also the radius of the sphere. The sphere is divided into $m$ horizontal slices, which divide each half circle between the north and south pole into $m$ arcs of equal lengths. This gives $m - 1$ horizontal circles, the *lines of latitude*. The two poles and all points of intersection of lines of longitude and lines of latitude are the vertices of polygons that we shall use as faces of the approximating polyhedron. These polygons are trapezoids except for those near the poles, which are triangles. It will be clear that the larger we choose $n$ and $m$ the better the approximation will be. However, computing time will also increase with growing $n$ and $m$, especially if we want hidden lines to be removed. The trapezoids on the sphere near the 'equator' (that is, those on the largest slice) will approximate squares if we choose

$$n = 2m$$

for we have $n$ points on each horizontal circle and $2m$ points on each vertical circle. Program SPHERE, listed in Section 3.4, generates such an approximated sphere. The user has to enter the values of $m$ and $n$ along with the radius of the sphere and the name of the output file. The center of the sphere will be the origin of the coordinate system and the poles lie on the $z$-axis. We obtain the sphere shown in Fig. 2.8 by using the programs SPHERE and D3D with $m = 10$ and $n = 20$.

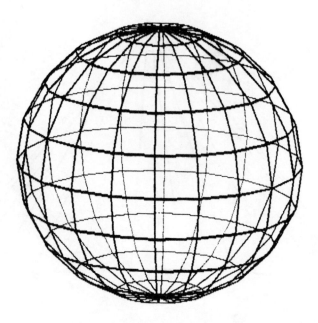

Fig. 2.8 Approximated sphere with m = 10, n = 20

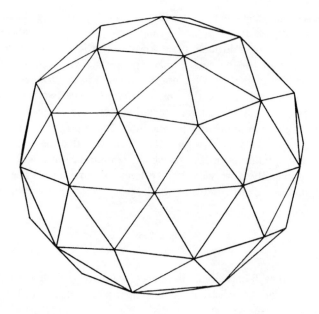

Fig. 2.9 Sphere approximated by 80 triangles

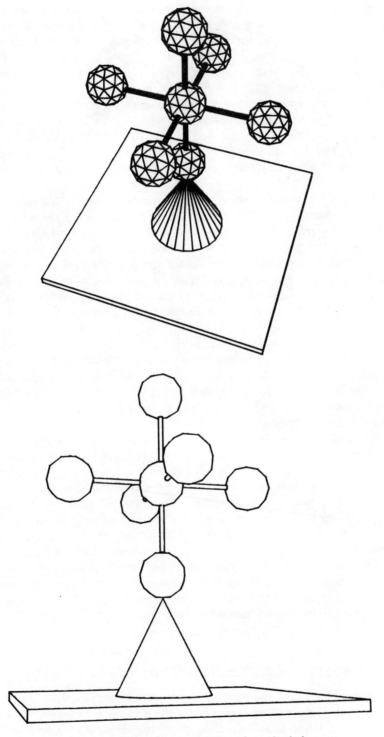

(a)

(b)

*Fig. 2.10 An object consisting of standard elements*

Although this picture looks nice, it is somewhat unsatisfactory that the elementary flat faces are not of about the same size. After all, for reasons of efficiency we want as few of these elementary areas as possible, provided that the object does not differ too much from a real sphere, so it is not efficient that there are so many small faces near the poles. Another possibly undesirable aspect is that (in images where the lines of longitude and of latitude are visible) the position of the viewpoint influences the image considerably. We will therefore consider an alternative method of approximating a sphere, namely by means of a polyhedron with 80 faces, which are triangles. In Section 3.6 we will discuss this object in greater detail; here we will simply use it. The file SPH80.DAT (generated by program SPH80, see Section 3.6) is all we have to use. The polyhedron in question is shown in Fig. 2.9. This image can be obtained by typing D3D SPH80.DAT and using the commands *H* and *P*.

Figures 2.10(a) and (b) show a combination of all standard elements discussed so far. At the bottom we have a square plate, with a cone placed on it in the middle. On top of this cone, we find the lowest of seven spheres, which are connected by six thin cylinders. The seven spheres are represented by polyhedra with 80 triangular faces. This image was obtained by reading file SPH80.DAT only once, namely for the sphere in the center. This sphere was 'copied' by a translation, to obtain the sphere in the foreground (with its center lying on the positive *x*-axis). A cylinder was read from a file (generated by program CYLINDER) only once, and 'moved' to its correct position between the first two spheres. In order to perform some rotations about the axes of the coordinate system, I had defined the points (1, 0, 0), (0, 1, 0), and (0, 0, 1) beforehand and assigned the numbers 1, 2, 3 to them, respectively. (Recall that point 0 is the origin of the coordinate system). Then I could rotate the sphere and the cylinder in the foreground about the *y*-axis, through 180°, to obtain the sphere and the cylinder in the background. Since the latest two spheres and the two cylinders have a consecutive sequence of vertex numbers, I could rotate these four elementary objects (in one operation) about the *z*-axis through 90°, to obtain the spheres and cylinders lying on the positive and the negative *y*-axis. Finally, a rotation of these two spheres and two cylinders through 90° about the *x*-axis produced those on the *z*-axis. For a complex object such as this one, it is wise to split it into two or more parts, and to store these separately in a file. In this example, I used two such files, one for the seven spheres with their connecting cylinders and one for the plate and the cone. Only when these two parts were completed did I combine them, reading first the former (that is, the more complex) part and then the latter (the plate and cone), which then had to be shifted downward, that is, with a negative *delta z*. Figure 2.10(b) shows the same object as Fig. 2.10(a), but seen from a different viewpoint and with a 'threshold' value of 35° to omit lines of intersection that do not really exist on the corresponding curved surfaces. It is a matter of taste whether we want such lines to be drawn or omitted; since we have many more line segments in Fig. 2.10(a) than we have in Fig. 2.10(b), the hidden-line computation takes much more time for the former than it does for the latter.

## 2.3   SOLIDS OF REVOLUTION AND CUTAWAY VIEWS

In the last section we have used some programs for special *solids of revolution*, namely a cylinder, a cone, and a sphere. These programs, written in the C programming language, are listed in Chapter 3. If you know little about the C language but are interested in it and want my advice, then, not surprisingly, I would recommend my book *C for Programmers*.

If learning C is beyond your ambitions, then you have two other options. First, if you can program in some other language, then you can use that to generate input files for D3D. After all, only the contents of these file matter, and D3D cannot find out how they have been prepared. So if, for example, you prefer BASIC or Pascal to C, you can use those languages instead. Second, you may not be able or willing to program at all. Even in this case, you can use D3D for interesting new objects, even if these cannot be composed of the available standard elements. An example of such an object is shown in Fig. 2.11. It is an incomplete solid of revolution, called a *cutaway view*. It arises from rotating Fig. 2.12 about the axis through an angle of 270°. This incomplete object can be used to have a clear view of the inner part of the corresponding complete object, which we would have obtained by a rotation through 360° instead of 270°.

It is not difficult to produce Fig. 2.11 using only D3D. We begin with defining the points 1 through 9, shown in Fig. 2.12 (using the viewpoint with $\rho = 1\,000\,000$, $\theta = 90°$, $\varphi = 90°$). The coordinates of these points are as follows:

|   | x | y | z |
|---|---|---|---|
| 1 | 0 | 0 | 0 |
| 2 | 10 | 0 | 0 |
| 3 | 10 | 0 | 2 |
| 4 | 10 | 0 | 4 |
| 5 | 6 | 0 | 4 |
| 6 | 2 | 0 | 6 |
| 7 | 2 | 0 | 8 |
| 8 | 0 | 0 | 8 |
| 9 | 0 | 0 | 2 |

Thus point 1 is the origin of the coordinate system and point 2 lies on the positive $x$-axis (pointing to the left in Fig. 2.12); all $y$-coordinates are zero, so we are working in the $xz$-plane. We do not want lines yet, so we actually begin with a version of Fig. 2.12 without any lines. Using command $T$, we then rotate all points except 1 and 2 about the $x$-axis through an angle of 15°. When requested, we enter the numbers 3 and 9 as lower and upper bounds, and, after selecting a rotation, we enter the numbers 1 and 2 as the points P and Q, required to determine the axis of rotation. In this and all following rotations we use the *Copy* option (not *Move*), so we will not mention this each time; nor will we keep mentioning the points 1 and 2 on the axis of rotation we are using. The number of each new point is obtained by increasing the corresponding old point number by 7, which gives the point numbers 10 through 16. This enables us to define seven faces as follows:

| F |   |   |   |
|---|---|---|---|
| 3 | -4 | 11 | -10. |
| 4 | 5 | 12 | 11. |
| 5 | 6 | 13 | 12. |
| 6 | -7 | 14 | -13. |
| 7 | 8 | 15 | 14. |
| 8 | -9 | 16 | -15. |
| 9 | 3 | 10 | 16. |

The minus signs prevent some line segments from being drawn. For example, line segment (11, 10) should not be visible as an edge in the final result, Fig. 2.11. Even though line segment (3, 4) is eventually to be drawn, it is treated here in the same way as (11, 10) in

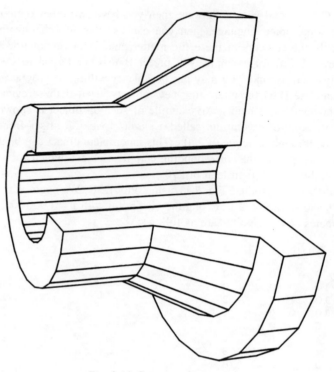

*Fig. 2.11 Cutaway view*

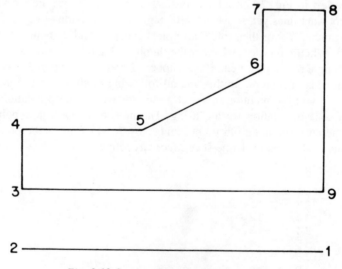

*Fig. 2.12 Section through axis of revolution*

view of subsequent copying operations. Except for some missing line segments we have now created what we will call a *sector* of 15°. This is to grow to a sector of 270°; although we could rotate and copy the sector of 15° seventeen times (which would yield 18 × 15° = 270°), we will obtain our result in only five rotations, as shown in Table 2.1.

Table 2.1 Rotations to extend a sector of 15° to one of 270°

| Lower bound | Upper bound | Angle of rotation | New point range | Resulting sector |
|---|---|---|---|---|
| 3  | 16  | 15°  | 17 – 30   | 30°  |
| 3  | 30  | 30°  | 31 – 58   | 60°  |
| 31 | 58  | 30°  | 59 – 86   | 90°  |
| 3  | 86  | 90°  | 87 – 170  | 180° |
| 87 | 170 | 90°  | 171 – 254 | 270° |

In each step we are rotating (and copying) a sector with an angle equal to the angle of rotation, mentioned in the third column. After these rotations we have to add a horizontal and a vertical bounding face, both passing through the axis of rotation:

```
F
 9   8   7   6   5   4   3.
248 249 250 251 252 253 254.
```

Recall that the vertices are to be given in counter-clockwise order when viewed from outside the object—hence a decreasing order for the first and an increasing order for the second of these two vertex-number sequences.

Only after command $H$, when hidden lines have been removed, do we have an image that pleases the eye, as shown in Fig. 2.11. The spherical coordinates of the viewpoint used here are $R = 50$, $\theta = 65°$, $\varphi = 70°$. During the process of constructing, the object is displayed as a wire-frame model, without some bounding faces. Since there are so many points, displayed point numbers are no good, nor are axes and bold lines, so before performing the transformations we had better use command $M$.

## 2.4   SMOOTH 3D CURVES

There is a mathematical method known as *B-spline* approximation, which can be used to obtain smooth curves in a very convenient way. We will use this method for curves in three dimensions, such as the one shown in Fig. 2.15. We can start with only a limited number of points, defined with program D3D. With command $W$ we write the coordinates of these points to a file, and this file is then read by a new program, CURVE3, listed in Section 3.8. This program generates a great many other points by B-spline interpolation; this technique will be discussed here only as far as user's aspects are concerned.

Program CURVE3 requests three pieces of information, to be entered on the keyboard:

1 The name of an input file
2 The name of an output file
3 An integer $N$, discussed below

Both the input and the output file are what we may call D3D-compatible, that is, they have the format of object files read and written by D3D. The integer $N$ is the number of intervals between two successive given points: with $m$ given points in the input file, the output file will contain $k$ points, where

$$k = (m - 3)N + 1$$

as we shall see at the end of this section.

Thanks to the D3D-compatibility of the files read and written by CURVE3, we can use program D3D both to prepare the input file for CURVE3 and to display the generated curve, stored in the output file:

$$D3D \longrightarrow file \longrightarrow CURVE3 \longrightarrow file \longrightarrow D3D$$

In the input file, only the first part, which lists the numbers and the coordinates of all points, is used by CURVE3. There may or may not be a second part, beginning with the word *Faces*; if present it is simply ignored. Actually, CURVE3 also ignores the point numbers, which means that, for example, the file

```
9      1.5    3.5    2.5
5      1.0    3.0    2.0
7      0.5    0.7    2.5
8      0.1    0.2    0.0
```

is equivalent to the file

```
1      1.5    3.5    2.5
2      1.0    3.0    2.0
3      0.5    0.7    2.5
4      0.1    0.2    0.0
```

as far as program CURVE3 is concerned. Fortunately, program D3D will write the points in increasing order of their numbers, so it will never produce the (possibly confusing) former file. I mention this only because you can make such a file with other means, such as a text editor or some program of your own, and then you need to know that the lines in the file are to appear in their proper order. Note that this is different for program D3D, for which point numbers in its input file are significant.

Figures 2.13, 2.14, and 2.15 were obtained in that order. Figure 2.13 shows the points 1 through 15, lying on a spring, along with line segments that connect them. Recall that such line segments can be given in object files as number pairs after the keyword *Faces*, or when using D3D, they are entered after command $F$, as, for example, in:

```
F
1    2.
2    3.
3    4.
```

As we have just seen, I might have omitted them, as far as program CURVE3 is concerned, but I introduced them only to make Fig. 2.13 as clear as possible. I then used a transformation

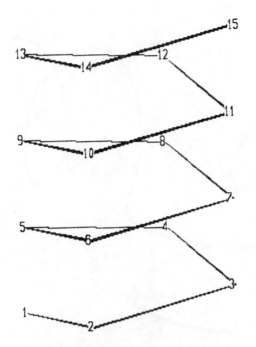

Fig. 2.13 Some points on a spring

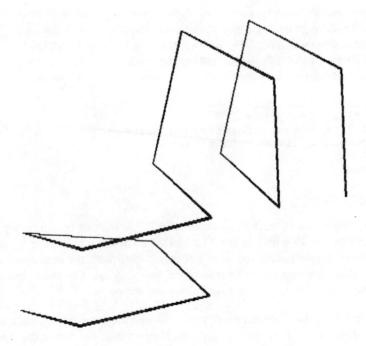

Fig. 2.14 Result after rotating points 9 through 15

*Fig. 2.15 Result of B-spline approximation*

(in the 'move' mode), namely a rotation of the point sequence with lower bound 9 and upper bound 15, through an angle of 90° and about the line through the points 7 and 8. The resulting object, shown in Fig. 2.14, was written to a file, say TEST.DAT. I then applied program CURVE3 to this file. After starting the program, three questions appear on the screen, which, together with their answers in our example, are shown below:

```
Input file:   TEST.DAT
Output file: TEST1.DAT
Enter N, the number of intervals between
two successive given points: 4
```

Finally, I typed

```
D3D TEST1.DAT
```

and used the commands *E* and *P* to obtain Fig. 2.15. Instead of only 15 points in file TEST.DAT, there are 49 points in file TEST1.DAT. They were obtained by means of the B-spline method, and although you need not be troubled with the mathematical details of this method, there are two points to remember; you may not like them, but they are the price we have to pay for the extreme smoothness of the curve:

1 In general, the curve does not exactly pass through the given points, but it only approx-imates them. The closer the given points are together, the better this approximation will be, so if some B-spline approximation is not good enough we can improve it by giving more points.

2  The very first point and the very last are not approximated. In our example, the end
   of the curve at the bottom in Fig. 2.15 approximates point 2, see Fig. 2.13, and the
   other end, at the top, approximates the second last point (point 14) of the broken line
   in Fig. 2.14. It will be clear that we need at least four points, say, A, B, C, D, to
   apply the B-spline method. In that case, the resulting curve would approximately lie
   between the points B and C. Although the points A and D are not approximated they
   do contribute to the approximating curve, so we cannot do without them.

Without using advanced mathematics we can now understand the formula

$$k = (m - 3)N + 1$$

mentioned above. There are $m$ given points, the first and the last of which are not approximated, so only $m - 2$ of them will approximately be connected by the curve. We first
imagine them to be connected by straight line segments; since the number of connections
is always 1 less than the number of connected points, there are only $m - 3$ of those line
segments. Each of them is divided into $N$ intervals, which altogether gives $(m - 3)N$ small
line segments. These connect the $k$ new points, and, again applying the rule that the number
of connections is one less than the number of connected points, we find the above expression
for $k$.

Note that what we have called a *curve* in this section is actually a sequence of $(m - 3)N$
straight line segments. By choosing $N$ large enough these line segments will be very small,
so that we can obtain very good approximations of real curves, as Fig. 2.15 demonstrates.

## 2.5   CABLES AND KNOTS

The three-dimensional curves of Section 2.4 are mathematical abstractions: we can regard
them as threads with diameter 0. We now want to transform them into real solid objects,
namely threads or *cables* with a diameter greater than 0. In the same way as we can imagine
a cylinder to be derived from a straight line (the cylinder axis) by giving the latter some
thickness, we will derive cables from 3D curves. The similarity between our cylinders and
our cables also applies to the way we will approximate the latter: as usual, a great number
of flat bounding faces will substitute for the curved cable surface.

As we did in the previous section, we will use a program which transforms one D3D-
compatible file into another. This program, CABLE, is listed in Section 3.9. Its input file can
best be generated by program CURVE3 (see Section 2.4), and its output file will normally
be read by program D3D, so altogether, we normally use the programs D3D, CURVE3,
CABLE, D3D, in that order. (Of course, we can display the curve before applying CABLE
to it, which means that program D3D would also be used in between CURVE3 and CABLE,
just to check that the curve is what we expect it to be.) Like CURVE3, program CABLE
asks us some questions, namely the names of the input and the output files, the number of
points that are to be placed on each circle, and the diameter of these circles. These circles
are similar to the base of a cylinder or a cone: if we have $n$ points on each circle, then each
cross section of the cable will be a regular polygon with $n$ sides. If we choose $n$ large, then
we may have a very good approximation of a cable, but we should not forget that eventually
we want hidden lines to be eliminated, which is a rather time-consuming process if there are
a great many bounding faces. As we have seen at the end of the previous section, program

CURVE3 produces $(m - 3)N$ small line segments, each of which will now expand to $n$ faces, so the number of faces that approximate the curved cable surface will be

$$(m - 3)Nn$$

where

    $m$ = the number of points that are given for B-spline approximation, that is, the number of points in the file read by program CURVE3;

    $N$ = the number of intervals between two successive points ($N$ is entered when running CURVE3);

    $n$ = the number of points on each cross section of the cable ($n$ is entered when running CABLE).

It is a good idea to begin with a rather small value of $n$, and to increase it later if the result should be unsatisfactory. With $n = 8$, I obtained a file, which, after reading it by program D3D, produced Fig. 2.16. So here the number of faces on the curved cable surface was:

$$(15 - 3) \times 4 \times 8 = 384$$

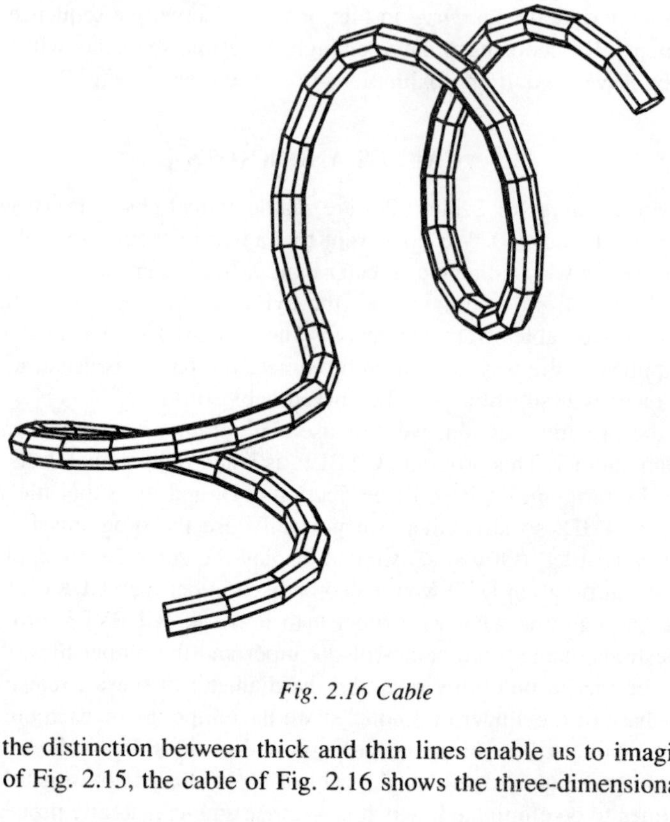

Fig. 2.16 Cable

Although the distinction between thick and thin lines enable us to imagine some 'depth' in the curve of Fig. 2.15, the cable of Fig. 2.16 shows the three-dimensional situation more clearly.

We can use the programs CURVE3 and CABLE to produce 3D pictures of *knots*. Consider, for example, Fig. 2.17 in connection with the following associated data file, to be used as input data for program CURVE3:

| | | | |
|----|-----|------|------|
| 1  | 0   | -100 | 12   |
| 2  | 0   | -70  | 10   |
| 3  | -15 | -30  | 8    |
| 4  | 15  | 0    | 15   |
| 5  | 0   | 20   | 22   |
| 6  | -15 | 30   | 0    |
| 7  | 0   | 20   | -22  |
| 8  | 15  | 0    | -15  |
| 9  | -15 | -30  | -8   |
| 10 | 0   | -70  | -50  |
| 11 | 0   | 0    | -100 |
| 12 | 0   | 70   | -50  |
| 13 | 15  | 30   | -8   |
| 14 | -15 | 0    | -15  |
| 15 | 0   | -20  | -22  |
| 16 | 15  | -30  | 0    |
| 17 | 0   | -20  | 22   |
| 18 | -15 | 0    | 15   |
| 19 | 15  | 30   | 8    |
| 20 | 0   | 70   | 10   |
| 21 | 0   | 100  | 12   |

Faces:

```
 1  2.
 2  3.
 3  4.
 4  5.
 5  6.
 6  7.
 7  8.
 8  9.
 9 10.
10 11.
11 12.
12 13.
13 14.
14 15.
15 16.
16 17.
17 18.
18 19.
19 20.
20 21.
```

We can obtain this file either by means of program D3D or by using a normal text editor, but we can also mix these methods: first, we use D3D to produce something like Fig. 2.17 (with $\theta = 0°$ and $\varphi = 90°$) but with all points still lying in the $yz$-plane; then we use a text editor to change the (zero) $x$-coordinates of all 21 points into their proper values. For example, the two points 4 and 18 initially have the same coordinates, namely $x = 0$, $y = 0$, $z = 15$. As point 4 should lie in the background, we give it the $x$-coordinate $-15$, whereas point 18, lying in the foreground, is given the $x$-coordinate 15. (Recall that the coordinate system is right-handed, so the positive $x$-axis in Fig. 2.17 points towards us.) Once we have

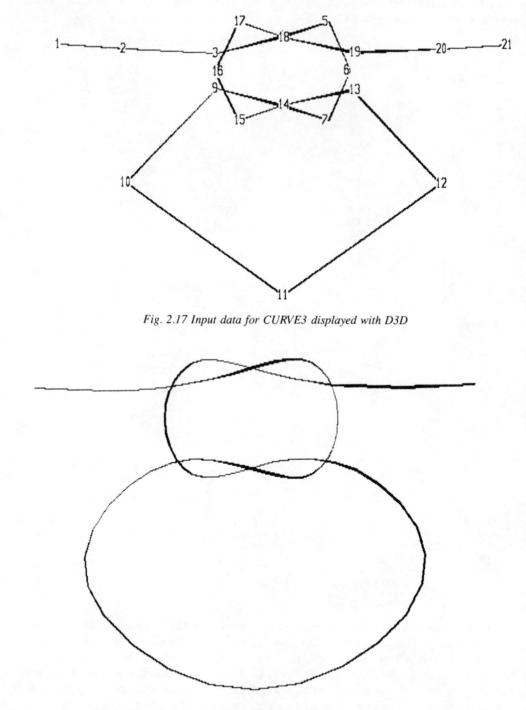

Fig. 2.17 Input data for CURVE3 displayed with D3D

Fig. 2.18 Result of CURVE3

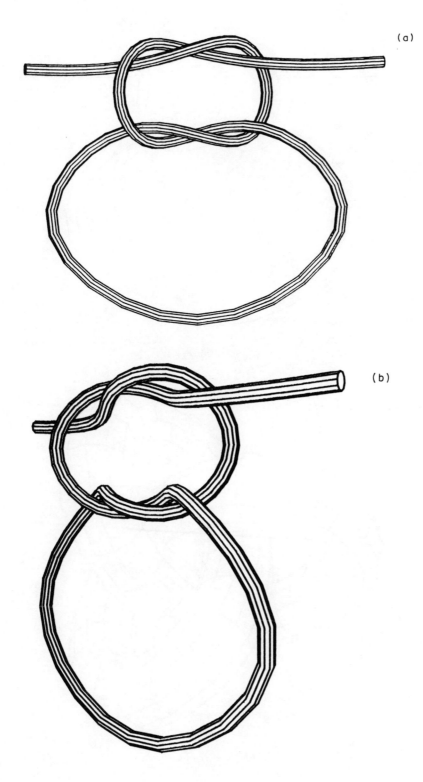

(a)

(b)

( c )

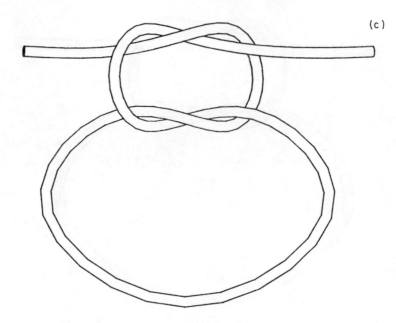

*Fig. 2.19 Reef knot*

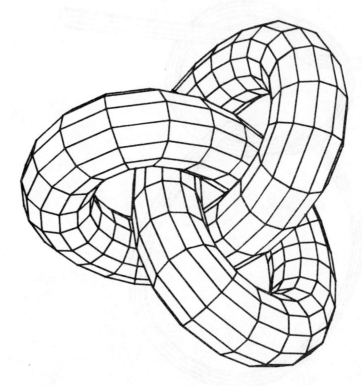

*Fig. 2.20 Knot after M.C. Escher*

done the somewhat (but not extremely!) tedious work of producing this file, the computer does the hard work of producing various pictures of a realistic reef knot. After applying program CURVE3 to this file, with, for example $N = 5$, we obtain Fig. 2.18, along with an associated object file. We then apply program CABLE to the latter file, which gives the final product, shown in Fig. 2.19(a), (b), (c). Here for each circle we have $r = 2$ as its radius and $n = 10$ as the number of points on it. For the three files involved, the associated picture is obtained by using program D3D; the latter program does in fact most of the work, namely the rather time-consuming process of hidden-line elimination (with command $H$). In cases like this it depends on the speed of your computer what values of $N$ and $n$ you can reasonably use. This work can be done on a machine with only an 8088 processor, but there will be an enormous improvement in speed if you switch to an IBM PC/AT with a mathematical co-processor. Though less dramatically, computing time is also influenced favorably by taking a rather large value for the 'threshold angle' $\alpha$, which causes certain artificial edges on curved surfaces to be omitted in the result. Here I have used $\alpha = 35°$ in Figs 2.19(a) and (b), and $\alpha = 50°$ in Fig. 2.19(c). Note that by using $\alpha = 35°$ the edges parallel to the axis of the cable are drawn, because we have $n = 10$, and

$$360°/n = 36° > 35°$$

Edges on cross sections have been omitted in Fig. 2.19(a) and (b) as a consequence of the rather large angle $\alpha = 35°$; they would have been drawn (as was done in Fig. 2.16) if the angle $\alpha$ had been equal to 0 or, equivalently, if the question about curved surfaces, which is displayed after our entering command $H$, had been answered in the negative.

Figure 2.20 shows another result (similar to one that M.C. Escher has drawn by hand!). It was produced essentially in the same way as those we have just been discussing. Starting with the following input data, program CURVE3 was executed, followed by the programs CABLE and D3D:

| | | | |
|---|---|---|---|
| 1 | 2 | 0 | 2 |
| 2 | 0 | 1.73 | -1 |
| 3 | -2 | 1.73 | 1 |
| 4 | 2 | 0 | 2 |
| 5 | 0 | -1.73 | 1 |
| 6 | -2 | 0 | 0 |
| 7 | 2 | 1.73 | 1 |
| 8 | 0 | 1.73 | 3 |
| 9 | -2 | 0 | 2 |
| 10 | 2 | 0 | 0 |
| 11 | 0 | 1.73 | -1 |
| 12 | -2 | 1.73 | 1 |

In contrast to Fig. 2.19, I have used $\alpha = 0°$, so that in Fig. 2.20 all edges have been displayed. As the programs CURVE3 and CABLE are intended for finite curves and cables, it is not obvious that the infinite 'cable' of Fig. 2.20 can be made in this way. As will be discussed in Section 3.8, there is no problem with CURVE3 in this regard. However, when giving the curve some thickness (in CABLE), we are using regular polygons instead of circles, and it is not to be expected that the vertices of the final polygon will exactly coincide with those of the first. I must therefore confess that the two ends of the cable shown in Fig. 2.20 do not meet perfectly, but that I chose the viewpoint such that the imperfect joint is hidden.

## 2.6   SQUARE SCREW THREAD

In this section we shall be dealing with a program that might be useful in mechanical engineering. It is about a screw thread with a square profile, as shown in Fig. 2.21(a) and (b). The program, called SCRTHR, produces an object file that can be read by D3D to produce a 3D view. Program SCRTHR is listed in Section 3.12. A screw thread is by no means a simple geometric object; nor will program SCRTHR be easy to understand. Fortunately, the program is very easy to use. It asks for the essential dimensions, namely, a major diameter $D$, a minor diameter $d$, a pitch $P$, and a desired length $L_0$, shown in Fig. 2.21(a). Actually, if the thread is really square, the sides of each square have length

$$0.5(D - d)$$

which is equal to half the pitch, so we have

$$P = D - d$$

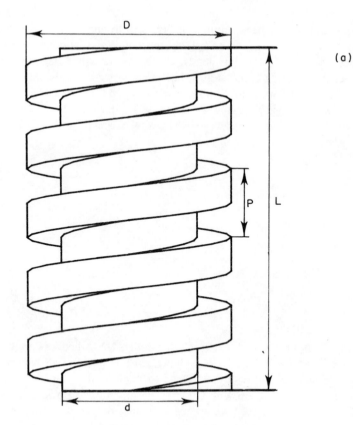

(a)

( b )

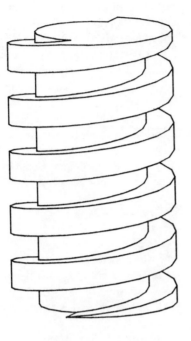

( c )

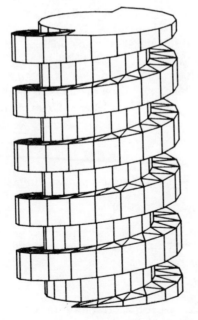

Fig. 2.21 Square screw thread

Thus, if the thread is really square, the pitch follows from the major and minor diameters and need therefore not be given separately. Program SCRTHR is a little more general in that it allows us to specify the pitch independently from the two diameters. In this way, it can also produce thread with a profile that is rectangular but not square.

As usual, curved surfaces are approximated by flat polygons. We therefore also have to give $k$, the number of steps in a *half* revolution. Recall that in Section 2.2 we have approximated the base of a cylinder by a regular polygon of 30 edges. A similar approximation here would require $k$ to be 15, since then we would have 30 steps in a full revolution, like we did with the cylinder. As screw thread is much more complex than a cylinder, we had better begin with some smaller value, say $k = 8$, and try to increase this later, if desirable.

If the screw is turned a full revolution, its advancement along its axis is $P$, the pitch. Since a full revolution takes $2k$ steps, the screw only advances

$$delta\ L = P\ /\ 2k$$

in each step. The real length $L$ will now be determined as the whole multiple of *delta L* that is nearest to the desired length $L_0$, so the difference between the real and the desired length will be less than half the value of *delta L*. Obviously, these two lengths will be exactly the same if the given value $L_0$ happens to be a multiple of *delta L*. For example, with a desired length $L_0 = 1.5$, a pitch $P = 0.25$, and ($k =$) 6 steps in a half revolution, we have

$$delta\ L = 0.25\ /\ (2 \times 6) = 1/48$$

and

$$L_0 = 1.5 = 72 \times (1/48)$$

so in this case the desired length $L_0$ is already a whole multiple of *delta L*, and the real length $L$ will therefore be equal to $L_0$.

Except for the dimensioning, which shows the meaning of $D$, $d$, $P$, $L$, both Fig. 2.21(a) and Fig. 2.21(b) were printed by program D3D on the basis of an object file produced by program SCRTHR. Here is a demonstration of the latter program to produce this very object file:

```
Major diameter: 3
Minor diameter: 2
If the thread really is to be square, we have:

   pitch = major - minor = 1.000

Then in one revolution, 'pitch' is the distance the
screw moves forward, so the imaginary 'square' has
sides of length

   h = pitch/2 = 0.500

Do you want a different pitch, so that the thread
will not be really square (but rectangular)? (Y/N): N
Desired length of the screw thread (not less than 0.500): 5
Number of steps taken in a half revolution: 10
The real length will be: 5.000
Name of output file: FIG2.21
```

If we had typed $Y$ in reply to the question about a different pitch, then we would have been asked another question, namely:

```
Pitch:
```

and we could then have entered a pitch independent of the major and minor diameters.

After generating the file FIG2.21 in this way, we can start program D3D, typing

```
D3D FIG2.21
```

For a complicated object like this screw thread, we will probably want only the hidden-line version of the perspective image; in cases like this, we had better use th in lines only on the initial screen. We will probably also want the bounding faces to approximate curved surfaces; the default threshold value of 35° will do. Figures 2.21(a) and (b) have been produced in this way, with the following spherical viewpoint coordinates:

(a) $\rho = 1000$, $\theta = 0°$, $\varphi = 90°$
(b) $\rho = 1000$, $\theta = 20°$, $\varphi = 80°$

Figure 2.21(c), produced with $\alpha = 0°$, shows how flat faces have been used to approximate curved surfaces. In Section 3.11 we will discuss this in greater detail.

## 2.7  EXPLODED VIEWS

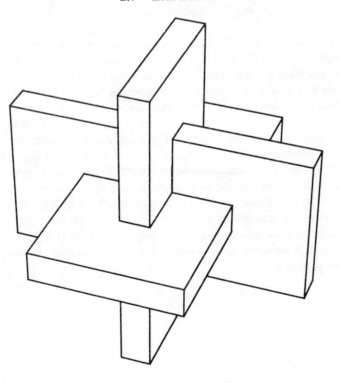

*Fig. 2.22 Object consisting of three parts*

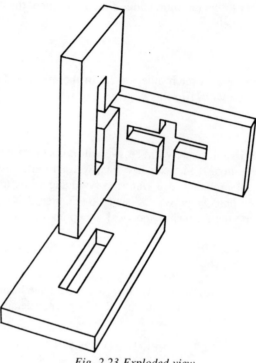

*Fig. 2.23 Exploded view*

Besides cutaway views, as shown in Fig. 2.11, we can use *exploded* views for complex objects. This technique is especially useful if an object consists of various parts and we want to show how to assemble these to form the complete object. For example, if it is given that the object shown in Fig. 2.22 consists of three parts, it will not be clear what these parts are, let alone how to put them together. The exploded view in Fig. 2.23 is very helpful for these purposes. It clearly shows the form of the three parts, and it suggests that we need only translate two of them to obtain the object of Fig. 2.22, which is indeed the case.

If you like, you can produce these two perspective views by using program D3D, as I did myself. As outer dimensions of the three parts, I used 40 × 20 × 4 (mm); the other dimensions follow from these. At first the three parts were in the same position, with their centers in the origin of the coordinate system. I used separate object files for the three parts, but I could derive the two objects that in Fig. 2.23 are in the foreground from the one in the background (which is the most complex) by omitting some of its vertices and updating its set of faces. Then I used some rotations to obtain Fig. 2.22. Finally, I obtained Fig. 2.23 by means of some translations.

*PART B*

# Writing Application Programs

# CHAPTER 3

## *Programs to Generate Input Files for Program D3D*

### 3.1 FUNCTION PROTOTYPES IN TURBO C

So far, we have been discussing three-dimensional design from the user's point of view. From now on we will primarily deal with programming aspects, which means that for users who are not familiar with programming the rest of this book may not be easy to read. However, even if you are such a user, you may appreciate the fact that all software discussed is given in source code, since this means that if you should want the programs to be modified you do not depend on the author but, instead, you can ask any experienced C programmer to adapt the programs according to your special wishes. If, on the other hand, you are interested primarily in programming aspects, you should not make the mistake of skipping over Chapters 1 and 2 of this book. After all, it is no good to discuss *how* programs do something if it is not perfectly clear *what* they do.

It would be nice if programming were as machine-independent as mathematics, for that would mean that all software we wrote would last forever. In practice, it is wise to avoid machine- and compiler-dependent aspects whenever we can, but, unfortunately, sometimes we cannot. This applies in particular to interactive graphics software, which, after all, is rather closely related to the hardware that is being used. Many important subjects in this book are system-independent, but some are not. In the last sentence, the rather vague term 'system' is used for the combination of the computer and the compiler that we are using. We shall present and discuss C programs running on the IBM PC or IBM PS/2. This machine, or one compatible with it, should have a color graphics adapter (CGA), an enhanced graphics adapter (EGA or VGA), or a Hercules graphics adapter (HGA). The resolutions used with these adapters are 640 × 200, 640 × 350, and 720 × 348, respectively. If you use essentially different hardware, you will probably not be able to run the programs in this book exactly as they are printed. However, many ideas and basic principles will be applicable to your situation, so you may regard my implementation of them on the IBM PC as just an example of how it can be done.

We shall use Turbo C throughout this book. If you want to use another C compiler for the IBM PC, some low-level routines may have to be modified, but it is most unlikely that such modifications should present serious difficulties.

This book uses the C programming language without explaining it. If you want to know more about it than you know at the moment you may try my book *C for Programmers*. (For more advanced programming techniques my book *Programs and Data Structures in C* may be useful, but the latter is no good if you are unfamiliar with C).

The C language is notorious for its pitfalls. This is mainly due to the absence of type checking and type conversion in situations where we would expect them. For example, if the first line of a function definition reads

```
double f(x) double x;
```

then the call $f(1)$ is incorrect because the integer argument 1 will not be converted to double-precision floating-point type. The call $f(1.0)$ would have been correct, since the constant 1.0 has the required type. What makes matters worse is that no type checking will take place in this case, so the compiler will accept this call, and during program execution we will obtain incorrect results. To overcome this type of trouble, the ANSI C Standards Committee has proposed a means of specifying parameter types in such a way that the compiler can perform the checks and conversions that we want. This implies a deviation from the original C language, defined by Kernighan and Ritchie (K & R) in *The C Programming Language*, so we might fear that adopting the ANSI standard might lead to all kinds of portability problems. Fortunately, many C compilers accept both the style of K & R and the proposed ANSI standard. An example of such a compiler is the one developed by Borland International, called *Turbo C*. In the Turbo C User's Guide much attention is paid to these two styles of programming. In Borland's terminology, the original K & R programs are said to be written in the *classic* style, to be distinguished from the *modern* style of the ANSI standard. Being a great admirer of K & R, I was very pleased with this terminology. The original C language really deserves the positive qualification 'classic', and I would be angry if it had been called 'obsolete'. On the other hand, we should not close our eyes to the fact that the C language is becoming very popular, which means that there are a great many beginners for whom a little help from the compiler in error checking would be extremely useful. Let us use an example to see what it is all about. In the classic style we can write:

```
/* CLASSIC */
double f();                    /* Declaration of f */

main()
{ printf("%3.1f", f(2.0));
}

double f(x) double x;  /* Definition of f  */
{ return 3.0 * x;
}
```

We must not replace 2.0 with 2 in this program, for that would not give the required output 6.0 but, instead, some incorrect value. In the modern style, we can write:

```
/* MODERN */
double f(double x);     /* Function prototype */

main()
{ printf("%3.1f", f(2.0));
}

double f(double x)      /* Function definition */
{ return 3.0 * x;
}
```

The way function $f$ is declared at the beginning of the program is an ANSI extension known as a *function prototype*. It tells the compiler not only (as a function declaration does in the classic style) that function $f$ returns a value of type *double*, but also that it expects an argument of that type. A compiler (that accepts the modern style) will check this and, if the argument has a different type, either give an error message or convert the given type to the type that is required.

Turbo C accepts both of the above programs CLASSIC and MODERN. If in the latter we write $f(2)$, then the *int* value 2 will be automatically converted to type *double*, as if we had written 2.0. In this extremely simple example, it may not be clear that function prototypes are useful. We should realize, however, that in large and complex programs, such as we shall be discussing in this book, type-conversion errors may take us several hours to find them if the compiler does not offer any help.

Large programs are usually split up into several modules. If we apply this modular approach to our simple example, the situation may be as follows:

Module 1:

```
/* MODERN */
double f(double x);   /* Function prototype */

main()
{ printf("%3.1f", f(2.0));
}
```

Module 2:

```
double f(double x)
{ return 3.0 * x;
}
```

When the compiler is dealing with module 1, then without the function prototype it would have no information about the definition of function $f$ (that is, the function itself), so this is a more obvious case where the function prototype is useful. It should also be noted that not only the *types* of function arguments but also their number are worthwhile to check. If in module 1 we replace $f(2.0)$ with $f()$, or with $f(2.0, 3.0, 4.0)$, the compiler will give an error message because the function prototype says that there should be exactly one argument. This would not be possible if we had replaced the function prototype with the line

```
double f();
```

which conforms to the classic style. In that case, the compiler would not complain, but there would be serious trouble during the execution of the compiled and linked program.

Users of Turbo C Version 1.0 who write their programs in the classic style are punished for this if they do not distinguish very carefully between the types *float* and *double*. Traditionally, function arguments of type *float* are 'widened' to type *double*. In this way, any incompatibility between *float* and *double* is resolved, for even if parameters are specified as *float*, the function in question will expect the corresponding arguments to be of type *double*. Thus, the normal convention is that internally both arguments and parameters have type *double* whenever they have floating-point type. Unfortunately, Turbo C Version 1.0 deviates from this principle, and takes the types of floating-point parameters and arguments very literally. This means that in the classic style we run into trouble if we combine a parameter of type *float* with a floating-point *constant* because floating-point constants are always of type *double*. With the modern style, there are no such troubles, for the function prototypes prescribe how arguments are to be converted into the type of the corresponding parameters. This seemed to me one of the most pressing arguments in favor of the modern style, especially as I did not know then that this was only a temporary problem. When I received Turbo C Version 1.5 (see also Section 4.3), I found that the compiler had been corrected, so that users of the classic style can now safely combine *float* arguments with *double* parameters and vice versa. Still, the modern style is advantageous to those users who have been lax in updating their compiler (and it would not surprise me if there were a great many of them). Finally, a function with *float* parameters, when written in the modern style, gives object code that is more efficient than that of the corresponding program in the classic style, because in the modern style the arguments need not be widened to type *double* and then 'narrowed' to type *float* again. You can notice the difference by compiling the following two functions separately:

```
void f(float x) { }      /* Modern  */

void f(x) float x; { }  /* Classic */
```

With Turbo C Version 1.5 and generating 8088 code for the 'huge' memory model, the lengths of the object modules are 143 and 188 bytes, respectively, so the modern style leads to more compact code.

Our discussion of function prototypes is not complete yet. First, parameter names may be omitted, so instead of

```
double f(float x);
```

we may write

```
double f(float);
```

However, the former form will often be preferred because the names of the parameters usually give us some idea what the function is about. Second, the keyword *void* may be useful. If function *f* has no parameters at all, we can write

```
double f(void);
```

This line will cause the compiler to give us an error message if we call function *f* with arguments. If, instead, we use the classic-style declaration

```
double f();
```

then the compiler will admit any number of arguments and not report any errors as far as that number is concerned, so the keyword *void* is really useful here.

We also need the keyword *void* to indicate that the function returns no value. We then write *void* (instead of *double*) in front of the function name, as in

```
void p(int i);

main()
{ p(3);
}

void p(int i)
{ printf("%d", i);
}
```

Omitting *void* in the first line (the function prototype) would result in a syntax error. If we have used it on this line, we have to use it also in the function definition itself, for otherwise the compiler would assume the function to return an *int* value (as required in the original C language defined in K & R), which would contradict the function prototype. This means that we could have omitted the second occurrence of *void* in this program, if, at the same time, we had replaced the first occurrence of it with *int*. As function *p* does not contain a return statement, the above solution is much nicer.

Turbo C allows us to use a classic-style function definition even if it is preceded by a function prototype, so we may write, for example,

```
int f(float x);   /* Modern function prototype   */
...
int f(x) float x; /* Classic function definition */
{ ...
}
```

In this case, error checking and argument conversion will take place the same way as in

```
int f(float x);   /* Modern function prototype */
...
int f(float x)    /* Modern function definition */
{ ...
}
```

Mixing classic and modern style is not particularly elegant. If we use the modern style consistently, we can simply write each function prototype as an exact copy of the first line of the corresponding function definition, except for the final semicolon, which occurs in the function prototype but must be omitted in the function definition. We therefore prefer the second of the above two forms to the first, and, from now on, we will consistently use the modern style.

We should be aware that in Turbo C we are using function prototypes as soon as we use standard header files, such as, for example, the well-known file *math.h*, included by the program line

```
#include <math.h>
```

With classic-style C compilers, the function *atan* is declared in this file as

```
double atan();
```

but in Turbo C we find the function prototype

```
double atan(double x);
```

in this file. By including *math.h* we implicitly include this function prototype in our own program, and the same applies to other header files, so in fact every Turbo C user uses function prototypes, possibly without knowing it. As for the function *atan*, a consequence of all this is that we may write

```
pi = 4.0 * atan(1);
```

instead of

```
pi = 4.0 * atan(1.0);
```

to compute an approximation of the value $\pi$, since the Turbo C compiler will convert the integer 1 to double precision floating point. However, for reasons of portability, it is wise to use the latter form rather than the former.

It might be considered a drawback that adopting the modern style prevents our programs from being accepted by compilers that require only classic-style programs. I have switched to the modern style myself only after considering the matter very carefully. After all, I have written five books (one in Dutch and four in English) that use the classic style throughout, and I would have preferred uniformity in style. So I first tried to stick to the classic style, but considering all that we have been discussing in this section I abandoned that idea, and decided to switch to the modern style. If you want to do the same, I would advise you to be consistent. Again, Turbo C can assist us in this by giving error messages if we forget some function prototype. In the 'integrated environment', we do this by selecting *Options*, then *Compiler*, then *Errors*, and finally *Less common errors*. Here the options *Call to function with no prototype* and *No declaration for function* are to be switched on. Incidentally, I have switched on most other options of the menus *Less common errors* and *Common errors* as well, for they include such useful things as signaling that a variable has been defined but is never used.

A function prototype is in fact a function declaration that is more complete than it would be in the classic style. This means that, like classic function declarations, we can group them together, and even combine them with program variables, such as $x$ in

```
float x, f(int i, char ch), g(void);
```

This line is equivalent to the three lines

```
float x;
float f(int i, char ch);
float g(void);
```

It should also be remembered that if in some program module we define a function in the modern style, and, in the same module, all calls to that function occur only *after* its definition, then a separate function prototype would be superfluous. Here is an example:

```
float f(float x) /* Function definition in modern style */
{ return x * x + x + 1;
}

main()
{ printf("%f", f(1))
}
```

Thanks to the modern style, the *int* argument 1 will be converted to type float, even though there is not a separate function prototype for $f$. Therefore, whenever I emphasize the general desirability of using function prototypes, I do not include cases like this, where the function definition already performs the task of a function prototype.

If you take my advice about instructing the Turbo C compiler to give messages in the case of missing function prototypes, then obviously you had better not omit such prototypes. This also applies to 'standard' functions such as *printf* and *exit*. The prototypes for such functions are included in header files. Thus, whenever we are using the function *printf* (which will almost always be the case), we begin the program with the line

```
#include <stdio.h>
```

Similarly, the function *exit* is declared in the header file *process.h*. It will now be clear why there are so many include-lines in the programs in this book. Recall that in the classic style we need not include a header file for functions that return an *int* value or no value at all. We now have to do this, but the extra amount of work is well spent, in particular if we sometimes suffer from the human habit of making mistakes. For example, with the modern style and the header file *stdio.h* included, the incorrect statement

```
printf('A');
```

will produce a clear error message, while in the classic style this serious error of writing 'A' instead of "A" would cause a very nasty problem during execution time, due to the fact that the ASCII value of 'A' (65) would be used as the begin address of a 'string' to be printed.

So much for the Turbo C compiler and language aspects. As there is much program text in this book, I thought it a good idea to discuss this important point in detail before we turn to the programs themselves, which you may perhaps like better than the present section.

## 3.2  CYLINDERS AND PRISMS

We will now consider some rather simple programs that produce files to be read by program D3D. The first is CYLINDER. We have dealt with the user's aspects of this program in Section 2.2, and we shall now have a look at the program text so that you will be able to write similar programs yourself.

```c
/* CYLINDER: Program to generate a cylinder
*/
#include <stdio.h>
#include <math.h>
#include <ctype.h>
#include <process.h>
main()
{ FILE *fp;
  char ch, str[50];
  float diam, r, h, delta, alpha, pi, rcos, rsin, half;
  int i, i1, n;
  pi = 4*atan(1.0);
  do
  { printf("Direction of axis? (X/Y/Z) ");
    ch = getchar(); ch = toupper(ch);
  } while (ch != 'X' && ch != 'Y' && ch != 'Z');
  printf("Diameter? "); scanf("%f", &diam); r = diam/2;
  printf("Altitude? "); scanf("%f", &h); half = h/2;
  printf("Number of polygon edges? "); scanf("%d", &n);
  printf("Name of output file? "); scanf("%s", str);
  fp = fopen(str, "w");
  if (fp == NULL) {printf("File problem"); exit(1);}
  delta = 2 * pi / n;
  for (i=1; i<=n; i++)
  { alpha = i * delta;
    rcos = r * cos(alpha); rsin = r * sin(alpha);
    if (ch == 'Z')
    { fprintf(fp, "%d %f %f %f\n", i, rcos, rsin, half);
      fprintf(fp, "%d %f %f %f\n", i+n, rcos, rsin, -half);
    } else
    if (ch == 'X')
    { fprintf(fp, "%d %f %f %f\n", i, half, rcos, rsin);
      fprintf(fp, "%d %f %f %f\n", i+n, -half, rcos, rsin);
    } else   /* ch == 'Y' */
    { fprintf(fp, "%d %f %f %f\n", i, rsin, half, rcos);
      fprintf(fp, "%d %f %f %f\n", i+n, rsin, -half, rcos);
    }
  }
  fprintf(fp, "Faces:\n");
  for (i=1; i<=n; i++)
    fprintf(fp, "%d%s", i,
    i == n ? ".\n" : i%10 ? " " : "\n");
  for (i=1; i<=n; i++)
    fprintf(fp, "%d%s", 2*n+1-i,
    i == n ? ".\n" : i%10 ? " " : "\n");
  for (i=1; i<=n; i++)
  { i1 = i==n ? 1 : i+1;
    fprintf(fp, "%d %d %d %d.\n", i, i+n, i1+n, i1);
  }
  fclose(fp);
}
```

Recall that we use a regular polygon instead of a circle as the base, which means that we are in fact dealing with a prism instead of a cylinder. This means that we can use this program not only for a cylinder but also for a prism, as long as its base is a regular polygon. This is demonstrated in Fig. 3.1, which shows how the vertices are numbered.

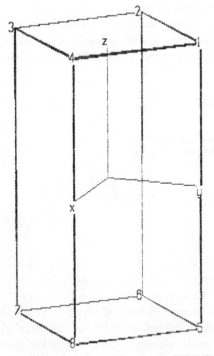

*Fig. 3.1 Prism as output of program CYLINDER*

A program statement such as

```
fprintf(fp, "%d%s", i,
i == n ? ".\n" : i%10 ? " " : "\n");
```

may not be immediately clear. It contains a nested conditional expression of the form

```
ppp ? aaa : qqq ? bbb : ccc
```

which associates as follows:

```
ppp ? aaa : (qqq ? bbb : ccc)
```

With some more program text we can instead use a conditional statement and increase program readability; in the above example this would lead to

```
if (i == n) fprintf(fp, "%d.\n", i); else
if (i % 10 != 0) fprintf(fp, "%d ", i); else
                 fprintf(fp, "%d\n", i);
```

Thus, after printing $i$ we give a period and a newline character if $i$ is equal to $n$; if not, then we give a space, except if $i$ is a multiple of 10, in which case we give a newline character. Both in the original form and in this extended version we will have at most ten vertex numbers on a line.

The rest of the program text will probably be clear, if it is considered in connection with Fig. 3.1. Remember that the vertex numbering should be clear in the first place if you want to understand a program like this or write a similar program of your own.

Here is a demonstration of how the prism of Fig. 3.1 can be obtained:

```
cylinder
Direction of axis? (X/Y/Z) z
Diameter? 10
Altitude? 15
Number of polygon edges? 4
Name of output file? fig3.1
```

We then type

```
d3d fig3.1
```

using command $M$ to indicate that we want the vertex numbers and the axes to be displayed and the entire screen to be used, and then command $P$ to print the result as shown in Fig. 3.1. Note that the sides of the bottom and the top squares are chords of the circles that would be approximated if a large number of edges had been chosen. In these squares the diagonals (not the sides) have the length 10 of the 'diameter' given above.

As file FIG3.1 is very small, we may as well have a look at it:

```
1 -0.000000  5.000000  7.500000
5 -0.000000  5.000000 -7.500000
2 -5.000000 -0.000000  7.500000
6 -5.000000 -0.000000 -7.500000
3  0.000000 -5.000000  7.500000
7  0.000000 -5.000000 -7.500000
4  5.000000  0.000001  7.500000
8  5.000000  0.000001 -7.500000
Faces:
1 2 3 4.
8 7 6 5.
1 5 6 2.
2 6 7 3.
3 7 8 4.
4 8 5 1.
```

### 3.3   CONES AND PYRAMIDS

Program CONE produces a cone approximated by a pyramid, which is similar to our approximation of a cylinder by a prism, as we did in the previous section.

```
/* CONE: Generating a cone.
*/
#include <math.h>
#include <stdio.h>
#include <process.h>
main()
```

```
{ FILE *fp;
  int n, i;
  float diam, r, h, delta, alpha, x, y, pi;
  char str[50];
  pi = 4.0 * atan(1.0);
  printf("Diameter of base circle? "); scanf("%f", &diam);

  r = diam/2;
  printf("Altitude? "); scanf("%f", &h);
  printf("Number of polygon edges? ");
  scanf("%d", &n);
  printf("Name of output file? "); scanf("%s", str);
  delta = 2*pi/n;
  fp = fopen(str, "w");
  if (fp == NULL) {printf("File problem"); exit(1);}
  for (i=1; i <= n; i++)
  { alpha = i * delta;
    x = r * cos(alpha); y = r *.sin(alpha);
    fprintf(fp, "%2d %f %f %f\n", i, x, y, 0.0);
  }
  fprintf(fp, "%2d %f %f %f\n", n+1, 0.0, 0.0, h);
  fprintf(fp, "Faces:\n");
  for (i=n; i>=1; i--) fprintf(fp, "%3d%s", i,
    (i==1 ? ".\n" : (i%10 == 1 ? "\n" : "")));
  for (i=1; i<=n; i++)
  fprintf(fp, "%2d %2d %2d.\n",
    i, (i == n ? 1 : i+1), n+1);
  fclose(fp);
}
```

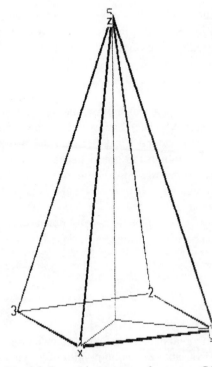

*Fig. 3.2 Pyramid as output of program CONE*

Here is a demonstration of this program to generate a file that program D3D can then read to produce Fig. 3.2:

```
Diameter of base circle? 10
Altitude? 15
Number of polygon edges? 4
Name of output file? fig3.2
```

Not all vertex numbers in Fig. 3.2 are printed in a clear way because the letters $x$, $y$, and $z$ near the end of the three positive axes are displayed later than these numbers: on the video screen the $x$, $y$, $z$ partially overwrite the vertex numbers 4, 1, and 5, respectively. We do not often display vertex numbers in the printed version, and if we do we can prevent the axes from being included; in that case the letters $x$, $y$, $z$ will not be printed either so that all vertex numbers will appear undamaged.

For the sake of completeness, here are the contents of file FIG3.2:

```
1 -0.000000 5.000000 0.000000
2 -5.000000 -0.000000 0.000000
3 0.000000 -5.000000 0.000000
4 5.000000 0.000001 0.000000
5 0.000000 0.000000 15.000000
Faces:
4 3 2 1.
1 2 5.
2 3 5.
3 4 5.
4 1 5.
```

Of course, it would be ridiculous to write a program only to generate this very simple file. However, if we wanted a more realistic approximation of a cone, as shown in Section 2.2, then program CONE would really be useful.

### 3.4   TRADITIONAL APPROXIMATION OF A SPHERE

In Section 2.2 we have used two ways of approximating a sphere, namely with program SPHERE and with file SPH80.DAT. The former will be the subject of this section. With program SPHERE we have $m$ horizontal slices between the two poles and $n$ lines of longitude, which are large circles through the poles. Instead of using $m = 10$ and $n = 20$ as we did in Section 2.2, we had better use an example with much smaller values, so that the vertex numbers can be printed clearly. With $m = 4$ and $n = 8$, program SPHERE, followed by D3D, gives the result shown in Fig. 3.3.

The method we are using is based on the well-known relations between rectangular coordinates $x$, $y$, $z$ and the spherical coordinates $R$, $\theta$, $\varphi$ for all points on the surface of a sphere with radius $R$ and center O:

$$x = R \sin \varphi \cos \theta$$
$$y = R \sin \varphi \sin \theta$$
$$z = R \cos \varphi$$

Lines of latitude (lying in horizontal planes) are obtained by taking $\varphi$ constant and $\theta$ variable; similarly, with constant $\theta$ and variable $\varphi$ we obtain lines of longitude (which are great circles through the poles).

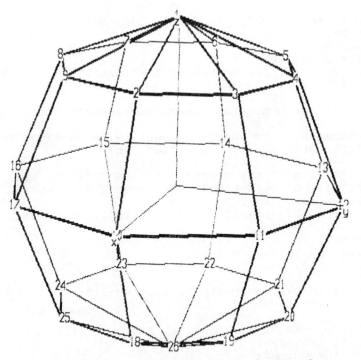

*Fig. 3.3 Sphere approximation with m = 4 and n = 8*

In program SPHERE, we use an integer variable $i$, which runs from 0 to $m$, and we number the vertices from top to bottom as follows:

$i = 0$ (north pole): 1

$i = 1$ (first line of latitude): 2, 3, ..., $n+1$

$i = 2$ (second line of latitude): $n+2$, $n+3$, ..., $2n+1$

$i = 3$ (third line of latitude): $2n+2$, $2n+3$, ..., $3n+1$

· · ·

$i = m-1$ (last line of latitude):

$$(m-2)n+2, (m-2)n+3, ..., (m-1)n+1$$

$i = m$ (south pole): $(m-1)n+2$

As approximating flat faces we have triangles near the poles and quadrangles everywhere else. (More specifically, these quadrangles are *trapezoids*, which means that they have two parallel sides.) With all this information (including Fig. 3.3) program SPHERE should be clear.

```
/* SPHERE: m slices, n points on each circle
*/
#include <stdio.h>
#include <math.h>
#include <process.h>
main()
{ FILE *fp;
  int i, j, m, n, nr, next, southpole;
```

```c
    double r, theta, phi, pi, delphi, deltheta,
      rsinphi, rcosphi, x, y, z;
    char str[30];
    pi = 4 * atan(1.0);
    printf("Enter m, the number of horizontal slices: ");
    scanf("%d", &m);
    printf(
"\nThere will be n points on each horizontal circle.\n");
    printf(
"It is recommended to choose n about twice as large as m.");
    printf("\nEnter n: "); scanf("%d", &n);
    delphi = pi/m; deltheta = 2*pi/n;
    printf("Radius of the sphere: "); scanf("%lf", &r);
    printf("Name of output file: "); scanf("%s", str);
    fp = fopen(str, "w");
    if (fp == NULL) {printf("File problem"); exit(1);}
    /* Vertex numbering:
        i=0:   1
        i=1:   2, 3, ..., n+1
        i=2:   n+2, n+3, ..., 2n+1
            ...
        i=m-1: (m-2)n+2, (m-2)n+3, ..., (m-1)n+1
        i=m:   (m-1)n+2
    */
    fprintf(fp, "%d %f %f %f\n", 1, 0.0, 0.0, r);   /* i = 0 */
    for (i=1; i<m; i++)
    { phi = i * delphi;
      rcosphi = r * cos(phi); rsinphi = r * sin(phi);
      for (j=0; j<n; j++)
      { nr = (i-1) * n + j + 2;
        theta = j * deltheta;
        x = rsinphi * cos(theta);
        y = rsinphi * sin(theta);
        z = rcosphi;
        fprintf(fp, "%d %f %f %f\n", nr, x, y, z);
      }
    }
    fprintf(fp, "%d %f %f %f\n", (m-1)*n+2, 0.0, 0.0, -r);
                                            /* i = m */
    fprintf(fp, "Faces:\n");
    for (j=2; j<=n+1; j++)
      fprintf(fp, "%d %d %d.\n", 1, j, (j<n+1 ? j+1 : 2));
    for (i=1; i<m-1; i++)
    { nr = (i-1) * n;
      for (j=2; j<=n+1; j++)
      { next = (j < n+1 ? j+1 : 2);
        fprintf(fp, "%d %d %d %d.\n",
                    nr+j, nr+n+j, nr+n+next, nr+next);
      }
    }
    southpole = (m-1)*n+2; nr = (m-2)*n;
    for (j=2; j<=n+1; j++)
      fprintf(fp, "%d %d %d.\n",
                  nr+j, southpole, (j<n+1 ? nr+j+1 : nr+2));
    fclose(fp);
}
```

## 3.5   REGULAR POLYHEDRA

A *polyhedron* is a solid whose bounding faces are polygons. If all sides of a polygon have the same length and if all the interior angles are equal the polygon is called *regular*. Analogously, a *polyhedron* is said to be *regular* if all its bounding faces are identical regular polygons. There are only five regular polyhedra, also called *Platonic solids*. They are shown in Fig. 3.4. Their main characteristics are listed below:

| Polyhedron | Faces | Edges | Vertices |
|---|---|---|---|
| Tetrahedron | 4 | 6 | 4 |
| Hexahedron (cube) | 6 | 12 | 8 |
| Octahedron | 8 | 12 | 6 |
| Dodecahedron | 12 | 30 | 20 |
| Icosahedron | 20 | 30 | 12 |

As an aside, it should be mentioned that these numbers satisfy Euler's theorem, which says that for any polyhedron we have:

```
Faces + Vertices = Edges + 2
```

Figure 3.4 has been produced by program D3D. It shows the five polyhedra in the same order as in the above table. For the dodecahedron and the icosahedron, shown in the bottom row, I have used separate programs to generate the object files. These programs are listed in Sections 3.5.4 and 3.5.5. Let us now have a look at the five regular polyhedra one by one.

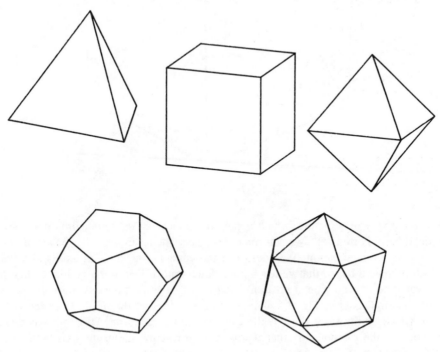

*Fig. 3.4 The five regular polyhedra: tetrahedron, hexahedron, octahedron; dodecahedron, icosahedron*

### 3.5.1  Tetrahedron

Although a tetrahedron has only four faces (which are equilateral triangles) drawing a 3D view of it is not a trivial matter. The easiest way of constructing it is to derive it from a cube, as shown in Fig. 3.5. Here the faces are inserted with command $F$, followed by the following four lines to define the four triangular faces:

```
1  3  6.
3  8  6.
1  6  8.
1  8  3.
```

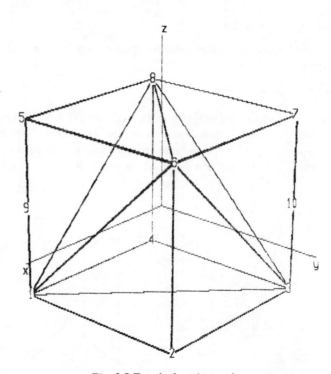

*Fig. 3.5 Tetrahedron in a cube*

This is not a very nice picture, which is due to the fact that the tetrahedron does not have a horizontal base. Fortunately, we can rotate an object about any axis (by means of command $T$) to improve this situation. We could use the edge 1-3 as such an axis and revolve the tetrahedron toward us, so that vertex 6 goes down until it lies in the $xy$-plane; then triangle 1-3-6 would be in a horizontal position. Actually, I have used the axis through the points 9 and 10, also indicated in Fig. 3.5. This line passes through the origin O of the coordinate system, which, at the same time, is the center of the tetrahedron. This center is therefore a fixed point of the rotation; in other words, after a rotation about the axis 9-10, the center of the tetrahedron still lies in O, which, for example, makes it easy for us to tell how to translate it in a next step (for example, in making Fig. 3.4). The angle $\alpha$ through which the rotation is to take place is shown in Fig. 3.6. It is the angle at vertex 11 of the right triangle with vertices 11, 2, and 6. Its opposite side (cube edge 2-6) has length 1, and its adjacent side (a half diagonal of a cube face) has length $\frac{1}{2}\sqrt{2}$. Thus, we have

$$\tan \alpha = 1/\tfrac{1}{2}\sqrt{2} = \sqrt{2}$$

Using a simple calculator, we find

$$\alpha = \arctan \sqrt{2} = 54.73561°$$

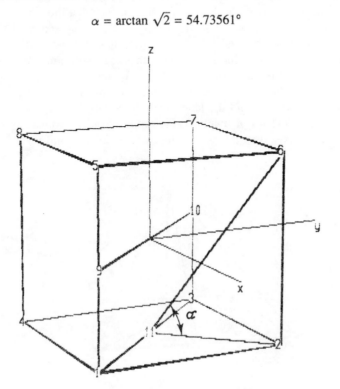

*Fig. 3.6 Angle $\alpha$ and axis 9-10, used in rotation*

We need this angle to perform the rotation we want; after deleting the points 5, 7, 2, 4 we then obtain the tetrahedron shown as the first object in Fig. 3.4.

### 3.5.2 Hexahedron

To be consistent with the other polyhedra, we are now employing the word *hexahedron* for what we normally call a *cube*. Of course, we already know how to construct a cube with D3D, so we need not discuss this in detail once more.

Recall that we can use D3D to build two objects separately and then load them one by one, applying a translation to one of them in order to place them beside each other, as we have discussed in Section 2.2. This is the way we can compose Fig. 3.4, building the five objects one by one and combining them only after we have obtained five object files. In each of these five files the center of the object is located in the origin O of the coordinate system. In this way we can use O as the fixed point in scaling operations, in such a way that the object to be scaled merely expands or shrinks, with its center remaining in its position.

Thus, we had better perform any scaling immediately after loading the object in question from its object file, and only then perform a translation.

### 3.5.3   Octahedron

As Fig. 3.4 illustrates, an octahedron has two vertices on either side of a square. Let us assign vertex numbers as shown in Fig. 3.7, and let us say that the sides of square 1-2-3-4 have length 1. Point 7 is the center of the square (and also the center of the octahedron), and point 8 is the midpoint of edge 4-1. Since point 5 lies on a perpendicular through point 7, all we need to know is the distance $h$ between these two points. We can now use the fact that all vertices of a regular polyhedron have the same distance to its center. Thus, for example, triangle 1-7-5 in Fig. 3.7 is an isosceles right triangle, so point 7 is just as far from point 5 as it is from point 1, and the latter distance is half the diagonal of square 1-2-3-4 (with sides of length 1). Thus, if point 7 is the origin of our coordinate system and point 5 lies on the positive $z$-axis, then the $z$-coordinate of the points 5 and 6 are $\frac{1}{2}\sqrt{2}$ and $-\frac{1}{2}\sqrt{2}$.

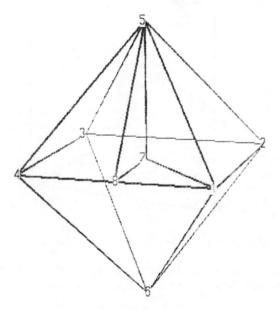

*Fig. 3.7 Octahedron*

It is a good idea to check that the faces of the object thus constructed are really equilateral triangles. We therefore first apply the Pythagorean theorem to triangle 8-7-5 to find the length of line segment 8-5. After squaring the lengths of the sides 8-7 and 7-5, the sum of these squares is

$$(\tfrac{1}{2})^2 + (\tfrac{1}{2}\sqrt{2})^2 \;=\; 3/4$$

According to Pythagoras, this is also the square of the length of line segment 8-5. We add the squared length of line segment 8-1 to it, to find

$$3/4 + (1/2)^2 = 1$$

which, again according to Pythagoras, must be the length of the edge 1-5. Thus, all edges of the object have length 1, which means that all eight bounding triangles of our object are equilateral and that the object is indeed an octahedron.

As we have $\frac{1}{2}\sqrt{2} \approx 0.707107$, the following object file can be used for the octahedron of Fig. 3.7 (without points 7 and 8):

```
1     0.5   0.5   0.000000
2    -0.5   0.5   0.000000
3    -0.5  -0.5   0.000000
4     0.5  -0.5   0.000000
5     0.0   0.0   0.707107
6     0.0   0.0  -0.707107
Faces:
  1 2 5.
  2 3 5.
  3 4 5.
  4 1 5.
  1 6 2.
  2 6 3.
  3 6 4.
  4 6 1.
```

### 3.5.4 Dodecahedron

As mentioned at the beginning of Section 3.5, a dodecahedron has 12 faces, 30 edges, and 20 vertices. Each of the 12 faces is a (regular) *pentagon*, that is, a polygon with five equal sides. As we have seen already in Section 1.5, Fig. 1.12, a dodecahedron fits in a cube; we can use this characteristic to construct it.

Before using pentagons to construct a dodecahedron, let us first have a look at pentagons themselves. In Fig. 3.8 we have one whose center is E; let us say that the five vertices of the pentagon lie on a circle with radius 1 and whose center is point E.

Figure 3.8 shows several important angles. From these and from EG = $R$ = 1, we find:

$$BE = \cos 36°$$
$$BG = \sin 36°$$

The angle of 36° (= $\pi/5$ radians) is an interesting one, because we have

$$2 \times 36° = 72°$$
$$\tfrac{1}{2} \times 36° = 18°$$
$$72° + 18° = 90°$$

This enables us to write cos 36° as a simple expression, namely

$$\cos 36° = (1 + \sqrt{5})/4$$

As D. E. Knuth shows in *The Art of Computer Programming*, Vol. 1, Solution of Exercise 19 of Section 1.2.8, we can prove this by introducing $u$ and $v$, defined as $u = \cos 72°$, $v = \cos 36°$.

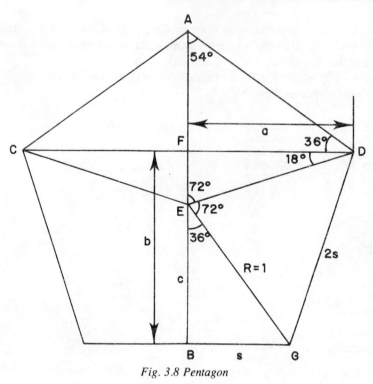

Fig. 3.8 Pentagon

Then we have

$$u = 2 \cos^2 36° - 1 = 2v^2 - 1$$
$$v = 1 - 2 \sin^2 18° = 1 - 2 \cos^2 72° = 1 - 2u^2$$

Hence

$$u + v = 2(v^2 - u^2) = 2(v + u)(v - u)$$

Dividing by $u + v$ gives

$$1 = 2(v - u) = 2\{v - (2v^2 - 1)\} = -4v^2 + 2v + 2$$

Thus we have to solve the quadratic equation

$$4v^2 - 2v - 1 = 0$$

which gives the desired result

$$v = (1 + \sqrt{5})/4$$

Actually, we will use the still more important constant

$$\tau = (1 + \sqrt{5})/2 = 1.6180339887\ldots$$

so that we have

$$\cos 36° = \tau/2$$

A nice characteristic of $\tau$ is that squaring it gives the same result as increasing it by 1:

$$\tau^2 = (1 + \sqrt{5})^2/4 = 1\tfrac{1}{2} + \tfrac{1}{2}\sqrt{5}$$

so we have

$$\tau^2 = \tau + 1 \tag{3.1}$$

Multiplying both sides of this equation by powers of $\tau$, we find

$$\tau^3 = \tau^2 + \tau$$
$$\tau^4 = \tau^3 + \tau^2$$
$$\tau^5 = \tau^4 + \tau^3$$

$$\ldots$$

Similarly, if we divide Eq. (3.1) by powers of $\tau$ we obtain

$$\tau = 1 + \tau^{-1}$$
$$1 = \tau^{-1} + \tau^{-2}$$
$$\tau^{-1} = \tau^{-2} + \tau^{-3}$$
$$\tau^{-2} = \tau^{-3} + \tau^{-4}$$

$$\ldots$$

Thus, each element of

$$\ldots, \tau^{-3}, \tau^{-2}, \tau^{-1}, 1, \tau, \tau^2, \tau^3 \ldots$$

is the sum of its two immediate predecessors.

It follows from all this that if we divide a line segment into two parts such that the larger part is $\tau$ times as long as the smaller part then the whole is $\tau$ times as long as the larger part. This principle is known as *golden section*.

Another important characteristic of $\tau$ is that any power of it can be written as $a\tau + b$, where $a$ and $b$ are integers:

$$\tau^2 = \tau + 1$$
$$\tau^3 = \tau^2 + \tau = 2\tau + 1$$
$$\tau^4 = \tau^3 + \tau^2 = 3\tau + 2$$
$$\tau^5 = \tau^4 + \tau^3 = 5\tau + 3$$
$$\tau^6 = \tau^5 + \tau^4 = 8\tau + 5$$

and so on. Also, we have:

$$\tau^{-1} = \tau - 1$$
$$\tau^{-2} = 1 - \tau^{-1} = 2 - \tau$$
$$\tau^{-3} = \tau^{-1} - \tau^{-2} = 2\tau - 3$$
$$\tau^{-4} = \tau^{-2} - \tau^{-3} = 5 - 3\tau$$
$$\tau^{-5} = \tau^{-3} - \tau^{-4} = 5\tau - 8$$

and so on.

Using Eq. (3.1), we can easily verify the identity

$$(a\tau + b)(a\tau - b - a) = a^2 - ab - b^2$$

which implies that (if $a$ and $b$ are not both zero) we have

$$\frac{1}{a\tau + b} = \frac{a\tau - b - a}{a^2 - ab - b^2}$$

Thus, any quotient $P(\tau)/Q(\tau)$, where $P(\tau)$ and $Q(\tau)$ are polynomials in $\tau$ with rational coefficients, can be written as a linear form $a\tau + b$, where $a$ and $b$ are rational numbers. This makes $\tau$ a nice constant to work with because if it occurs in complicated expressions we have a good chance of simplifying them.

All this may seem to be a digression from our subject (the pentagon), but it is not. For one thing, any two diagonals of a pentagon that intersect in an interior point divide each other according to the golden section! We will not use this, but, as Fig. 3.8 shows, if we draw some auxiliary lines in a pentagon, there are many angles of 36°, 72°, 18°, and 54° (= 36° + 18°). We can now write

$$c = \cos 36° = \tau/2$$
$$s = \sin 36° = \sqrt{(1 - c^2)} = \sqrt{(1 - \tau^2/4)} = \sqrt{\{1 - (\tau + 1)/4\}}$$
$$= \tfrac{1}{2}\sqrt{(3 - \tau)}$$
$$\cos 72° = 2c^2 - 1 = \tfrac{1}{2}\tau^2 - 1 = \tfrac{1}{2}(\tau + 1) - 1 = (\tau - 1)/2$$

and, using the letters A through F as indicated in Fig. 3.8, we have

$$AB = AE + EB = 1 + \cos 36° = 1 + \tau/2$$
$$EF = ED \times \cos 72° = (\tau - 1)/2$$
$$b = BF = BE + EF = \cos 36° + \cos 72° = \tau/2 + (\tau - 1)/2$$
$$= \tau - \tfrac{1}{2}$$
$$a = CF = FD = ED \times \sin 72° = 1 \times 2 \times \cos 36° \times \sin 36° = \tau s$$

(We simply keep in mind that we can replace $s$ with $\tfrac{1}{2}\sqrt{(3 - \tau)}$ in expressions such as $\tau s$.)

We now consider Fig. 3.9, which is a front view of a dodecahedron in a cube, as shown in Fig. 1.12 in perspective. Here AB, present also in Fig. 3.8, appears in its true length $1 + \tau/2$. It is the hypotenuse of the right triangle ABH, which we can use to compute the half edge $h$ of the cube. Using Pythagoras, we have:

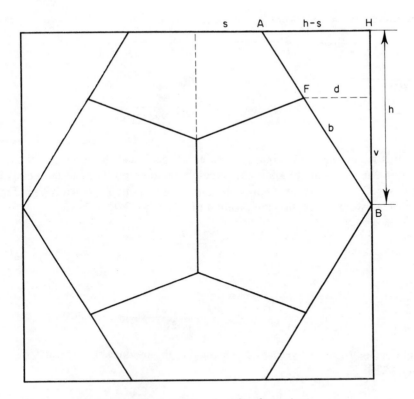

*Fig. 3.9 Dodecahedron in cube (front view)*

$$AH^2 + BH^2 = AB^2$$
$$(h - s)^2 + h^2 = (1 + \tau/2)^2$$
$$2h^2 - 2sh + s^2 = (1 + \tau/2)^2$$
$$2h^2 - 2sh + (3 - \tau)/4 = 1 + \tau + \tau^2/4$$
$$2h^2 - 2sh + (3 - \tau)/4 = 1 + \tau + (\tau + 1)/4$$
$$4h^2 - 4sh - 3\tau - 1 = 0$$
$$h = [4s + \sqrt{\{16s^2 + 16(3\tau + 1)\}}]/8$$
$$= [4s + \sqrt{\{4(3 - \tau) + 16(3\tau + 1)\}}]/8$$
$$= \{2s + \sqrt{(11\tau + 7)}\}/4$$

which we can still simplify by using

$$\tau^4 = 3\tau + 2$$
$$\tau^6 = 8\tau + 5$$

Thus we have

$$\sqrt{(11\tau + 7)} = \sqrt{(\tau^6 + \tau^4)} = \tau^2\sqrt{(\tau^2 + 1)} = (\tau + 1)\sqrt{(\tau + 2)}$$

which gives

$$h = \frac{2s + (\tau + 1)\sqrt{(\tau + 2)}}{4}$$

With this result, we know both the size of the cube and the positions of the points A and B in it. We also want to know the three-dimensional positions of the points C and D, shown in Fig. 3.8. They lie on a horizontal line through point F, shown both in Fig. 3.8 and in Fig. 3.9, so we will first find the position of F. In Fig. 3.9, we have

$$\frac{v}{b} = \frac{h}{\tau/2 + 1}$$

Thus

$$v = \frac{2bh}{\tau + 2} = \frac{2(\tau - 1/2)h}{\tau + 2} = (\tau - 1)h$$

(The latter equality can be verified by calculating the product of $\tau + 2$ and $\tau - 1$, and by using Eq. 3.1.)

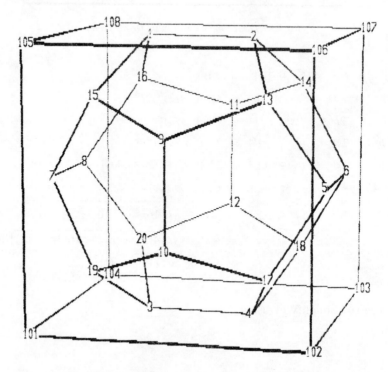

Fig. 3.10 Point numbering in dodecahedron and cube

Using both this expression for $v$ and

$$\frac{d}{v} = \frac{h - s}{h}$$

(see Fig. 3.9), we obtain

$$d = (\tau - 1)(h - s)$$

The positions of C and D (see Fig. 3.8) are now easy to find, since they lie on the line which is perpendicular to the plane of Fig. 3.9 and passes through F, and we have computed CF and DF above as $a = \tau s$.

Thanks to symmetry, all other vertices of the dodecahedron follow from those we have been discussing. Program DODECA shows this in detail; it generates an object file for both the dodecahedron and the cube, as displayed in Fig. 3.10. The $x$-, $y$-, and $z$-axes have been omitted in this illustration to avoid any additional complexity, but they have the usual directions, that is, they have the directions of the edges 103-102, 101-102, and 102-106, respectively, and the origin lies in the center of the cube. Vertex 2 in Fig. 3.10 corresponds to point A in Figs. 3.8 and 3.9, and so on. We can easily dispose of the cube by deleting the vertices in the range 101-108, if we want only the dodecahedron itself. This is the case, for example, if we want an object file to combine it with the other regular polyhedra, as shown in Fig. 3.4.

```
/* DODECA: This program constructs a dodecahedron and a cube
                in which it fits.
*/
#include <stdio.h>
#include <math.h>

main()
{ float s, a, h, v, d, tau;
    static float x[21], y[21], z[21]; /* Initially 0 */
    int i;
    FILE *fp;
    tau = (sqrt(5.0) + 1)/2;      /*  tau = 2 * cos(pi/5)  */
    /* Sometimes the letter phi is used instead of tau */
    s = sqrt(3 - tau)/2 ;         /* s = sin (pi/5)   */
    a = tau * s;
    h = (2*s+(tau+1)*sqrt(tau+2))/4;  /* Half edge of cube */
    v = (tau - 1) * h;
    d = (tau - 1) * (h - s);

    printf("The twelve faces of the dodecahedron are\n");
    printf("pentagons, each fitting in a circle with\n");
    printf("radius 1.\n");
    printf("The sides of these pentagons have length %f.\n",
            2*s);
    printf(
"The dodecahedron fits in a cube with edges of length");
        printf(" %f.\n", 2*h);
    x[5] = x[7] = s;
    x[6] = x[8] = -s;
    x[9] = x[10] = h;
```

```
      x[11] = x[12] = -h;
      x[13] = x[15] = x[17] = x[19] = a;
      x[14] = x[16] = x[18] = x[20] = -a;
      y[1] = y[3] = -s;
      y[2] = y[4] = s;
      y[5] = y[6] = h;
      y[7] = y[8] = -h;
      y[13] = y[14] = y[17] = y[18] = h-d;
      y[15] = y[16] = y[19] = y[20] = -(h-d);
      z[1] = z[2] = h;
      z[3] = z[4] = -h;
      z[9] = z[11] = s;
      z[10] = z[12] = -s;
      z[13] = z[14] = z[15] = z[16] = v;
      z[17] = z[18] = z[19] = z[20] = -v;
      fp = fopen("dodeca.dat", "w");
      for (i=1; i<=20; i++)
         fprintf(fp, "%3d %f %f %f\n", i, x[i], y[i], z[i]);

      /* The cube in which the dodecahedron fits will have the
         vertex numbers 101, 102, ..., 108:
      */
      fprintf(fp, "101 %f %f %f\n",   h, -h, -h);
      fprintf(fp, "102 %f %f %f\n",   h,  h, -h);
      fprintf(fp, "103 %f %f %f\n",  -h,  h, -h);
      fprintf(fp, "104 %f %f %f\n",  -h, -h, -h);
      fprintf(fp, "105 %f %f %f\n",   h, -h,  h);
      fprintf(fp, "106 %f %f %f\n",   h,  h,  h);
      fprintf(fp, "107 %f %f %f\n",  -h,  h,  h);
      fprintf(fp, "108 %f %f %f\n",  -h, -h,  h);

      fprintf(fp, "Faces:\n");
      fprintf(fp, " 1 15   9 13   2.\n");
      fprintf(fp, " 1   2 14 11 16.\n");
      fprintf(fp, " 5   6 14   2 13.\n");
      fprintf(fp, " 7 15   1 16   8.\n");
      fprintf(fp, "19 10   9 15   7.\n");
      fprintf(fp, "10 17   5 13   9.\n");
      fprintf(fp, "20   8 16 11 12.\n");
      fprintf(fp, "18 12 11 14   6.\n");
      fprintf(fp, " 3   4 17 10 19.\n");
      fprintf(fp, " 4 18   6   5 17.\n");
      fprintf(fp, " 3 20 12 18   4.\n");
      fprintf(fp, " 3 19   7   8 20.\n");
      /* The cube edges are entered as loose line segments:
      */
      fprintf(fp, "101 102.\n102 103.\n103 104.\n104 101.\n");
      fprintf(fp, "105 106.\n106 107.\n107 108.\n108 105.\n");
      fprintf(fp, "101 105.\n102 106.\n103 107.\n104 108.\n");
      fclose(fp);
   }
```

### 3.5.5  Icosahedron

As Fig. 3.11 shows, we can place an *icosahedron* in such a position that ten of its vertices are also the vertices of two horizontal pentagons. Let us refer to the remaining two vertices as the north pole (at the top) and the south pole (at the bottom), and let us use the term *axis* for the line through these poles. The center O of the icosahedron will be the origin of our coordinate system, and the axis of the icosahedron will coincide with the $z$-axis. The two pentagons just mentioned will have the same size as the bounding faces of the dodecahedron, discussed in Section 3.5.4. Thus, either of them has a circumradius 1, and the sides of the pentagons will have length $2s$, where

$$s = \sin 36°$$

Each side of our pentagons is also an edge of the icosahedron, so these edges, too, have length $2s$. As Fig. 3.11 shows, the lower horizontal pentagon can be derived from the upper one by both a rotation through $36°$ about the axis and a vertical translation. This means that the only remaining problem to be solved is to find the $z$-coordinates of the two pentagons and of the two poles. In Fig. 3.12 we find the same pentagon as the upper one in Fig. 3.11; instead of vertex numbers 2, 3, 4, 5, 6, we are now using the letters A, B, C, D, E. Point F is the center of pentagon ABCDE, O is the center of the entire icosahedron, N is the north pole, and M is the midpoint of CN. We now want to find $h$ and $r$, indicated in Fig. 3.12.

As NFC is a right triangle, we can apply the Pythagorean theorem to it to find the value of $h = $ FN, expressed in $s$ ($= \sin 36°$):

$$FN^2 = CN^2 - CF^2$$
$$h^2 = (2s)^2 - 1^2$$
$$h = \sqrt{(4s^2 - 1)}$$

Using $\tau = (1 + \sqrt{5})/2$ again (see Section 3.5.4), and also using

$$s = \tfrac{1}{2}\sqrt{(3 - \tau)}$$
$$s^2 = (3 - \tau)/4$$

we can express $h$ in $\tau$ as well:

$$h = \sqrt{(2 - \tau)} = \sqrt{(\tau^{-2})} = \tau^{-1} = \tau - 1$$

In order to find $r = $ ON, we observe that triangle NMO is similar to triangle NFC. Thus we have

$$\frac{s}{r} = \frac{h}{2s}$$

which gives

$$r = \frac{2s^2}{h} = \frac{(3 - \tau)/2}{\tau - 1} = \tau - \tfrac{1}{2}$$

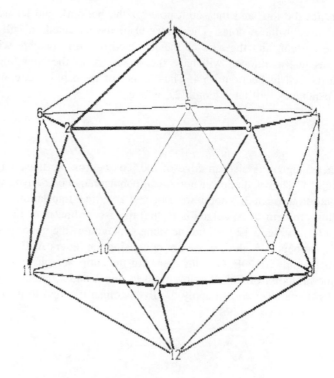

*Fig. 3.11 Point numbering in icosahedron*

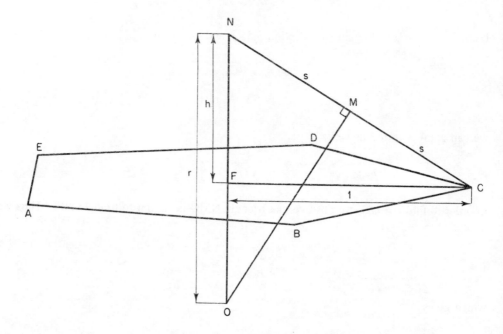

*Fig. 3.12 Pentagon and north pole of icosahedron*

The $z$-coordinate of all points in pentagon ABCDE is

$$r - h = (\tau - \tfrac{1}{2}) - (\tau - 1) = \tfrac{1}{2}$$

This means that the two horizontal pentagons lie a distance 1 apart; in other words, their distance is equal to the circumradius of the pentagons.

Referring to the vertex numbering shown in Fig. 3.11, we have found that the vertices 2, 3, 4, 5, 6 have 0.5 ($= r - h$) as their $z$-coordinates. Similarly, we have $z = -0.5$ for the vertices 7, 8, 9, 10, 11. The two poles, 1 and 12, have $z$-coordinates $r = \tau - \tfrac{1}{2}$ and $-r = -(\tau - \tfrac{1}{2})$, respectively, and for these two vertices we have $x = y = 0$. As for the $x$- and $y$-coordinates of the vertices 2, ..., 11, we use the fact that they lie on horizontal circles with radius 1. Thus, for appropriate angles $\alpha$, they are equal to $\cos \alpha$ and $\sin \alpha$, respectively. We will choose this angle $\alpha$ as follows:

| Vertex | $\alpha$ |
|--------|----------|
| 2 | $-36°$ |
| 3 | $36°$ |
| 4 | $108°$ |
| 5 | $180°$ |
| 6 | $252°$ |
| 7 | $0°$ |
| 8 | $72°$ |
| 9 | $144°$ |
| 10 | $216°$ |
| 11 | $288°$ |

All this is used in program ICOSA, listed below. It generates an object file that enables program D3D to produce Fig. 3.11.

```c
/* ICOSA: Icosahedron: a regular polyhedron with
            20 boundary faces, which are equilateral
            triangles.
*/
#include <stdio.h>
#include <math.h>
#define p(i, x, y, z) fprintf(fp,"%d %f %f %f\n",i,x,y,z)
#define face(i, j, k) fprintf(fp, "%d %d %d.\n", i, j, k)

main()
{ FILE *fp;
  int i;
  double s, pi, r, alpha, tau;
  pi = 4 * atan(1.0);
  tau = (sqrt(5.0) + 1)/2;  /* tau = 2 * cos(pi/5);        */
  s = sin(pi/5);            /* pi/5 radians = 36 degrees */
  r = tau - 0.5;
  printf("Ten of the twelve vertices of the icosahedron\n");
  printf(
"lie on two horizontal pentagons, either of which\n");
  printf("fits in a circle with radius 1.\n");
  printf("These two pentagons lie a distance 1 apart.\n");
  printf("The edges have length %f.\n", 2*s);
  printf(
"The icosahedron fits in a sphere with radius %f.\n", r);
  fp = fopen("icosa.dat", "w");
```

```
p(1, 0.0, 0.0, r); /* North pole */
for (i=0; i<5; i++)
{ alpha = -pi/5 + i * pi/2.5;
                        /* In degrees: -36 + i * 72 */
  p(2+i, cos(alpha), sin(alpha), 0.5);
}
for (i=0; i<5; i++)
{ alpha = i * pi/2.5;
  p(7+i, cos(alpha), sin(alpha), -0.5);
}
p(12, 0.0, 0.0, -r);   /* South pole */
fprintf(fp, "Faces:\n");
for (i=0; i<5; i++) face(1, 2+i, i<4 ? 3+i : 2);
for (i=0; i<5; i++) face(2+i, 7+i, i<4 ? 3+i : 2);
for (i=0; i<5; i++)
                face(7+i, i<4 ? 8+i : 7, i<4 ? i+3 : 2);
  for (i=0; i<5; i++) face(i+7, 12, i<4 ? i+8 : 7);
}
```

It should perhaps be mentioned that there is another way of constructing an icosahedron. This very elegant method is based on three mutually perpendicular rectangles, similar to the three parts that form the object shown in Fig. 2.22. In Fig. 3.11 we can use, for example, the rectangles

```
2-6-9-8,
1-4-12-11,
3-7-10-5
```

for this purpose. These are so-called *golden* rectangles: their sides are in the ratio $1 : \tau$. If we take these rectangles parallel to the axes of our coordinate system, then the position of the icosahedron will be different from the one shown in Fig. 3.11. It is strongly recommended to use this method as an exercise and to write an alternative program that generates an icosahedron.


## 3.6   SPHERE APPROXIMATION WITH 80 TRIANGLES

The five regular polyhedra have too few faces to be used as approximations of a sphere. However, we can use an icosahedron as a basis for another object that has 80 triangular faces. We have briefly discussed this object in Section 2.2; it is shown in Figs. 2.9 and 2.10.

As Fig. 3.13 shows, we can divide a triangle into four smaller triangles by using the midpoint of each side and connecting neighboring points. Applying this literally to the 20 equilateral triangles of an icosahedron would be no good, for then we would not really increase the number of planes in which all bounding faces lie.

Instead of using the midpoints D, E, F (see Fig. 3.13) themselves, we will use their central projections onto the surface of the sphere we want to approximate. Let this sphere have radius 1 and center O (the origin of the coordinate system). Then the vertices A, B, C of the large triangles lie at a distance 1 from O, but the points D, E, F lie at a somewhat smaller distance, $d$, from O. We will now extend the line segments OD, OE, OF (which have length $d$), to obtain OD', OE', OF', such that these latter three line segments have length 1. For example, we have

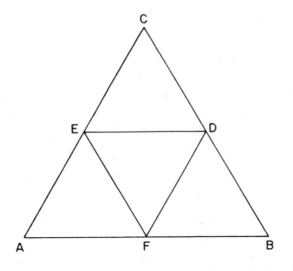

Fig. 3.13 Triangle divided into four smaller triangles

$$x_{D'} = x_D/d$$
$$y_{D'} = y_D/d$$
$$z_{D'} = z_D/d$$

Instead of the midpoints D, E, F, we will use D', E', F', and instead of the original triangle ABC we will use the four smaller triangles AF'E', F'BD', E'D'C, F'D'E'.

Program SPH80 is based on program ICOSA of Section 3.5.5. The same twelve vertices are computed first, but we now divide the coordinates by a factor $r$, in order to approximate a unit sphere (rather than a sphere with radius $r$). As each side of a large (equilateral) triangle is also a side of an adjacent triangle, we would generate each midpoint twice if we did not take special measures. We therefore keep track of all edges the midpoint of which we have computed, so that all midpoints will occur only once in the object file. The program text itself shows further details.

```
/* SPH80: Polyhedron with 80 triangular faces to
      approximate a sphere.
      It is based on an icosahedron, which is a regular
      polyhedron with 20 equilateral triangles as bounding
      faces. Instead of each of these triangles, four
      smaller triangles are used, which gives 20 x 4 = 80
      of these smaller triangles (not equilateral).
      For each equilateral triangle of the icosahedron
      the midpoints of its three sides are projected onto
      the sphere in which the icosahedron fits.
      We obtain the four smaller triangles by
      connecting neighboring points.
*/
```

```c
#include <stdio.h>
#include <math.h>
#include <process.h>

void point(int i, float x, float y, float z);
void subdivide(int A, int B, int C);
void storeface(int i, int j, int k);
void midpnt(int B, int C, int *pP, float x, float y,
                                            float z);

int npoints;
struct {float x, y, z;} pnt[43];

int nface=0;
struct {int i, j, k;} fc[80];

int nedge=0;
struct {int i, j, P;} edges[120];

FILE *fp;

main()
{ int i, l;
  double pi, r, alpha, tau;
  pi = 4 * atan(1.0);
  tau = (sqrt(5.0) + 1)/2;  /* tau = 2 * cos(pi/5)   */
  r = tau - 0.5;
  printf("A sphere (with radius 1) is approximated\n");
  printf("by an object with 80 triangular bounding\n");
  printf("faces. The results are written to the\n");
  printf(
  "object file SPH80.DAT (which can be read by D3D).\n");
  fp = fopen("SPH80.DAT", "w");
  point(1, 0.0, 0.0, 1.0); /* North pole */
  for (i=0; i<5; i++)
  { alpha = -pi/5 + i * pi/2.5;
                    /* In degrees: -36 + i * 72 */
    point(2+i, cos(alpha)/r, sin(alpha)/r, 0.5/r);
  }
  for (i=0; i<5; i++)
  { alpha = i * pi/2.5;
    point(7+i, cos(alpha)/r, sin(alpha)/r, -0.5/r);
  }
  point(12, 0.0, 0.0, -1.0); /* South pole */
  npoints = 12;
  for (i=0; i<5; i++) subdivide(1, 2+i, i<4 ? 3+i : 2);
  for (i=0; i<5; i++) subdivide(2+i, 7+i, i<4 ? 3+i : 2);
  for (i=0; i<5; i++)
            subdivide(7+i, i<4 ? 8+i : 7, i<4 ? i+3 : 2);
  for (i=0; i<5; i++) subdivide(i+7, 12, i<4 ? i+8 : 7);
  fprintf(fp, "Faces:\n");
  for (l=0; l<80; l++)
    fprintf(fp, "%d %d %d.\n", fc[l].i, fc[l].j, fc[l].k);
  fclose(fp);
}

void midpnt(int B, int C, int *pP, float x, float y,
                                            float z)
```

```
/*   Point (x, y, z) is midpoint of BC.
     If it is a new vertex, store it and write it to the
     object file, using a new vertex number. If not, find
     its vertex number.
     The vertex number is to be assigned to *pP anyway.
*/
{ int tmp, e;
  if (C < B) {tmp = B; B = C; C = tmp;}
  /* B, C in increasing order, for the sake of uniqueness */
  for (e=0; e<nedge; e++)
     if (edges[e].i == B && edges[e].j == C) break;
  if (e == nedge)   /* Not found, so we have a new vertex */
  { edges[e].i = B; edges[e].j = C;
    edges[e].P = *pP = ++npoints;
    nedge++;
    point(*pP, x, y, z);
  } else *pP = edges[e].P;
                 /* Edge BC has been dealt with before, so
                    the vertex is not new
                 */
}

void point(int i, float x, float y, float z)
{ fprintf(fp, "%d %f %f %f\n", i, x, y, z);
  pnt[i].x = x; pnt[i].y = y; pnt[i].z = z;
}

void subdivide(int A, int B, int C)
/* Divide triangle ABC into four smaller triangles
*/
{ float xP, yP, zP, xQ, yQ, zQ, xR, yR, zR;
  int P, Q, R;
  static float d = -1;
     /* d is equal to -1 only before the first call
        of this function; after this, d will have its
        correct value (between 0 and 1), namely the distance
        between any midpoint and the center of the sphere.
        We project all midpoints onto the sphere (with
        radius 1) by dividing their coordinates by d.
     */
  xP = (pnt[B].x + pnt[C].x)/2;
  yP = (pnt[B].y + pnt[C].y)/2;
  zP = (pnt[B].z + pnt[C].z)/2;

  xQ = (pnt[C].x + pnt[A].x)/2;
  yQ = (pnt[C].y + pnt[A].y)/2;
  zQ = (pnt[C].z + pnt[A].z)/2;

  xR = (pnt[A].x + pnt[B].x)/2;
  yR = (pnt[A].y + pnt[B].y)/2;
  zR = (pnt[A].z + pnt[B].z)/2;

  if (d < 0) d = sqrt(xP*xP + yP*yP + zP*zP);
                                 /* 0 < d < 1 */
  xP /= d; yP /= d; zP /= d;
  xQ /= d; yQ /= d; zQ /= d;
  xR /= d; yR /= d; zR /= d;
```

```
    midpnt(B, C, &P, xP, yP, zP);
    midpnt(C, A, &Q, xQ, yQ, zQ);
    midpnt(A, B, &R, xR, yR, zR);

    storeface(A, R, Q);
    storeface(R, B, P);
    storeface(Q, P, C);
    storeface(Q, R, P);
}

void storeface(int i, int j, int k)
{  fc[nface].i = i;
   fc[nface].j = j;
   fc[nface].k = k;
   nface++;
}
```

We have already seen several perspective views of the constructed object (see Figs. 2.9 and 2.10). Figure 3.14 shows a top view of it. Recall that vertex number 1 denotes the north pole; in this view we see the vertices of the five original triangles 1-2-3, 1-3-4, 1-4-5, 1-5-6, 1-6-2, and how each of these has been replaced with four smaller triangles.

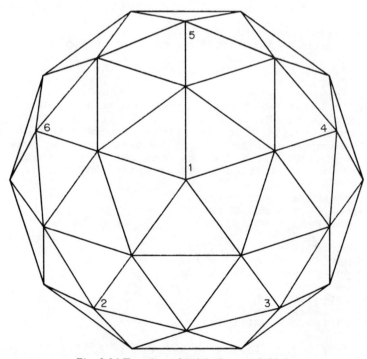

*Fig. 3.14 Top view of polyhedron with 80 faces*

The principle we have just been using can be applied to our new object once again. This means that the number of triangular faces is again multiplied by 4, so that there are 320 of them. It will be a good exercise for you to work this out!

## 3.7 THREE-DIMENSIONAL ROTATIONS

In Section 1.8.1 we have discussed some user's aspects of rotations in three-dimensional space. It is now time to deal with the software with which such rotations can be achieved. From the programmer's point of view, rotations will be performed by means of two functions, *initrotate* and *rotate*. With the former, we give detailed information about the rotation so that a *rotation matrix* can be generated. This is done only once for each rotation, no matter how many points are to be rotated. The latter function performs the actual work; it is to be called for each point to be rotated.

In order to specify a rotation we have to give a directed axis and an angle $\alpha$. The rotation will then take place about that axis and through the angle $\alpha$. For the directed axis we will use a point A, with coordinates $x_A$, $y_A$, $z_A$, and a vector

$$\mathbf{v} = [v_1, \ v_2, \ v_3]$$

Then the directed axis is the line through point A with the direction of vector $\mathbf{v}$. If we would turn a (normal) screw in the same way as our rotation through the angle $\alpha$ (assuming $\alpha$ to be positive), then the screw would move along the axis in the direction of vector $\mathbf{v}$.

The functions *initrotate* and *rotate* are quite easy to use. Consider, for example, program GENROTA, which is a general program for any 3D rotation; it reads an object file (in D3D format) and writes a similar output file. The names of these files, point A, vector $\mathbf{v}$, and angle $\alpha$ are entered on the keyboard:

```
/* GENROTA: A general program to rotate a set of points.
   After compilation it is to be linked together with the
   module TRAFO.OBJ.
*/
#include <stdio.h>
#include <math.h>
#include <process.h>
void initrotate(double xA, double yA, double zA,
    double v1, double v2, double v3, double alpha);
void rotate(double x, double y, double z,
    double *px1, double *py1, double *z1);

main()
{ FILE *fp1, *fp2;
  double xA, yA, zA, v1, v2, v3, alphadeg, alpha,
         x, y, z, x1, y1, z1, pi;
  char str[30];
  int nr, ch, n=0;
  printf("Input file:  "); scanf("%s", str);
  fp1 = fopen(str, "r");
  printf("Output file: "); scanf("%s", str);
  fp2 = fopen(str, "w");
  if (fp1 == NULL || fp2 == NULL)
  { printf("File problem"); exit(1);
  }
  printf("Enter xA, yA, zA: ");
  scanf("%lf %lf %lf", &xA, &yA, &zA);
  printf("Enter v1. v2, v3: ");
```

```
    scanf("%lf %lf %lf", &v1, &v2, &v3);
    printf("Enter alpha (in degrees): ");
    scanf("%lf", &alphadeg);
    pi = 4 * atan(1.0);
    alpha = alphadeg * pi/180; /* alpha in radians */
    initrotate(xA, yA, zA, v1, v2, v3, alpha);
    while (
    fscanf(fp1, "%d %lf %lf %lf", &nr, &x, &y, &z) == 4)
    { rotate(x, y, z, &x1, &y1, &z1); n++;
        fprintf(fp2, "%d %f %f %f\n", nr, x1, y1, z1);
    }
    while (ch = getc(fp1), ch != EOF) putc(ch, fp2);
    fclose(fp1); fclose(fp2);
    printf("Ready! %d points rotated\n", n);
}
```

Let us use a prism, given by the following object file, for a demonstration:

```
1 1.000000 0.000000 0.000000
2 1.000000 2.000000 0.000000
3 0.000000 2.000000 0.000000
4 0.000000 0.000000 0.000000
5 1.000000 0.000000 3.000000
6 1.000000 2.000000 3.000000
7 0.000000 2.000000 3.000000
8 0.000000 0.000000 3.000000
Faces:
  1 2 6 5.
  2 3 7 6.
  3 4 8 7.
  1 4 8 5.
  5 6 7 8.
  1 4 3 2.
```

With $x_A = 0.5$, $y_A = 1$, $z_A = 0$, $v_1 = 0$, $v_2 = 0$, $v_3 = 1$, $\alpha = 75°$, this file is transformed into a new one which describes the same prism rotated through 75° about its vertical axis. Both the original and the rotated prisms are shown in Fig. 3.15.

Program GENROTA has to be linked together with the (compiled) module TRAFO.OBJ. If you have never linked modules together with Turbo C, you should know that you can use a so-called *project file*, say GENROTA.PRJ, which in our example contains only two lines of text, namely

GENTRAFO
TRAFO

Then you have to select the option P and to enter the name of the project file and everything will work. We will use the module TRAFO for several applications, so it is a good idea to compile it only once. The following module, with file name TRAFO.C, is compiled and the resulting object file is called TRAFO.OBJ. Once this has been done, it will not be recompiled; nor do we have to duplicate the source text in all programs where rotations are involved.

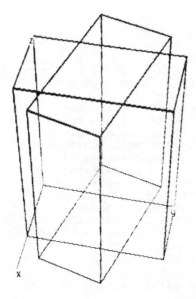

*Fig. 3.15 Prism before and after rotation*

```
/* TRAFO: Three-dimensional transformations   */

#include <math.h>

double r11, r12, r13, r21, r22, r23,
  r31, r32, r33, r41, r42, r43;

void initrotate(double a1, double a2, double a3,
         double v1, double v2, double v3, double alpha)
/* Computation of the rotation matrix

              | r11   r12   r13   0 |
      R =     | r21   r22   r23   0 |
              | r31   r32   r33   0 |
              | r41   r42   r43   1 |

   to be used as [x1  y1   z1   1] = [x   y   z   1] R,
   see function 'rotate'.
   Point (x1, y1, z1) is the image of (x, y, z).
   The rotation takes place about the axis
      (a1, a2, a3)+lambda(v1, v2, v3)
   and through the angle alpha.
*/
{ double rho, theta, cal, sal, cph, sph, cth, sth,
     cph2, sph2, cth2, sth2, pi, cal1;
  cal = cos(alpha); sal = sin(alpha);
  cal1 = 1.0-cal;
  rho = sqrt(v1*v1+v2*v2+v3*v3);
  pi = 4.0 * atan(1.0);
  if (rho == 0.0) {theta=0.0; cph=1.0; sph=0.0;} else
  { if (v1 == 0.0)
       theta = (v2 >= 0.0 ? 0.5*pi : 1.5*pi);
    else
```

```
    { theta = atan(v2/v1);
        if (v1 < 0) theta += pi;
    }
    cph = v3/rho; sph = sqrt(1.0 - cph*cph);
    /* cph = cos(phi), sph = sin(phi)   */
 }
 cth = cos(theta); sth = sin(theta);
 cph2 = cph*cph; sph2 = 1.0 - cph2;
 cth2 = cth*cth; sth2 = 1.0 - cth2;
 r11 = (cal*cph2+sph2)*cth2+cal*sth2;
 r12 = sal*cph+call*sph2*cth*sth;
 r13 = sph*(cph*cth*call-sal*sth);
 r21 = sph2*cth*sth*call-sal*cph;
 r22 = sth2*(cal*cph2+sph2)+cal*cth2;
 r23 = sph*(cph*sth*call+sal*cth);
 r31 = sph*(cph*cth*call+sal*sth);
 r32 = sph*(cph*sth*call-sal*cth);
 r33 = cal*sph2+cph2;
 r41 = a1-a1*r11-a2*r21-a3*r31;
 r42 = a2-a1*r12-a2*r22-a3*r32;
 r43 = a3-a1*r13-a2*r23-a3*r33;
}

void rotate(double x, double y, double z,
        double *px1, double *py1, double *pz1)
{ *px1 = x*r11+y*r21+z*r31+r41;
  *py1 = x*r12+y*r22+z*r32+r42;
  *pz1 = x*r13+y*r23+z*r33+r43;
}
```

If you are familiar with matrix multiplication, then the following explanation will help you to understand the functions *initrotate* and *rotate*. The latter computes the image vector $\mathbf{x'}$ by post-multiplying the original vector $\mathbf{x}$ by a general rotation matrix $R_{\text{GEN}}$:

$$\mathbf{x'} = \mathbf{x}\, R_{\text{GEN}}$$

where

$$\mathbf{x} = [x\ y\ z\ 1]$$
$$\mathbf{x'} = [x'\ y'\ z'\ 1]$$

$$R_{\text{GEN}} = \begin{bmatrix} r_{11} & r_{12} & r_{13} & 0 \\ r_{21} & r_{22} & r_{23} & 0 \\ r_{31} & r_{32} & r_{33} & 0 \\ r_{41} & r_{42} & r_{43} & 1 \end{bmatrix}$$

The task of function *initrotate* is to compute this matrix as a product of other matrices:

$$R_{\text{GEN}} = T^{-1}\, R^*\, T$$

where $T$ is a *translation matrix*, which contains the coordinates of the given point A:

$$T = \begin{bmatrix} 1 & 0 & 0 & 0 \\ 0 & 1 & 0 & 0 \\ 0 & 0 & 1 & 0 \\ x_A & y_A & z_A & 1 \end{bmatrix}$$

$$T^{-1} = \begin{bmatrix} 1 & 0 & 0 & 0 \\ 0 & 1 & 0 & 0 \\ 0 & 0 & 1 & 0 \\ -x_A & -y_A & -z_A & 1 \end{bmatrix}$$

Before performing the rotation, the object is shifted to O by $T^{-1}$, which is also a translation matrix. Then the rotation about an axis through O (in the direction of **v**) through the angle $\alpha$ takes place, which is taken care of by matrix $R^*$, and, finally, the rotated object is shifted back by means of matrix $T$. We still have to discuss matrix $R^*$. This $4 \times 4$ matrix is derived from the $3 \times 3$ matrix $R$ simply by adding a unit column vector and a unit row vector to the latter; so symbolically we may write

$$R^* = \begin{bmatrix} \cdot & \cdot & \cdot & 0 \\ \cdot & \cdot & \cdot & 0 \\ \cdot & \cdot & \cdot & 0 \\ 0 & 0 & 0 & 1 \end{bmatrix}$$

where the nine dots represent the elements of matrix $R$, which is now the remaining missing link. It is found as a product of five other $3 \times 3$ matrices:

$$R = R_z^{-1} R_y^{-1} R_v R_y R_z$$

The one in the middle, $R_v$, performs the actual rotation through the angle $\alpha$:

$$R_v = \begin{bmatrix} \cos \alpha & \sin \alpha & 0 \\ -\sin \alpha & \cos \alpha & 0 \\ 0 & 0 & 1 \end{bmatrix}$$

As follows immediately from this matrix, $R_v$ performs a rotation about the z-axis, whereas a rotation about the directed axis through O in the direction of **v** is needed. This explains the other four matrices; they deal with coordinate transformations, as we will briefly discuss.

First of all, we need the spherical coordinates of the endpoint $(v_1, v_2, v_3)$ of vector **v** (assuming that the starting point of this vector is O). Nearly at the beginning of this book, in Fig. 1.2, the meaning of the spherical coordinates $\rho, \theta, \varphi$ is shown. They are related to the endpoint of vector **v** as follows:

$$v_1 = \rho \sin \varphi \cos \theta$$
$$v_2 = \rho \sin \varphi \sin \theta$$
$$v_3 = \rho \cos \varphi$$

Unfortunately, we do not want to derive $v_1, v_2, v_3$ from $\rho, \theta, \varphi$, but it is the other way round. We therefore need the inverse equations, which are more complex in that logical decisions are involved:

$$\rho = \sqrt{(v_1^2 + v_2^2 + v_3^2)}$$

If $\rho = 0$ (which should not occur), we set $\theta = \varphi = 0$. Otherwise

$$\theta = \begin{cases} \arctan (v_2/v_1) & \text{if } v_1 > 0 \\ \pi + \arctan (v_2/v_1) & \text{if } v_1 < 0 \\ \pi/2 & \text{if } v_1 = 0 \text{ and } v_2 \geq 0 \\ 3\pi/2 & \text{if } v_1 = 0 \text{ and } v_2 < 0 \end{cases}$$

$$\varphi = \arccos (v_3\rho)$$

We can now change the coordinate system such that **v**, the axis of rotation, will lie on the new positive $z$-axis. We begin with a rotation of the $x$- and the $y$-axes about the $z$-axis through an angle $\theta$. If a point had to be transformed in this way, then the rotation matrix would be

$$R_z = \begin{bmatrix} \cos \theta & \sin \theta & 0 \\ -\sin \theta & \cos \theta & 0 \\ 0 & 0 & 1 \end{bmatrix}$$

Since we are using a coordinate transformation we need the inverse of this matrix, which is

$$R_z^{-1} = \begin{bmatrix} \cos \theta & -\sin \theta & 0 \\ \sin \theta & \cos \theta & 0 \\ 0 & 0 & 1 \end{bmatrix}$$

(You can easily verify this with a simple example in 2D space: moving the $y$-axis a distance $d$ to the right changes the $x$-coordinates of all points in the same way as if, instead, those points had been moved a distance $d$ to the left.)

In the next step, we rotate the (new) $x$- and $z$-axes about the (new) $y$-axis through an angle $\varphi$, for which we need the matrix

$$R_y^{-1} = \begin{bmatrix} \cos \varphi & 0 & \sin \varphi \\ 0 & 1 & 0 \\ -\sin \varphi & 0 & \cos \varphi \end{bmatrix}$$

This gives a new $z$-axis, which has the direction of vector **v**, so we can now use matrix $R_v$, shown above. After this the coordinate system has to be transformed back in its original position. For this we use first the matrix

$$R_y = \begin{bmatrix} \cos \varphi & 0 & -\sin \varphi \\ 0 & 1 & 0 \\ \sin \varphi & 0 & \cos \varphi \end{bmatrix}$$

and then the matrix $R_z$, shown above where we were discussing matrix $R_z^{-1}$.

In principle, the work of computing $R$ as a product of the five given matrices could be done by the computer, but as this would be done with numbers instead of expressions, it would involve quite a lot of unnecessary work. After all, the final matrix $R$ is less complex than the intermediate results and if we have $R$ available, expressed in $\theta$, $\varphi$, and $\alpha$, we can use this immediately rather than performing all those matrix multiplications each time. I therefore did this work in the conventional way, using a large sheet of paper and inventing abbreviations such as $s_\alpha$ for sin $\alpha$ to keep the extremely long formulas within reasonable limits. Fortunately, a good many simplifications are possible. The result is used in the function *initrotate*, occurring in the module TRAFO.

## 3.8 B-SPLINE SPACE CURVES

In Section 2.4 we have been using program CURVE3 to approximate a sequence of points in 3D space. We will now discuss this program itself, along with the B-spline method on which it is based. It is strongly recommended to read Section 2.4 once again (as I did myself when writing the present section!).

With $m$ given points, there are $m - 1$ intervals, but only $m - 3$ of these correspond to portions of the B-spline curve. Let us call such a portion a *curve segment*, or, more briefly, a *segment*. For example, in Fig. 3.16, where we have $m = 10$, the entire curve consists of $10 - 3 = 7$ curve segments, corresponding to the line segments 2-3, 3-4, 4-5, 5-6, 6-7, 7-8, 8-9.

A difficulty in B-spline approximation is that we cannot tell one segment from the other because the entire curve is so smooth! In Fig. 3.16, we see that the first segment begins near point 2, so it must end near point 3, where the second segment begins, but we cannot precisely see the point where that transition takes place. Yet it is necessary to remember

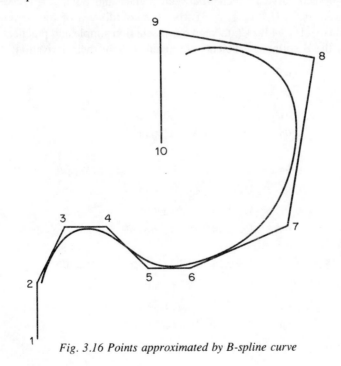

*Fig. 3.16 Points approximated by B-spline curve*

that there are such boundary points, for otherwise we cannot understand the underlying mathematical functions.

Incidentally, Fig. 3.16 was produced as follows. I first used D3D to define the points 1 through 10 and to draw the nine connecting straight line segments. I used what we may call a *front view*, which means that $\rho$ is very large, $\theta = 0°$, and $\varphi = 90°$, and, with cursor control, I defined the ten points in the $yz$-plane. Then I applied program CURVE3 to the object file, say PNT10.DAT, and entered $N = 20$ as the number of intervals between each two successive points. This resulted in an output file to which I applied program D3D again. Finally, with command $R$ and not clearing the screen, I loaded the original file PNT10.DAT, to display also the given ten points and the straight line segments between them. Only the point numbers were written by hand because otherwise the numbers of all the (141) interpolation points on the curves would also have been displayed, which would have resulted in a mess. (This example shows that a 3D curve-fitting program can be used for 2D curve fitting: the ten given points lie in the $yz$-plane and so does the resulting curve.)

As for the underlying mathematical functions mentioned above, these are polynomials of degree 3, in parametric form:

$$
\begin{aligned}
x &= a_3 t^3 + a_2 t^2 + a_1 t + a_0 \\
y &= b_3 t^3 + b_2 t^2 + b_1 t + b_0 \\
z &= c_3 t^3 + c_2 t^2 + c_1 t + c_0
\end{aligned}
\tag{3.2}
$$

Since there are $m - 3$ curve segments, as discussed above, we also have $m - 3$ sets of cubic functions (each 'set' consisting of a function for $x$, one for $y$, and one for $z$). In each curve segment, lying between point $i$ and point $i + 1$, the variable $t$ ranges from 0 to 1, that is, for $t = 0$ we have the endpoint near point $i$ and for $t = 1$ we approximate point $i + 1$.

Also for each such curve segment (between point $i$ and point $i + 1$), we can compute the coefficients $a_j$, $b_j$, $c_j$ ($j = 0, 1, 2, 3$) from the coordinates of four neighboring points, namely the points $i-1, i, i+1, i+2$; to keep our discussion simple and practical, the following expressions for the B-spline coefficients are given without their derivation:

$$
\begin{aligned}
a_3 &= (-x_{i-1} + 3x_i - 3x_{i+1} + x_{i+2})/6 \\
a_2 &= (x_{i-1} - 2x_i + x_{i+1})/2 \\
a_1 &= (-x_{i-1} + x_{i+1})/2 \\
a_0 &= (x_{i-1} + 4x_i + x_{i+1})/6
\end{aligned}
$$

$$
\begin{aligned}
b_3 &= (-y_{i-1} + 3y_i - 3y_{i+1} + y_{i+2})/6 \\
b_2 &= (y_{i-1} - 2y_i + y_{i+1})/2 \\
b_1 &= (-y_{i-1} + y_{i+1})/2 \\
b_0 &= (y_{i-1} + 4y_i + y_{i+1})/6
\end{aligned}
\tag{3.3}
$$

$$
\begin{aligned}
c_3 &= (-z_{i-1} + 3z_i - 3z_{i+1} + z_{i+2})/6 \\
c_2 &= (z_{i-1} - 2z_i + z_{i+1})/2 \\
c_1 &= (-z_{i-1} + z_{i+1})/2 \\
c_0 &= (z_{i-1} + 4z_i + z_{i+1})/6
\end{aligned}
$$

Note that these three sets of four equations are similar.

In (3.2) we regard $x$, $y$, and $z$ as polynomials in $t$ and in (3.3) we find the coefficients of these polynomials. For the sake of completeness, and in view of what we are going to discuss in Section 3.9, it ought to be mentioned that if, in (3.2), we replace the symbols $a_3$ and so on with the corresponding expressions given in (3.3), then we can re-arrange the resulting expressions to obtain

$$x = F_{-1}(t)\, x_{i-1} + F_0(t)\, x_i + F_1(t)\, x_{i+1} + F_2(t)\, x_{i+2}$$
$$y = F_{-1}(t)\, y_{i-1} + F_0(t)\, y_i + F_1(t)\, y_{i+1} + F_2(t)\, y_{i+2} \qquad (3.4)$$
$$z = F_{-1}(t)\, z_{i-1} + F_0(t)\, z_i + F_1(t)\, z_{i+1} + F_2(t)\, z_{i+2}$$

in which we find the following *blending functions*:

$$F_{-1}(t) = (-t^3 + 3t^2 - 3t + 1)/6$$
$$F_0(t) = (3t^3 - 6t^2 + 4)/6 \qquad (3.5)$$
$$F_1(t) = (-3t^3 + 3t^2 + 3t + 1)/6$$
$$F_2(t) = t^3/6$$

In program CURVE3, $x$, $y$, and $z$ are computed according to (3.2), which is more efficient than applying the equivalent equations (3.4). The latter, however, show more clearly that each new point $(x, y, z)$ is computed as a linear combination of the given four points in the neighborhood and that the coefficients (that is, the blending functions) depend on $t$.

```
/* CURVE3: B-spline curve fitting in three dimensions.
   The program reads an input file and writes an output
   file, which are both compatible with program D3D, so we
   can use the following scheme:

D3D  --> input file  -->  CURVE3  -->  output file  -->  D3D

   The input file contains lines with point numbers i and
   three-dimensional coordinates of the m points P(i)
   (i = 1, 2, ..., m). Any section beginning with the word
   'Faces' in the file is ignored. The program writes the
   three-dimensional coordinates of the k points
   Q(j) (j = 1, 2, ..., k) in the output file (each
   coordinate triple preceded by a point number j), where
   k = (m-3)N + 1.
   The value of N is read from the keyboard. (N is the
   number of intervals between two successive points P(i)
   and P(i+1).
   Point Q(1) is an approximation of P(2);
   point Q(N+1) is an approximation of P(3);
   point Q(2N+1) is an approximation of P(4);
   ...
   point Q(k) is an approximation of P(m-1).
*/
#include <stdio.h>
#include <alloc.h>
#include <process.h>
```

```
main()
{ char infil[30], outfil[30];
  int m=0, k, N, i, j, first=0;
  float *x, *y, *z, X, Y, Z, t, xdum, ydum, zdum,
    xA, xB, xC, xD, yA, yB, yC, yD, zA, zB, zC, zD,
    a0, a1, a2, a3, b0, b1, b2, b3, c0, c1, c2, c3;
  FILE *fpin, *fpout;
  printf("Input file:  "); scanf("%s", infil);
  printf("Output file: "); scanf("%s", outfil);
  printf("Enter N, the number of intervals between\n");
  printf("two successive given points: "); scanf("%d", &N);
  fpin = fopen(infil, "r");
  if (fpin == NULL)
  { printf("File not available"); exit(1);
  }
  while (
  fscanf(fpin, "%*d %f %f %f", &xdum, &ydum, &zdum) >0) m++;
  fclose(fpin); fpin = fopen(infil, "r");
  x = (float *)malloc((m+1) * sizeof(float));
  y = (float *)malloc((m+1) * sizeof(float));
  z = (float *)malloc((m+1) * sizeof(float));
  if (z == NULL) {printf("Not enough memory"); exit(1);}
  for (i=1; i<=m; i++)
    fscanf(fpin, "%*d %f %f %f", x+i, y+i, z+i);
  fclose(fpin);
  fpout = fopen(outfil, "w");
  for (i=2; i<m-1; i++)
  { xA=x[i-1]; xB=x[i]; xC=x[i+1]; xD=x[i+2];
    yA=y[i-1]; yB=y[i]; yC=y[i+1]; yD=y[i+2];
    zA=z[i-1]; zB=z[i]; zC=z[i+1]; zD=z[i+2];

    a3=(-xA+3*(xB-xC)+xD)/6.0;
    a2=(xA-2*xB+xC)/2.0;
    a1=(xC-xA)/2.0;
    a0=(xA+4*xB+xC)/6.0;

    b3=(-yA+3*(yB-yC)+yD)/6.0;
    b2=(yA-2*yB+yC)/2.0;
    b1=(yC-yA)/2.0;
    b0=(yA+4*yB+yC)/6.0;

    c3=(-zA+3*(zB-zC)+zD)/6.0;
    c2=(zA-2*zB+zC)/2.0;
    c1=(zC-zA)/2.0;
    c0=(zA+4*zB+zC)/6.0;

    for (j=first; j<=N; j++)
    { t = (float)j/(float)N;
      X = ((a3*t+a2)*t+a1)*t+a0;
      Y = ((b3*t+b2)*t+b1)*t+b0;
      Z = ((c3*t+c2)*t+c1)*t+c0;
      fprintf(fpout, "%d %f %f %f\n", (i-2)*N+j+1, X, Y, Z);
    }
    first = 1;
  }
```

```
    fprintf(fpout, "Faces:\n"); k = (m-3)*N+1;
    for (j=1; j<k; j++) fprintf(fpout, "%d %d.\n", j, j+1);
    fclose(fpout);
}
```

Before finishing this section, let me point out that it is quite easy to obtain a smooth curve that is *closed*. As normally a B-spline curve will begin near the second point (point 2) and end near the second last point (point $m - 1$), these two points should coincide. Also, point 1 should coincide with point $m - 2$ and point 3 with point $m$, as shown schematically in:

$$
\begin{array}{cccccc}
& 1 & & 2 & 3 & 4 & . & . & . & . & . & . & . & . & . \\
& & & & & & & & & & & & & & & . \\
. & . & . & . & . & . & . & . & . & . & . & . & m-2 & m-1 & m & & . \\
. & & & & & & & & & & & & & & & & & . \\
. & & & & & & & & & & & & & & & & & . \\
. & . & . & . & . & . & . & . & . & . & . & . & . & . & . & . & . & .
\end{array}
$$

Thus, there should be two coinciding line segments.

It may also be worthwhile to note that two or more successive points are allowed to coincide. This can be used as a means to 'pull' a curve to a given point; this technique is useful especially if, in the case of an open curve, we want the given endpoints (points 1 and $m$) to be approximated. For example, we can give the very first point the numbers 1, 2, 3, which will force the curve to begin exactly in this point. At first sight this may seem strange, since according to the equations (3.4) each computed point $(x, y, z)$ is derived from four given points, so we may think that we can guarantee the curve to start at point 1 only if it coincides with the points 2, 3, *and* 4. However, according to (3.4), the coefficient of point 4 would be $F_2(t)$, and (3.5) shows that this coefficient is zero if $t = 0$, which is indeed the case for the very first computed point. Thus, only the points 1, 2, and 3 effectively contribute to the position of this point, and if these three points are in fact one point, then the curve will start at it.

### 3.9  CABLES

After our preparations in Sections 3.7 and 3.8, we are now in a position to develop a program to generate 'cables', as discussed in Section 2.5. Our C functions *initrotate* and *rotate*, discussed in Section 3.7, will be extremely useful for this purpose.

With a space curve given as a sequence of points, preferably generated by program CURVE3 (see Section 3.8), we will use these points as centers of circles. The radius $R$ of the circles is entered on the keyboard, and so is $n$, the number of points on each circle. (As usual, each circle will be approximated by a regular polygon with $n$ vertices.) The $n$ vertices of the first polygon will be computed in a special way, entirely different from the way those of the other polygons are obtained. Let us denote the first three given points on the curve by $C_0$, $C_1$, $C_2$. Point $C_1$ will be the center of the first circle, $C_2$ that of the second, and so on, so there will be no circle with the very first point, $C_0$, as its center.

We begin by using the points $C_0$ and $C_2$ to obtain the axis of the first circle (with center $C_1$). The equation of the plane $\alpha$ in which this circle lies can be expressed in the coordinates $x_i$, $y_i$, $z_i$ of the three points $C_i$ $(i = 0, 1, 2)$:

$$ax + by + cz = d$$

where

$$
\begin{aligned}
a &= x_2 - x_0 \\
b &= y_2 - y_0 \\
c &= z_2 - z_0 \\
d &= ax_1 + by_1 + cz_1
\end{aligned}
$$

Since $\mathbf{n} = [a, b, c]$ is the vector starting at $C_0$ and ending at $C_2$, the line through $C_1$ and with the same direction as $\mathbf{n}$ is the axis of the circle we are interested in. We can find some vector $\mathbf{r} = [r_x, r_y, r_z]$ perpendicular to this axis:

$$
\begin{aligned}
r_x &= b, \; r_y = -a, \; r_z = 0 & \text{if } |a| \geq \delta \text{ or } |b| \geq \delta \\
r_x &= 0, \; r_y = c, \; r_z = -b & \text{if } |a| < \delta \text{ and } |b| < \delta
\end{aligned}
$$

where $\delta$ is some small positive number, say $10^{-5}$. Vector $\mathbf{r}$ has been chosen such that its inner product with $\mathbf{n}$ is zero; the above logical decision prevents us from obtaining a vector $\mathbf{r}$ whose length is (almost) 0.

After computing

$$
L = \sqrt{(r_x^2 + r_y^2 + r_z^2)}
$$

we can use the point with the following coordinates as the first point on the circle in question:

$$
\begin{aligned}
x[0] &= x_1 + Rr_x/L \\
y[0] &= y_1 + Rr_y/L \\
z[0] &= z_1 + Rr_z/L
\end{aligned}
$$

As we want $n$ points on each circle, we use

$$
\theta = 2\pi/n
$$

and find the other $n - 1$ points on the circle, each time rotating the previous point about the axis of the circle and through the angle $\theta$. Complex as this task is, all we have to do is call our functions *initrotate* and *rotate*; first we call *initrotate* with, in this order, $x_1, y_1, z_1,$ $a, b, c, \theta$ as its arguments, and then we perform the following for-loop:

```
for (i=1; i<n; i++)
    rotate(x[i-1], y[i-1], z[i-1], x+i, y+i, z+i);
```

(Recall that in the C language the expression $x + i$ denotes the address of the array element $x[i]$, so we might have used the expression $\&x[i]$ instead.)

We now have to compute the remaining circles, and we will do this by deriving the $n$ points on each new circle from those on the immediately preceding circle. Let us use the letter A for the center of this preceding circle (briefly called *circle A*) and B for that of the new circle (*circle B*). (Thus, immediately after constructing the very first circle, we have A $= C_1$ and B $= C_2$.) Let us denote the axis of circle A by $l$. If B lies on $l$, then the $n$ points of circle B can be obtained by a simple translation of the corresponding points on circle A;

all we have to do is add $x_B - x_A$, $y_B - y_A$, and $z_B - z_A$ to the coordinates of the $n$ points on circle A.

Things are not so simple if B does not lie on $l$. In this case we can obtain circle B by rotating circle A, or, more accurately, by rotating the $n$ points of circle A such that their new positions are the desired points of circle B. We can use our functions *initrotate* and *rotate* once again provided that we can supply an axis and an angle of rotation. Note that this rotation is essentially different from the one we have been using to find $n - 1$ points on the first circle. We now consider three planes, shown in Fig. 3.17, namely:

Plane $\alpha$ in which circle A lies;
Plane $\beta$ through line $l$ and point B;
Plane $\gamma$ through the midpoint M of line segment AB and perpendicular to that line segment.

For plane $\alpha$ we have the equation

$$ax + by + cz = d$$

that is, we have computed the values $a$, $b$, $c$, and $d$ for the first circle (with center $C_1$). We shall discuss how to find similar values for the other circles shortly.

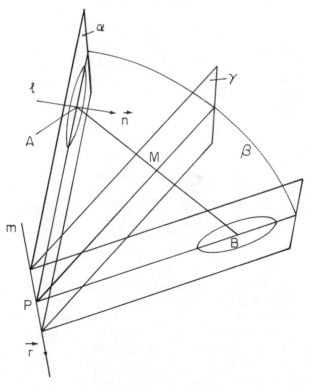

Fig. 3.17 Rotating circle A to obtain circle B

For plane $\beta$, we use a parametric representation rather than an equation. We know that this plane passes through point A and that it is parallel to the vectors $[a, b, c]$ and **AB**. This leads to the following representation for plane $\beta$, in which $\lambda$ and $\mu$ are parameters:

$$[x\ y\ z] = [x_A\ y_A\ z_A] + \lambda[a\ b\ c] + \mu[x_B - x_A\ y_B - y_A\ z_B - z_A]$$

Plane $\gamma$ is perpendicular to vector **AB**, which means that we can use

$$
\begin{aligned}
d_x &= x_B - x_A \\
d_y &= y_B - y_A \\
d_z &= z_B - z_A
\end{aligned}
$$

as coefficients in its equation. It passes through the midpoint M of AB. Thus, with

$$
\begin{aligned}
x_M &= (x_A + x_B)/2 \\
y_M &= (y_A + y_B)/2 \\
z_M &= (z_A + z_B)/2 \\
d_0 &= d_x\,x_M + d_y\,y_M + d_z\,z_M
\end{aligned}
$$

we find the following equation for $\gamma$:

$$d_x x + d_y y + d_z z = d_0$$

The planes $\alpha$, $\beta$ and $\gamma$ have one point of intersection, which we call P; this can now be computed. Then the line $m$ through P and perpendicular to plane $\beta$ is the axis of rotation we need, and the angle APB (that is, the angle between the lines AP and BP) is the desired angle of rotation. We shall use the letter $\varphi$ for this angle. Actually, we need a *directed* axis; in other words, besides point P we want a vector **v**, in such a way that if we regard **v** as lying on line $m$, we have to rotate circle A through the angle $\varphi$ about **v** in the positive sense (corresponding to the direction of **v** like the movement of a normal screw). This vector **v** is found as the vector product of the vectors **PA** and **PB**:

$$\mathbf{v} = \mathbf{PA} \times \mathbf{PB}$$

We can also use the vectors **PA** and **PB** to derive the angle $\varphi$ from their inner product, using

$$\mathbf{PA} \cdot \mathbf{PB} = PA \times PB \times \cos\varphi$$

where PA and PB are the lengths of the vectors **PA** and **PB**.

After rotating circle A to obtain circle B, we must not forget to generate also a new vector $[a\ b\ c]$, perpendicular to circle B, since in the next step circle B will act as the old circle A and then we will have to use new values of $a$, $b$, and $c$. Although it is often convenient to place the starting point of a vector elsewhere, we now place it at the origin O of the coordinate system, and we are then interested in the new point $(a', b', c')$, obtained by rotating point $(a, b, c)$ about vector **v**, which this time also has O as its starting point. Thus, the new values of the program variables $a$, $b$, $c$ are obtained as follows:

```
initrotate(0.0, 0.0, 0.0, v1, v2, v3, phi);
rotate(a, b, c, &a, &b, &c);
```

Further details about the computation of P, v, and $\varphi$ can be found in program CABLE.

```
/* CABLE: This program reads a file that represents a
          space curve, and it writes a file that represents
          a cable. The circular cable section will be
          a regular polygon with n vertices; it approximates
          a circle with radius R. Both n and R are read
          from the keyboard.
          The program is to be linked together with the
          module TRAFO, in which the functions
          'initrotate' and 'rotate' are defined.
*/
#include <stdio.h>
#include <math.h>
#include <alloc.h>
#include <process.h>

void initrotate(double a1, double a2, double a3,
                double v1, double v2, double v3, double alpha);
void rotate(double x, double y, double z,
            double *px1, double *py1, double *pz1);

int zero(double x);

double *getdouble(int n);

double *enlarge(double *px, int N);

void ermes(char *s);

main()
{ char infil[30], outfil[30];
  int i, n, j, m, jn, jn0, k, tablesize;
  double R, *x, *y, *z, xC0, yC0, zC0, xC1, yC1, zC1,
    xC2, yC2, zC2, *xC, *yC, *zC,
    a, b, c, d, rx, ry, rz, pi, theta, Len,
    *getdouble(), *enlarge(),
    xA, yA, zA, xB, yB, zB, dx, dy, dz, d0, c1, c2, c0,
    xM, yM, zM, e1, e2, e0, denom, lambda, mu, xP, yP, zP,
    xAP, yAP, zAP, xBP, yBP, zBP, v1, v2, v3,
    cosphi, phi;
  FILE *fpin, *fpout;
  printf("Input file:  "); scanf("%s", infil);
  fpin = fopen(infil, "r");
  if (fpin == NULL)
     ermes("File not available");
  if
  (fscanf(fpin, "%*d %lf %lf %lf", &xC0, &yC0, &zC0) != 3 ||
   fscanf(fpin, "%*d %lf %lf %lf", &xC1, &yC1, &zC1) != 3 ||
   fscanf(fpin, "%*d %lf %lf %lf", &xC2, &yC2, &zC2) != 3)
        ermes("Input file incorrect");
  printf("Output file: "); scanf("%s", outfil);
```

```
fpout = fopen(outfil, "w");
printf("How many points on each circle? ");
scanf("%d", &n);
printf("Radius: "); scanf("%lf", &R);
a=xC2-xC0; b=yC2-yC0; c=zC2-zC0; d=a*xC1+b*yC1+c*zC1;
/* First circle has center (xC1, yC1, zC1), radius R, and
   it lies in plane ax + by + cz = d
*/
x = getdouble(n); y = getdouble(n); z = getdouble(n);
if (zero(a) && zero(b)) {rx=0; ry=c; rz=-b;}
                   else {rx=b; ry=-a; rz=0;}
Len=sqrt(rx*rx+ry*ry+rz*rz);
rx/=Len; ry/=Len; rz/=Len;
/* (rx, ry, rz) is a unit vector perpendicular to
   (a, b, c)
*/
x[0]=xC1+rx*R; y[0]=yC1+ry*R; z[0]=zC1+rz*R;
pi=4.0*atan(1.0);
theta=2*pi/n;
/* Computation of n points on the first circle: */
initrotate(xC1, yC1, zC1, a, b, c, theta);
for (i=1; i<n; i++)
   rotate(x[i-1], y[i-1], z[i-1], x+i, y+i, z+i);
/* Count number of circles
   (number of points minus 1 read from input file):   */
m = 2;
while (
fscanf(fpin, "%*d %lf %lf %lf", &xC0, &yC0, &zC0) == 3)
                                                   m++;
tablesize = m*n;
x = enlarge(x, tablesize);
y = enlarge(y, tablesize);
z = enlarge(z, tablesize);
fclose(fpin); fpin = fopen(infil, "r");        /* Rewind */
fscanf(fpin, "%*d %lf %lf %lf", &xC0, &yC0, &zC0);
                                            /* Skip */
xC = getdouble(m);
yC = getdouble(m);
zC = getdouble(m);
for (j=0; j<m; j++)
   fscanf(fpin, "%*d %lf %lf %lf", xC+j, yC+j, zC+j);
/* (xC[0], yC[0], zC[0]) is now the center of the given
   circle, lying in plane ax + by + cz =d, and with radius
   R. The n relevant points on this circle have already
   been computed; their coordinates are
   x[0], y[0], z[0], ..., x[n-1], y[n-1], z[n-1].
   The other m-1 circles will be derived from this first
   one by means of rotations.
*/
fclose(fpin);
for (j=1; j<m; j++)
{ jn=j*n; jn0=jn-n;
  xA=xC[j-1]; yA=yC[j-1]; zA=zC[j-1];
  xB=xC[j];   yB=yC[j];   zB=zC[j];
  dx=xB-xA; dy=yB-yA; dz=zB-zA;
  c1=a*a+b*b+c*c;
```

```
c2=a*dx+b*dy+c*dz;
c0=d-a*xA-b*yA-c*zA;
xM=0.5*(xA+xB); yM=0.5*(yA+yB); zM=0.5*(zA+zB);
d0=dx*xM+dy*yM+dz*zM;
e1=dx*a+dy*b+dz*c;
e2=dx*dx+dy*dy+dz*dz;
e0=d0-dx*xA-dy*yA-dz*zA;
denom=c1*e2-c2*e1;
if (fabs(denom) < 1e-12)
{ /* Direction does not change.
      Instead of using a point P infinitely far
      away, we perform a simple translation:
  */
  for (i=0; i<n; i++)
  { x[jn+i] = x[jn0+i] + dx;
    y[jn+i] = y[jn0+i] + dy;
    z[jn+i] = z[jn0+i] + dz;
  }
} else
  /* Direction changes.
      The polygon will be rotated through the angle phi
      about vector v passing through point P:
  */
{ lambda=(c0*e2-c2*e0)/denom;
  mu=(c1*e0-c0*e1)/denom;
  xP=xA+lambda*a+mu*dx;
  yP=yA+lambda*b+mu*dy;
  zP=zA+lambda*c+mu*dz;
  /* Point P (of intersection of three planes) is
      center of rotation
  */
  xAP=xA-xP; yAP=yA-yP; zAP=zA-zP;
  xBP=xB-xP; yBP=yB-yP; zBP=zB-zP;
  v1=yAP*zBP-yBP*zAP;
  v2=xBP*zAP-xAP*zBP;
  v3=xAP*yBP-xBP*yAP;
  /* (v1, v2, v3) is direction of axis of rotation */
  cosphi=(xAP*xBP+yAP*yBP+zAP*zBP)/
          sqrt((xAP*xAP+yAP*yAP+zAP*zAP)*
              (xBP*xBP+yBP*yBP+zBP*zBP));
  phi = (cosphi == 0 ? 0.5*pi :
      atan(sqrt(1.0-cosphi*cosphi)/cosphi));
  /* phi is the angle of rotation */
  initrotate(xP, yP, zP, v1, v2, v3, phi);
  for (i=0; i<n; i++)
    rotate(x[jn0+i], y[jn0+i], z[jn0+i],
          x+jn+i, y+jn+i, z+jn+i);
  initrotate(0.0, 0.0, 0.0, v1, v2, v3, phi);
  rotate(a, b, c, &a, &b, &c);
}
  d=a*xC[j]+b*yC[j]+c*zC[j];
}
if (fpout == NULL) ermes("Problem with output file");
for (k=0; k<m*n; k++)
  fprintf(fpout, "%d %f %f %f\n", k+1, x[k], y[k], z[k]);
fprintf(fpout, "Faces:\n");
```

```
    for (k=n-1; k>=0; k--) fprintf(fpout, " %d", k+1);
    fprintf(fpout, ".\n");

    for (k=(m-1)*n; k<m*n; k++) fprintf(fpout, " %d", k+1);
    fprintf(fpout, ".\n\n");

    for (j=1; j<m; j++)
    { jn=j*n+1; jn0=jn-n;
      for (i=0; i<n-1; i++)
      { fprintf(fpout, " %d %d %d.\n", jn+i+1, -(jn0+i),
          jn0+i+1);
        fprintf(fpout, " %d %d %d.\n", jn0+i, -(jn+i+1),
          jn+i);
      }
      fprintf(fpout, " %d %d %d.\n\n", jn, -(jn0+n-1), jn0);
      fprintf(fpout, " %d %d %d.\n\n", jn0+n-1, -jn, jn+n-1);
    }
    fclose(fpout);
}

int zero(double x)
{ return fabs(x) < 1e-5;
}

double *getdouble(int n)
{ double *p;
  p = (double *)malloc(n * sizeof(double));
  if (p == NULL) ermes("Not enough memory");
  return p;
}

double *enlarge(double *px, int N)
{ px = (double *)realloc(px, N*sizeof(double));
  if (px == NULL) ermes("Not enough memory");
  return px;
}

void ermes(char *s)
{ printf(s); exit(1);
}
```

For demonstrations of program CABLE, please refer to Section 2.5, Figs. 2.16, 2.19, and 2.20.

## 3.10   B-SPLINE SURFACES

In Section 3.8 we have been dealing with space curves, the points of which have coordinates $x(t)$, $y(t)$, $z(t)$, where $t$ is a parameter. We will now consider surfaces, the points of which have coordinates $x(u, v)$, $y(u, v)$, $z(u, v)$ where $u$ and $v$ are two independent parameters. We will again use B-spline approximation. Apart from the fact that two parameters are involved, this subject will be similar to B-spline curves. Instead of a sequence of $m$ given points, we are now given a set of $nm$ points, which we can arrange in a table as follows:

$$
\begin{array}{cccc}
P_{11} & P_{12} & \ldots & P_{1m} \\
P_{21} & P_{22} & \ldots & P_{2m} \\
\cdot & \cdot & \ldots & \cdot \\
\cdot & \cdot & \ldots & \cdot \\
\cdot & \cdot & \ldots & \cdot \\
P_{n1} & P_{n2} & \ldots & P_{nm}
\end{array}
$$

We shall use the notions *horizontal* and *vertical* with reference to the rows and columns of this table; for example, we may say that $P_{1m}$ is the rightmost point on the first horizontal line.

Actually, our program will read a normal object file in D3D format, in which the points are given in the above order $P_{11}$, $P_{12}$, ..., $P_{nm}$. The program will read $m$ and $n$ from the keyboard, and expect a file in which the point numbers range from 1 to $mn$. Thus, point $P_{ij}$ in the above table has number

$$k = (i - 1)m + j$$

in the input file. We can also interpret the above table of points $P_{ij}$ as two sets of curves: for each 'horizontal' curve, $i$ is constant and $j$ ranges from 1 to $m$, and for each 'vertical' curve, $j$ is constant and $i$ ranges from 1 to $n$. As we know, in the B-spline approximation process the very first and the very last point on a curve, though used in the computation, are not approximated. The same applies to the points $P_{ij}$ in the above table for which $i = 1$ or $i = n$, and to those for which $j = 1$ or $j = m$. For the computation of the grid points on a surface 'rectangle' we now need four points in both directions, which altogether gives the following sixteen points:

$$
\begin{array}{cccc}
P_{i-1,j-1} & P_{i-1,j} & P_{i-1,j+1} & P_{i-1,j+2} \\
P_{i,j-1} & P_{i,j} & P_{i,j+1} & P_{i,j+2} \\
P_{i+1,j-1} & P_{i+1,j} & P_{i+1,j+1} & P_{i+1,j+2} \\
P_{i+2,j-1} & P_{i+2,j} & P_{i+2,j+1} & P_{i+2,j+2}
\end{array}
$$

All these points will be used to approximate the 'rectangle' in the middle (with $P_{i,j}$ at its top-left and $P_{i+1,j+1}$ at its bottom-right corner). This rectangle in the middle will be divided into $N \times M$ small surface elements (such that we count $N$ elements in the vertical and $M$ elements in the horizontal direction). Our program will read $M$ and $N$ from the keyboard.

With the formulae for the four functions $F_{-1}$, $F_0$, $F_1$, $F_2$, given in (3.5) (see Section 3.8), we replace the formulae (3.4) with their two-dimensional counterparts; since these formulae for $x$, $y$, and $z$ have identical structures, we give only the one for $x$ below:

$$
\left.
\begin{aligned}
x = {} & F_{-1}(u)F_{-1}(v)x_{i-1,i-1} + F_{-1}(u)F_0(v)x_{i-1,i} \\
& + F_{-1}(u)F_1(v)x_{i-1,i+1} + F_{-1}(u)F_2(v)x_{i-1,i+2} \\[6pt]
& + F_0(u)F_{-1}(v)x_{i,i-1} + F_0(u)F_0(v)x_{i,i} \\
& + F_0(u)F_1(v)x_{i,i+1} + F_0(u)F_2(v)x_{i,i+2} \\[6pt]
& + F_1(u)F_{-1}(v)x_{i+1,i-1} + F_1(u)F_0(v)x_{i+1,i} \\
& + F_1(u)F_1(v)x_{i+1,i+1} + F_1(u)F_2(v)x_{i+1,i+2} \\[6pt]
& + F_2(u)F_{-1}(v)x_{i+2,i-1} + F_2(u)F_0(v)x_{i+2,i} \\
& + F_2(u)F_1(v)x_{i+2,i+1} + F_2(u)F_2(v)x_{i+2,i+2}
\end{aligned}
\right\} \quad (3.6)
$$

Recall that in Section 3.8 we did not actually use (3.4), but rather the equivalent form (3.2), which contains polynomials in $t$. We can do a similar thing here, and rewrite (3.6) in such a way that we have sums of sixteen terms in which the following products occur:

$$u^3v^3, \ u^3v^2, \ u^3v, \ u^3, \ u^2v^3, \ u^2v^2, \ u^2v, \ u^2, \ uv^3, \ uv^2, \ uv, \ u, \ v^3, \ v^2, \ v, \ 1$$

The coefficients in these terms will be rather complex formulae, which I will omit here to avoid duplicated work: they have been used in program BSPLSURF and can be found there.

```
/* BSPLSURF: B-spline surface.
   This program expects a D3D object file in which a grid
   of points is defined. The program asks the user to enter
   m and n: there must be exactly mn points in the file,
   numbered 1, 2, ..., mn. It is assumed that these points
   are arranged in a grid as follows:

      1            2        ...        m
     m+1          m+2       ...       2m
    2m+1         2m+2       ...       3m
      .            .        ...        .
      .            .        ...        .
      .            .        ...        .
  (n-1)m+1    (n-1)+2       ...       mn

   Neither m nor n must be less than 4. The position of the
   points in 3D space is free: no two points need have the
   same x-, y-, or z-coordinates.
   If the object file contains a section beginning with
   "Faces:", then this section is ignored.
   Two integers M and N are to be entered; they denote
   numbers of intervals used in the surface-fitting process.
   There will be M intervals between the points 1 and 2, and
   N intervals between the points 1 and m+1, and so on.
   The B-spline curved surface that approximates the given
   points is written to an output file in D3D format.
*/
#include <stdio.h>
#include <process.h>
#include <alloc.h>
main()
{ FILE *fp1, *fp2;
  char str[30];
  float *xx, *yy, *zz, x, y, z, v, u, u2, u3,
     a00, a01, a02, a03,
     a10, a11, a12, a13,
     a20, a21, a22, a23,
     a30, a31, a32, a33,
     b00, b01, b02, b03,
     b10, b11, b12, b13,
     b20, b21, b22, b23,
     b30, b31, b32, b33,
     c00, c01, c02, c03,
     c10, c11, c12, c13,
     c20, c21, c22, c23,
     c30, c31, c32, c33,
     x00, x01, x02, x03,
```

```
        x10,  x11,  x12,  x13,
        x20,  x21,  x22,  x23,
        x30,  x31,  x32,  x33,
        y00,  y01,  y02,  y03,
        y10,  y11,  y12,  y13,
        y20,  y21,  y22,  y23,
        y30,  y31,  y32,  y33,
        z00,  z01,  z02,  z03,
        z10,  z11,  z12,  z13,
        z20,  z21,  z22,  z23,
        z30,  z31,  z32,  z33;

    int size, i, j, m, n, M, N, mn, l, k, I, J,
        A, B, C, ii, jj, nn, mm, P,
        h00,  h01,  h02,  h03,
        h10,  h11,  h12,  h13,
        h20,  h21,  h22,  h23,
        h30,  h31,  h32,  h33;

    do
    { printf("Enter m and n (both at least 4): ");
      scanf("%d %d", &m, &n);
    } while (m < 4 || n < 4);
    printf("Input file:    "); scanf("%s", str);
    fp1 = fopen(str, "r");
    printf("Output file:    "); scanf("%s", str);
    fp2 = fopen(str, "w");
    if (fp1 == NULL || fp2 == NULL)
    { printf("File problem"); exit(1);
    }
    mn = m * n; size = (mn+1) * sizeof(float);
    xx = malloc(size); yy = malloc(size); zz = malloc(size);
    for (l=0; l<mn; l++)
    { if (fscanf(fp1, "%d %f %f %f", &k, &x, &y, &z) != 4)
      { printf("Too few points in file"); exit(1);
      }
      if (k < 1 || k > mn)
      { printf("Point number %d incorrect", k); exit(1);
      }
      xx[k] = x; yy[k] = y; zz[k] = z;
    }
    fclose(fp1);
    printf("Enter M and N: "); scanf("%d %d", &M, &N);
    /* Let us imagine that we have n rows of m points,
       which gives (n-1) * (m-1) rectangles. Among these,
       only (n-3) * (m-3) rectangles will be approximated.
       We consider each of these rectangles to be divided
       into M x N tiny rectangles, which we will call
       'elements'.
       There will be A points in the output file for each
       horizontal grid line:
    */
    A = (m-3) * M + 1;
    printf("  i    j\n");
    for (i=2; i<=n-2; i++)
    for (j=2; j<=m-2; j++)
```

```
{ h11 = (i-1) * m + j;
  h10 = h11-1; h12 = h10+2; h13 = h10+3;
  h00 = h10-m; h01 = h00+1; h02 = h00+2; h03 = h00+3;
  h20 = h10+m; h21 = h20+1; h22 = h20+2; h23 = h20+3;
  h30 = h20+m; h31 = h30+1; h32 = h30+2; h33 = h30+3;

  printf("%3d %3d\n", i,  j); /* Show that we are busy */

  /* Here the 16 points are numbered as follows:

  P00  P01  P02  P03
  P10  P11  P12  P13
  P20  P21  P22  P23
  P30  P31  P32  P33

  The inner region, within P11, P12, P21, P22, will be
  approximated in this step (with the current values of
  i and j).
  */

  x00 = xx[h00]; y00 = yy[h00]; z00 = zz[h00];
  x01 = xx[h01]; y01 = yy[h01]; z01 = zz[h01];
  x02 = xx[h02]; y02 = yy[h02]; z02 = zz[h02];
  x03 = xx[h03]; y03 = yy[h03]; z03 = zz[h03];

  x10 = xx[h10]; y10 = yy[h10]; z10 = zz[h10];
  x11 = xx[h11]; y11 = yy[h11]; z11 = zz[h11];
  x12 = xx[h12]; y12 = yy[h12]; z12 = zz[h12];
  x13 = xx[h13]; y13 = yy[h13]; z13 = zz[h13];

  x20 = xx[h20]; y20 = yy[h20]; z20 = zz[h20];
  x21 = xx[h21]; y21 = yy[h21]; z21 = zz[h21];
  x22 = xx[h22]; y22 = yy[h22]; z22 = zz[h22];
  x23 = xx[h23]; y23 = yy[h23]; z23 = zz[h23];

  x30 = xx[h30]; y30 = yy[h30]; z30 = zz[h30];
  x31 = xx[h31]; y31 = yy[h31]; z31 = zz[h31];
  x32 = xx[h32]; y32 = yy[h32]; z32 = zz[h32];
  x33 = xx[h33]; y33 = yy[h33]; z33 = zz[h33];

  a33 = (x00-x03-x30+x33
        +3*(-x01+x02-x10+x13+x20-x23+x31-x32)
        +9*(x11-x12-x21+x22))/36;

  a32 = (-x00-x02+x30+x32 + 2*(x01-x31)
        + 3*(x10+x12-x20-x22) + 6*(-x11+x21))/12;

  a31 = (x00-x02-x30+x32 + 3*(-x10+x12+x20-x22))/12;

  a30 = (-x00-x02+x30+x32 + 3*(x10+x12-x20-x22)
        + 4*(-x01+x31) + 12*(x11-x21))/36;

  a23 = (-x00+x03-x20+x23 + 2*(x10-x13)
        + 3*(x01-x02+x21-x22) + 6*(x12-x11))/12;
```

$$a22 = (x00+x02+x20+x22 + 2*(-x01-x10-x12-x21))/4 + x11;$$

$$a21 = (x02-x00-x20+x22 + 2*(x10-x12))/4;$$

$$a20 = (x00+x02+x20+x22 - 2*(x10+x12) \\ + 4*(x01+x21) - 8*x11)/12;$$

$$a13 = (x00-x03-x20+x23 + 3*(x02-x01+x21-x22))/12;$$

$$a12 = (-x00-x02+x20+x22 + 2*(x01-x21))/4;$$

$$a11 = (x00-x02-x20+x22)/4;$$

$$a10 = (-x00-x02+x20+x22 + 4*(-x01+x21))/12;$$

$$a03 = (x03-x00-x20+x23 + 3*(x01-x02+x21-x22) \\ + 4*(x13-x10) + 12*(x11-x12))/36;$$

$$a02 = (x00+x02+x20+x22 - 2*(x01+x21) \\ + 4*(x10+x12) - 8*x11)/12;$$

$$a01 = (x02-x00-x20+x22 + 4*(x12-x10))/12;$$

$$a00 = (x00+x02+x20+x22 + 4*(x01+x10+x12+x21) \\ + 16*x11)/36;$$

$$b33 = (y00-y03-y30+y33 \\ +3*(-y01+y02-y10+y13+y20-y23+y31-y32) \\ +9*(y11-y12-y21+y22))/36;$$

$$b32 = (-y00-y02+y30+y32 + 2*(y01-y31) \\ + 3*(y10+y12-y20-y22) + 6*(-y11+y21))/12;$$

$$b31 = (y00-y02-y30+y32 + 3*(-y10+y12+y20-y22))/12;$$

$$b30 = (-y00-y02+y30+y32 + 3*(y10+y12-y20-y22) \\ + 4*(-y01+y31) + 12*(y11-y21))/36;$$

$$b23 = (-y00+y03-y20+y23 + 2*(y10-y13) \\ + 3*(y01-y02+y21-y22) + 6*(y12-y11))/12;$$

$$b22 = (y00+y02+y20+y22 + 2*(-y01-y10-y12-y21))/4 + y11;$$

$$b21 = (y02-y00-y20+y22 + 2*(y10-y12))/4;$$

$$b20 = (y00+y02+y20+y22 - 2*(y10+y12) \\ + 4*(y01+y21) - 8*y11)/12;$$

$$b13 = (y00-y03-y20+y23 + 3*(y02-y01+y21-y22))/12;$$

$$b12 = (-y00-y02+y20+y22 + 2*(y01-y21))/4;$$

$$b11 = (y00-y02-y20+y22)/4;$$

```
b10 = (-y00-y02+y20+y22 + 4*(-y01+y21))/12;

b03 = (y03-y00-y20+y23 + 3*(y01-y02+y21-y22)
      + 4*(y13-y10) + 12*(y11-y12))/36;

b02 = (y00+y02+y20+y22 - 2*(y01+y21)
      + 4*(y10+y12) - 8*y11)/12;

b01 = (y02-y00-y20+y22 + 4*(y12-y10))/12;

b00 = (y00+y02+y20+y22 + 4*(y01+y10+y12+y21)
      + 16*y11)/36;


c33 = (z00-z03-z30+z33
      +3*(-z01+z02-z10+z13+z20-z23+z31-z32)
      +9*(z11-z12-z21+z22))/36;

c32 = (-z00-z02+z30+z32 + 2*(z01-z31)
      + 3*(z10+z12-z20-z22) + 6*(-z11+z21))/12;

c31 = (z00-z02-z30+z32 + 3*(-z10+z12+z20-z22))/12;

c30 = (-z00-z02+z30+z32 + 3*(z10+z12-z20-z22)
      + 4*(-z01+z31) + 12*(z11-z21))/36;

c23 = (-z00+z03-z20+z23 + 2*(z10-z13)
      + 3*(z01-z02+z21-z22) + 6*(z12-z11))/12;

c22 = (z00+z02+z20+z22 + 2*(-z01-z10-z12-z21))/4 + z11;

c21 = (z02-z00-z20+z22 + 2*(z10-z12))/4;

c20 = (z00+z02+z20+z22 - 2*(z10+z12)
      + 4*(z01+z21) - 8*z11)/12;

c13 = (z00-z03-z20+z23 + 3*(z02-z01+z21-z22))/12;

c12 = (-z00-z02+z20+z22 + 2*(z01-z21))/4;

c11 = (z00-z02-z20+z22)/4;

c10 = (-z00-z02+z20+z22 + 4*(-z01+z21))/12;

c03 = (z03-z00-z20+z23 + 3*(z01-z02+z21-z22)
      + 4*(z13-z10) + 12*(z11-z12))/36;

c02 = (z00+z02+z20+z22 - 2*(z01+z21)
      + 4*(z10+z12) - 8*z11)/12;

c01 = (z02-z00-z20+z22 + 4*(z12-z10))/12;

c00 = (z00+z02+z20+z22 + 4*(z01+z10+z12+z21)
      + 16*z11)/36;
```

```
/* In the output file we will be using point numbers k,
   which are to be computed from the controlled
   variables i, j, I, J.
   In each rectangle, determined by the pair
   (i, j) and to be divided into N x M elements,
   we use I, counting up to N, and J, counting up to M.
   To avoid duplicated points, I and J normally start at
   1, except for the lowest values (2) of i and j: then
   I and J start at 0, respectively. (Of all rectangles
   that are to be divided into elements, the one with
   i=j=2 is the leftmost rectangle at the top.)
   If I=0 (which implies i=2), then k = (j-2)M + J + 1,
   otherwise k = A + (i-2)NA + (I-1)A + (j-2)M + J + 1.
   This means that in either case we have:

       k = {(i-2)N + I}A + {(j-2)M + 1} + J

   (A is the total number of mesh points on a horizontal
   row.)
*/
B = (j-2)*M+1;
for (I = (i == 2 ? 0 : 1); I <= N; I++)
{ u = (float)I/N; u2 = u*u; u3 = u2*u;
  C = ((i-2)*N+I)*A + B;
  for (J = (j == 2 ? 0 : 1); J <= M; J++)
  { k = C + J;
    v = (float)J/M;
    x = ((a03*v+a02)*v+a01)*v+a00+
        u*(((a13*v+a12)*v+a11)*v+a10)+
        u2*(((a23*v+a22)*v+a21)*v+a20)+
        u3*(((a33*v+a32)*v+a31)*v+a30);

    y = ((b03*v+b02)*v+b01)*v+b00+
        u*(((b13*v+b12)*v+b11)*v+b10)+
        u2*(((b23*v+b22)*v+b21)*v+b20)+
        u3*(((b33*v+b32)*v+b31)*v+b30);

    z = ((c03*v+c02)*v+c01)*v+c00+
        u*(((c13*v+c12)*v+c11)*v+c10)+
        u2*(((c23*v+c22)*v+c21)*v+c20)+
        u3*(((c33*v+c32)*v+c31)*v+c30);
    fprintf(fp2, "%d %f %f %f\n", k, x, y, z);
  }
}
}
fprintf(fp2, "Faces:\n");
nn = (n - 3) * N;
mm = A - 1;          /* mm = (m - 3) * M */
for (ii=0; ii<nn; ii++)
for (jj=0; jj<mm; jj++)
{ P = ii * A + jj + 1;
  /* We have to divide each (nearly rectangular) surface
     element into two triangles to ensure that the points
     that will be used as vertices of polygons really lie
     in the same plane. The minus sign in, for example,
```

```
             P -Q R will prevent D3D from drawing line segment PQ.
             Since either face of each triangle may be visible, we
             specify its vertices both counter-clockwise and
             clockwise:
          */
          fprintf(fp2, "%d %d %d.\n", P, -(P+A+1), P+1);
          fprintf(fp2, "%d %d %d.\n", P+A+1, -P, P+A);
          fprintf(fp2, "%d %d %d.\n", P, -(P+A+1), P+A);
          fprintf(fp2, "%d %d %d.\n", P+A+1, -P, P+1);
      }
      fclose(fp2);
  }
```

Figure 3.19 has been made by program D3D on the basis of a file produced by program BSPLSURF. The input data for the latter program contains 42 points, some of which coincide. We have discussed the idea of assigning more than one number to one point for curve fitting at the end of Section 3.8, and this idea can also be applied to surfaces. Consider the following table, with $n = 6$ and $m = 7$:

| 1 | 2 | 3 | 4 | 5 | 6 | 7 |
|---|---|---|---|---|---|---|
| 8 | 9 | 10 | 11 | 12 | 13 | 14 |
| 15 | 16 | 17 | 18 | 19 | 20 | 21 |
| 22 | 23 | 24 | 25 | 26 | 27 | 28 |
| 29 | 30 | 31 | 32 | 33 | 34 | 35 |
| 36 | 37 | 38 | 39 | 40 | 41 | 42 |

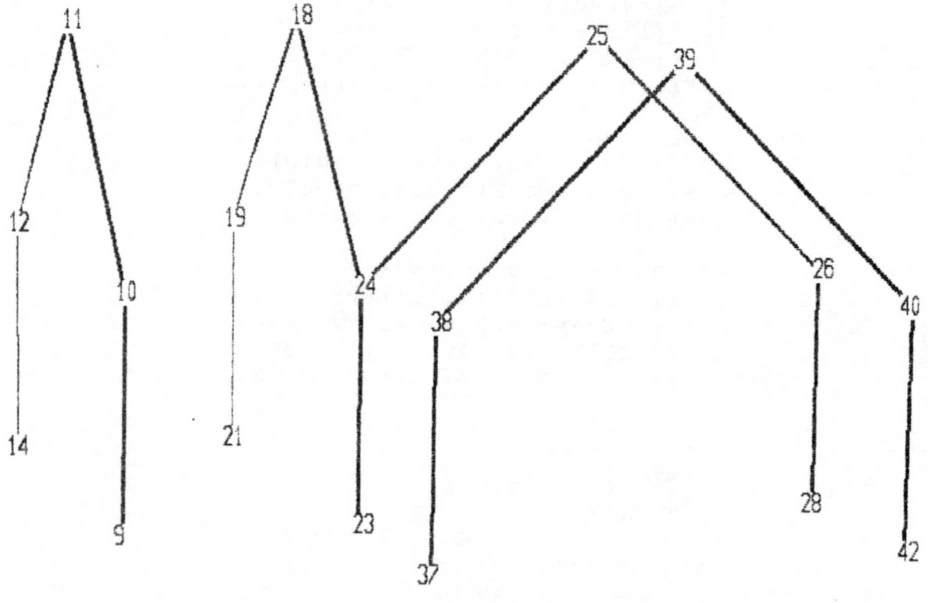

Fig. 3.18 Input file for BSPLSURF, displayed by D3D

Each row in this table corresponds to a broken line in Fig. 3.18. However, the first row denotes the same points as the second, and the points of the fifth row coincide with those of the sixth. Besides, the first point in each row coincides with the second and the sixth with the seventh. With two or more coinciding points, D3D displays only the highest number. For example, in Fig. 3.18 point number 9 also denotes the points 1, 2, 8. (Note that applying this idea of coinciding points is by no means essential; if you think this only a annoying complication you can use only distinct points, but remember that the first and the last point on each curve will not be approximated.) The points numbers 16 and 17 are also missing in Fig. 3.18; these two points coincide with the points 23 and 24, for quite a different reason. I constructed Fig. 3.18 by using the *Transform* command; the broken line indicated by the numbers 23, 24, 25, 26, 28 was obtained by rotating the one on which point 18 lies through 90° about the axis (24, 23), which means that the points 15, 16, 17 coincide with the points 22, 23, 24. Using $N = M = 3$ resulted in a file with 130 points, displayed by program D3D in Fig. 3.19.

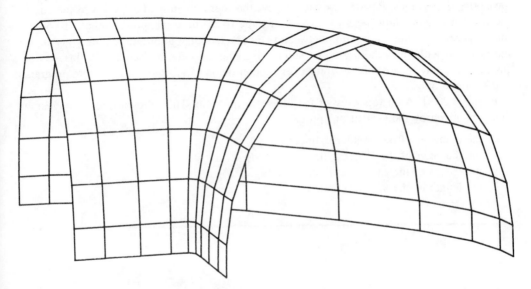

*Fig. 3.19 Result of B-spline surface fitting*

The highest point number 130, just mentioned, offers us a good opportunity to check the relation between $n, m, N, M, i, j$ on the one hand and the highest absolute point number k, appearing in the output file, on the other. In general, we have

$$k = \{(i - 2)N + I\}A + (j - 2)M + 1 + J$$

where the value

$$A = (m - 3)M + 1$$

is the number of points in the output file that lie on one 'horizontal' line. In the example of Fig. 3.19 we have

$$m = 7, n = 6, M = 3, N = 3$$
$$A = (7 - 3) \times 3 + 1 = 13$$

Since $i$ and $j$ are used in for-loops where their maximum values are $n - 2$ and $m - 2$, respectively, and the maximum values of $I$ is $N$ and that of $J$ is $M$, we find the largest value of $k$ by using $i = 4, j = 5, I = 3, J = 3$, which gives

$$k = \{(4 - 2) \times 3 + 3\} \times 13 + (5 - 2) \times 3 + 1 + 3 = 130$$

## 3.11   INTERSECTING CYLINDERS

Figure 1.13 in Section 1.5 has shown us some images of an object consisting of two intersecting cylinders, sometimes called a *tee-joint*. We will now discuss a program that generates a file for such an object. With this program we can produce not only the file EXAMPLE3.DAT, mentioned in Section 1.3, but also files for similar constructions which have other dimensions. Besides, we can improve the approximation of cylinders by increasing the number of bounding faces (obviously at the cost of more computing time). If you are more interested in the intersection between two cylinders than in programming, you can use the program without bothering about some programming details discussed in this section. Instead, you may regard this section as yet another demonstration of how to write programs that generate object files.

Figure 3.20 shows a top view of the object in question. The following four dimensions are to be given by the user of our program:

$d$, the diameter of the smaller cylinder
$D$, the diameter of the larger cylinder ($D < d$)
$l$, the length of the smaller cylinder (see Fig. 3.20)
$L$, the length of the larger cylinder ($L > d$)

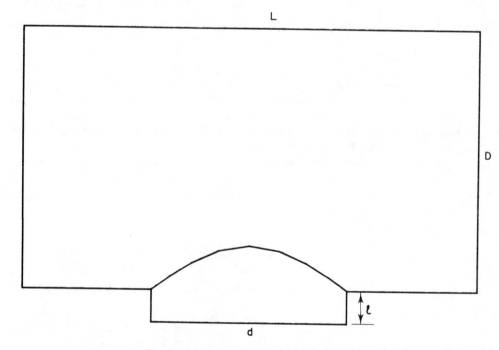

*Fig. 3.20 Top view of intersecting cylinders*

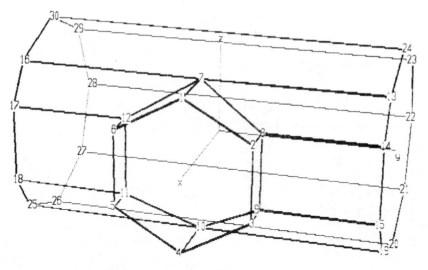

*Fig. 3.21 Perspective view of intersecting cylinders (n = 3)*

(Note that the terms *small* and *large* should not be taken too literally here, since the length *l* of the 'smaller' cylinder may be larger than the other three dimensions.)

We shall place the origin O of the coordinate system in the point of intersection of the two cylinder axes. The *y*-axis will coincide with the axis of the larger cylinder and the (positive) *x*-axis with that of the smaller cylinder, as shown in Fig. 3.21.

As usual, we will approximate the circular cross sections of the two cylinders by polygons. Normally, such polygons are *regular*. Here, this will be the case for the smaller cylinder, but it will not apply to the larger one. This is because we want the parallel lines on the smaller cylinder to intersect those on the larger cylinder. For example, in Fig. 3.21 the front face of the smaller cylinder is approximated by a hexagon, with point 2 as one of its vertices. The line through this point parallel to the *x*-axis intersects the larger cylinder in point 8, and line segment 8-14 is used as an edge on the larger cylinder. Thus, the positions of the vertices 13, 14, 15, 19 in Fig. 3.21 follow from those of the vertices 1, 2, 3, 4 on the smaller cylinder, and the former four points will therefore not lie equally far apart, as Fig. 3.22 shows.

The user of our program (TCYL) will enter *n*, the number of points on *half* the smaller circle, so in Fig. 3.21 we have *n* = 3. (Obviously, *n* will be chosen greater than 3 in practice.) On the larger circle, we know the position of vertex 13, which determines the angle $\alpha$, shown in Fig. 3.22. Then we divide the supplement of $\alpha$ into *n* equal portions, which altogether gives 2*n* sectors, each with an angle

$$\theta = \frac{180° - \alpha}{n}$$

and *n* sectors of unequal size for the remaining angle 2$\alpha$.

Instead of Fig. 3.22 we had better use Fig. 3.23, which is more general in its vertex numbering. The vertices on the front end of the smaller cylinder are numbered 1, 2, ..., 2*n*. The next 2*n* numbers (2*n* + 1, 2*n* + 2, ..., 4*n*) are assigned to the vertices on the intersection

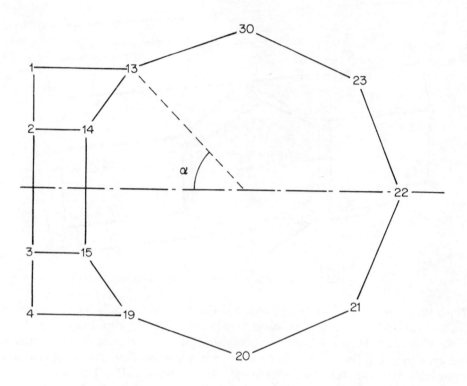

*Fig. 3.22 Side view of intersecting cylinders (n = 3)*

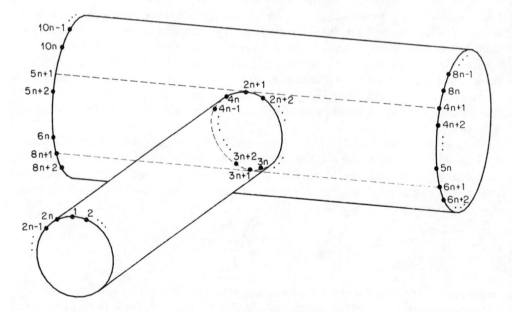

*Fig. 3.23 Vertex numbering in intersecting cylinders*

of the two cylinders. Then we have the vertices $4n + 1$, $4n + 2$, ..., $5n$, which lie on the right-hand flat face of the larger cylinder. The corresponding points on the left-hand face have the numbers $5n + 1$, $5n + 2$, ..., $6n$. Finally, we assign numbers to the remaining points on these two flat faces: $6n + 1$, $6n + 2$, ..., $8n$ for the right-hand, and $8n + 1$, $8n + 2$, ..., $10n$ for the left-hand face.

Finding the rectangular coordinates of all these vertices is a rather simple task; it is more difficult to find correct general expressions for the vertex numbers of each face, especially because not all parts of the larger cylinder can be dealt with in the same way.

There is a rather tricky point associated with the option of omitting 'artificial' edges in the final result, where hidden lines have been omitted, as shown in Fig. 1.13(b) and (c) and discussed in Section 1.5. This option works correctly only if such an edge is given twice in the object file and if two such occurrences of the same edge are given in terms of the *same vertex-number pairs*. For example, since the line segment 7-13 in Fig. 3.21 is an edge of the polygon 8-14-13-7, we had better not combine the two line segments 16-7 and 7-13 into one side of the rectangle 16-13-24-30, but, instead, we should represent this rectangle by the five-sided (degenerated) polygon 13-24-30-16-7. This explains the two faces with five vertex numbers in the object file.

Program TCYL contains comments that indicate the various parts of the object surface. With these comments, in connection with Fig. 3.23, the program text should be clear.

```c
/* TCYL: Preprocessor for D3D, to draw a T-shaped object
         consisting of two intersecting cylinders.
*/
#include <stdio.h>
#include <math.h>
#include <process.h>
#include <alloc.h>

void wri(int a);
void wr4(int a, int b, int c, int d);
void endcode(void);

FILE *fp;

main()
{ char filnam[30];
   int i, n, n2, n3, n4, n5, n6, n8, n9, n10,
      tablelength;
   float a, b, l, L, D, d, R, r, alpha, theta, delta,
      *x, *y, *z, pi, beta;
   pi = 4.0 * atan(1.0);
   printf(
"\n--------------------------- length L, diameter D\n");
   printf("                       |\n");
   printf("                       |\n");
   printf("                       | length l, diameter d\n");
   printf("                       |\n");
   printf("                       |\n\n");

   do
   { printf("\n(d < D,   d < L)\n\n");
      printf("Enter d, D, l, L in that order: \n");
      scanf("%f %f %f %f", &d, &D, &l, &L);
   } while (d >= D || d >= L);
```

```
    R = D/2; r = d/2; a = 1 + R; b = L/2;
    printf(
 "\nThe circular boundary face with diameter d will be\n");
    printf(
    "approximated by a regular polygon of 2n sides.\n\n");
    printf("Enter n: "); scanf("%d", &n);
    printf("Name of output file: "); scanf("%s", filnam);
    fp = fopen(filnam, "w");
    if (fp == NULL) {printf("File problem"); exit(1);}
    n2 = 2*n; n3 = 3*n; n4 = 4*n; n5 = 5*n;
    n6 = 6*n; n8 = 8*n; n9 = 9*n; n10 = 10*n;
    tablelength = (n10 + 1) * sizeof(float);
    x = (float *)malloc(tablelength);
    y = (float *)malloc(tablelength);
    z = (float *)malloc(tablelength);
    if (z == NULL) {printf("Not enough memory"); exit(1);}
    theta = pi/n;
    for (i=1; i<=n2; i++)
    { x[i] = a;
      y[i] = r*sin((i-1)*theta);
      z[i] = r*cos((i-1)*theta);
    }
    for (i=n2+1; i<=n4; i++)
    { y[i] = y[i-n2]; z[i] = z[i-n2];
      x[i] = sqrt(R*R - z[i]*z[i]);
    }
    for (i=n4+1; i<=n5; i++)
    { x[i] = x[i-n2]; y[i] = b; z[i] = z[i-n2];
    }
    for (i=n5+1; i<=n6; i++)
    { x[i] = x[i-n]; y[i] = -b; z[i] = z[i-n];
    }
    alpha = atan(z[n4+1]/x[n4+1]);
    delta = (pi - alpha)/n;
    for (i=n6+1; i<=n8; i++)
    { beta = alpha + (i-n6-1)*delta;
      x[i] = R * cos(beta); y[i] = b; z[i] = -R * sin(beta);
    }
    for (i=n8+1; i<=n10; i++)
    { x[i] = x[i-n2]; y[i] = -b; z[i] = z[i-n2];
    }
    for (i=1; i<=n10; i++)
      fprintf(fp, "%d %f %f %f\n", i, x[i], y[i], z[i]);

    fprintf(fp, "\nFaces:\n");

    /* Smaller cylinder, curved surface: */
    for (i=1; i<n2; i++) wr4(i, i+1, i+n2+1, i+n2);
    wr4(n2, 1, n2+1, n4);

    /* Larger cylinder, pieces on curved surface to the right
       of smaller cylinder; from top to bottom: */
    for (i=n2+1; i<n3; i++) wr4(i, i+1, i+n2+1, i+n2);
    wr4(n3, n3+1, n6+1, n5);

    /* Larger cylinder, pieces on curved surface to the left
       of smaller cylinder; from bottom to top: */
```

```
   wr4(n3+2, n6, n8+1, n3+1);
   for (i=n3+3; i<=n4; i++) wr4(i, n9+2-i, n9+3-i, i-1);
   wr4(n2+1, n5+1, n5+2, n4);

   /* Larger cylinder, large rectangular pieces on curved
      surface, starting near the smaller cylinder's lowest
      point:
   */
   wri(n6+2); wr4(n6+1, n3+1, n8+1, n8+2);
   for (i=n6+3; i<=n8; i++) wr4(i, i-1, i+n2-1, i+n2);
   wri(n4+1); wr4(n8, n10, n5+1, n2+1);

   /* Flat front surface of smaller cylinder: */
   for (i=n2; i>0; i--) wri(i);
   endcode();

   /* Right-hand flat surface of larger cylinder:        */
   for (i=n4+1; i<=n5; i++) wri(i); /* Front portion      */
   for (i=n6+1; i<=n8; i++) wri(i); /* Remaining portion */
   endcode();

   /* Left-hand flat surface of larger cylinder:         */
   for (i=n6; i>n5; i--) wri(i);      /* Front portion      */
   for (i=n10; i>n8; i--) wri(i);     /* Remaining portion */
   endcode();
   fclose(fp);
}

void wri(int a)
{ fprintf(fp, " %d", a);
}

void wr4(int a, int b, int c, int d)
{ fprintf(fp, " %d %d %d %d.\n", a, b, c, d);
}

void endcode(void)
{ fprintf(fp,".\n");
}
```

### 3.12   A PROGRAM FOR SQUARE SCREW THREAD

We will now deal with program SCRTHR, used in Section 2.6. Recall that it produces an object file for a square screw thread, as shown in Fig. 2.21. We will not reiterate the discussion of Section 2.6, but rather focus on the vertex numbering and the approximation of the curved surfaces by flat faces.

Let us begin with the terminology we shall be using. Recall that we are given a major diameter $D$, and a minor diameter $d$; in the program (as in mathematics) we normally prefer a radius to a diameter, so we define

$$R = D/2, \qquad r = d/2$$

The *axis* of the screw thread will coincide with the positive $z$-axis, which implies that the screw is in a vertical position.

We will distinguish:

1 The *outer surface*, all points of which lie at a distance $R$ from the axis of the screw.
2 The *inner surface*, all points of which lie at a distance $r$ from the axis.

3　The *top face*, a flat surface lying in the plane $z = L$.

4　The *bottom face*, a flat surface lying in the $xy$-plane ($z = 0$).

5　The *upper flank*, a curved surface, partly visible in Fig. 3.24, which connects the inner and outer surfaces.

6　The *lower flank*, a curved surface, similar to the upper flank and partly visible in Fig. 3.25.

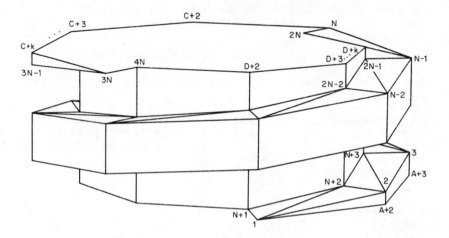

*Fig. 3.24 Screw thread approximated by flat faces; perspective top view*

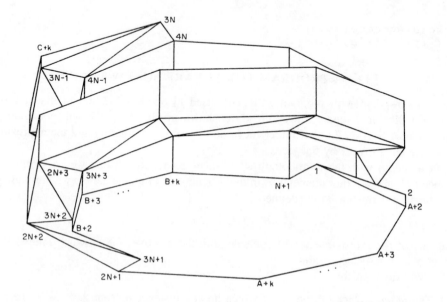

*Fig. 3.25 Screw thread approximated by flat faces; perspective bottom view*

In our screw thread, each curved, non-horizontal edge is a so-called *helix*. As for the approximation process, the user of SCRTHR has to enter $k$, the number of steps taken in a half revolution, which ensures that

$$n = 2k$$

the number of steps in a full revolution, is even. Since the given pitch is equal to the forward movement of the screw in a full revolution, that is, in $n$ steps, the $z$-coordinate increases by

$$delta\ L\ =\ \frac{pitch}{n}$$

if we follow a helix one step. The given length $L_0$ is then rounded to the nearest whole multiple of *delta L*, which is called $L$. We will often be using the constant

$$N\ =\ \frac{L}{delta\ L}\ +\ 1$$

which denotes the number of vertices on each helix. We number these vertices as follows (see Figs. 3.24 and 3.25), from bottom to top:

$1, 2, \ldots, N$:
Helix 1, the intersection of the outer surface and the upper flank;

$N+1, N+2, \ldots, 2N$:
Helix 2, the intersection of the inner surface and the upper flank;

$2N+1, 2N+2, \ldots, 3N$:
Helix 3, the intersection of the outer surface and the lower flank;

$3N+1, 3N+2, \ldots, 4N$:
Helix 4, the intersection of the inner surface and the lower flank.

Besides the four helixes, we have to consider the top and the bottom faces, on either of which we find two half circles, one with radius $R$ and the other with radius $r$. On each of these four half circles there are $k - 1$ points which still have to be assigned vertex numbers because they do not lie on a helix. With the abbreviations

$$A\ =\ 4N\ -\ 1$$
$$B\ =\ A\ +\ k\ -\ 1\ =\ 4N\ +\ k\ -\ 2$$
$$C\ =\ B\ +\ k\ -\ 1\ =\ 4N\ +\ 2k\ -\ 3$$
$$D\ =\ C\ +\ k\ -\ 1\ =\ 4N\ +\ 3k\ -\ 4$$

we do this as shown in Figs. 3.24 and 3.25:

$A+2, A+3, \ldots, A+k$:
Remaining points on the intersection of the outer surface and the bottom face;

$B+2, B+3, \ldots, B+k$:
Remaining points on the intersection of the inner surface and the bottom face;

$C+2, C+3, \ldots, C+k$:
Remaining points on the intersection of the outer surface and the top face;

$D+2, D+3, \ldots, D+k$:
Remaining points on the intersection of the inner surface and the top face.

Starting at the bottom, the first 180° and the last 180° of the outer surface is to be dealt with somewhat differently from the rest (which we shall call the *middle part*), and the same applies to the inner surface. We approximate the middle parts of both the outer and the inner surfaces by parallelograms, each of which has two vertical sides. The first part of the outer surface is the triangle with vertex numbers 1, $A+2$, 2. Then there are $k-1$ trapezoids: they have two vertical sides of unequal lengths. This is similar for the final 180°; the very last part of the outer surface is the triangle with vertices $3N$, $C+k$, $3N-1$. Similar conditions apply for the inner surface, which begins with the triangle $B+2$, $3N+2$, $3N+1$ and ends with the triangle $D+k$, $2N-1$, $2N$.

It might surprise you that the upper and the lower flanks in Figs. 3.24 and 3.25 show a division into triangles: using quadrangles instead may seem simpler and more natural. Actually, I must confess that in the first version of my program I made the same mistake. An attempt to specify, for example, the surface part 1, 2, $N+2$, $N+1$, shown in Fig. 3.24, as one polygon results in an error message from D3D, complaining that not all vertices of an alleged polygon lie in the same plane. This can be explained as follows. The vertices 1 and $N+1$ have the same $z$-coordinates ($z = 0$) and so have the vertices 2 and $N+2$ ($z = pitch/n$). Thus the two lines $(1, N+1)$ and $(2, N+2)$ lie in two different horizontal planes. This means that these two horizontal lines would be parallel if the four points mentioned lay in the same plane (since any non-horizontal plane will have parallel lines of intersection with two horizontal planes). Clearly, the two horizontal lines in question are not parallel, so the four points in question do not lie in the same plane. This also proves that, contrary to what you might expect, the two line segments $(1, 2)$ and $(N+1, N+2)$ are not parallel (the former having a smaller slope than the latter).

Finally, the bottom and the top faces are non-convex polygons, each of which can be specified as one bounding face. Apart from some discontinuities in their vertex numbers, they are not difficult, especially not if you can use Figs. 3.24 and 3.25. Obviously, I did not have these illustrations when I started thinking about writing program SCRTHR, nor did I have a real model or photograph of a flat-ended screw thread, so it took me quite a while to sketch the shape of these two end faces. With the above point numbering, program SCRTHR is rather simple. It might be instructive to mention that at first I used an entirely different point numbering and wrote a program so complicated that I could not understand it myself later when I needed it to write this book. However, the program worked correctly, so I could produce some pictures such as Fig. 3.24. Using these, I chose the above vertex numbering and designed an entirely new program, SCRTHR, as it is listed here.

```
/* SCRTHR:   Screw-thread
*/
#include <stdio.h>
#include <math.h>
#include <ctype.h>
#include <alloc.h>
#include <process.h>
```

```
struct point {float x, y, z;} *p;
FILE *fp;

void p1(int i);
void p1e(int i);
void p3e(int i, int j, int k);
void p4e(int i, int j, int k, int l);
void pr(int a, int b);

main()
{ int i, j, n, N, N2, N3, N4, k, steps, A, B, C, D;
  double pi, theta, phi, R, r, deltaL,
      major, minor, pitch, h, L, L0, offset;
  char str[30], ch;
  pi = 4 * atan(1.0);
  printf("Major diameter: "); scanf("%lf", &major);
  printf("Minor diameter: "); scanf("%lf", &minor);
  printf(
  "If the thread really is to be square, we have:\n");
  printf("\n    pitch = major - minor = %5.3f\n\n",
  pitch = major - minor);
  printf(
  "Then in one revolution, 'pitch' is the distance the\n");
  printf(
  "screw moves forward, so the imaginary 'square'\n");
  printf("has sides of length\n");
  printf("\n    h = pitch/2 = %5.3f\n\n", pitch/2);
  printf(
  "Do you want a different pitch, so that the thread\n");
  printf(
  "will not be really square (but rectangular)? (Y/N): ");
  scanf("%s", str);
  ch = toupper(str[0]);
  if (ch == 'Y')
  { printf("Pitch: "); scanf("%lf", &pitch);
  }
  h = pitch/2;
  printf("Desired length of the screw thread ");
  printf("(not less than %5.3f): ", h);
  scanf("%lf", &L0);
  if (L0 < h) L0 = h; /* At least a half revolution */
  printf("Number of steps taken in a half revolution: ");
  scanf("%d", &k);
  n = 2 * k;
  deltaL = pitch/n;
  steps = (int)(L0/deltaL + 0.5); N = steps + 1;
  N2 = 2*N; N3 = 3*N; N4 = 4*N;
  L = steps * deltaL;
  printf("The real length will be: %5.3f\n", L);
  printf("Name of output file: "); scanf("%s", str);
  fp = fopen(str, "w");
  theta = pi/k;
  R = major/2; r = minor/2;
  A = 4 * N - 1;
  B = A + k - 1;
  C = B + k - 1;
  D = C + k - 1;
```

```c
p = (struct point *)malloc((D+k+1)*sizeof(struct point));
if (p == NULL) {printf("Not enough memory"); exit(1);}
for (i=1; i<=N; i++)    /* Outer helix on upper flank */
{ phi = (i-1)*theta;
  p[i].x = R * cos(phi);
  p[i].y = R * sin(phi);
  p[i].z = (i-1) * deltaL;
}
for (i=N+1; i<=N2; i++)    /* Inner helix on upper flank */
{ p[i].x = p[i-N].x * r/R;
  p[i].y = p[i-N].y * r/R;
  p[i].z = p[i-N].z;
}
for (i=N2+1; i<=N3; i++)   /* Outer helix on lower flank */
{ p[i].x = -p[i-N2].x;
  p[i].y = -p[i-N2].y;
  p[i].z = p[i-N2].z;
}
for (i=N3+1; i<=N4; i++)   /* Inner helix on lower flank */
{ p[i].x = p[i-N].x * r/R;
  p[i].y = p[i-N].y * r/R;
  p[i].z = p[i-N].z;
}
for (i=A+2; i<=A+k; i++)
                    /* Outer half circle in bottom plane */
{ phi = (i-A-1)*theta;
  p[i].x = R * cos(phi);
  p[i].y = R * sin(phi);
  p[i].z = 0;
}
for (i=B+2; i<=B+k; i++)
                    /* Inner half circle in bottom plane */
{ p[i].x = -p[i-B+A].x * r/R;
  p[i].y = -p[i-B+A].y * r/R;
  p[i].z = 0;
}
offset = steps * theta;
while (offset > 2*pi) offset -= 2*pi;
for (i=C+2; i<=C+k; i++)
                    /* Outer half circle in top plane */
{ phi = offset + (i-C-1)*theta;
  p[i].x = R * cos(phi);
  p[i].y = R * sin(phi);
  p[i].z = L;
}
for (i=D+2; i<=D+k; i++)
                    /* Inner half circle in top plane */
{ p[i].x = -p[i-D+C].x * r/R;
  p[i].y = -p[i-D+C].y * r/R;
  p[i].z = L;
}
for (i=1; i<=D+k; i++)
  fprintf(fp, "%4d %f %f %f\n",
                i, p[i].x, p[i].y, p[i].z);

fprintf(fp, "Faces:\n");
```

```
/* z = 0: */
p1(N2+1); pr(A+k, A+2); p1(1); p1(N+1);
pr(B+k, B+2); p1e(N3+1);

/* z = L: */
p1(N); pr(C+2, C+k); p1(N3); p1(N4);
pr(D+2, D+k); p1e(N2);

/* First 180 degrees (at the bottom) */

/* Outer surface: */
p3e(1, A+2, 2);
for (j=2; j<k; j++) p4e(A+j, A+j+1, j+1, j);
p4e(A+k, N2+1, k+1, k);

/* Inner surface: */
p3e(B+2, N3+2, N3+1);
for (j=2; j<k; j++) p4e(B+j+1, N3+j+1, N3+j, B+j);
p4e(N+1, N3+k+1, N3+k, B+k);

/* Final 180 degrees (at the top) */

/* Outer surface: */
p3e(N3, C+k, N3-1);
for (j=2; j<k; j++) p4e(C+k-j+2, C+k-j+1, N3-j, N3-j+1);
p4e(C+2, N, N3-k, N3-k+1);

/* Inner surface: */
p3e(D+k, N2-1, N2);
for (j=2; j<k; j++) p4e(D+k-j+2, D+k-j+1, N2-j, N2-j+1);
p4e(D+2, N4, N2-k, N2-k+1);

/* Middle part */

/* Outer surface: */
for (j=1; j<N-k; j++) p4e(N2+j, N2+j+1, k+j+1, k+j);

/* Inner surface: */
for (j=1; j<N-k; j++) p4e(N+j, N+j+1, N3+k+j+1, N3+k+j);

/* Upper flank: */
for (j=1; j<N; j++)
{ p3e(j, N+j+1, N+j);
  p3e(N+j+1, j, j+1);
}

/* Lower flank: */
for (j=1; j<N; j++)
{ p3e(N3-j+1, N4-j, N4-j+1);
  p3e(N4-j, N3-j+1, N3-j);
}
fclose (fp);
}

void p1(int i)
{ fprintf(fp, " %d", i);
}
```

```
void p1e(int i)
{ fprintf(fp, " %d.\n", i);
}

void p3e(int i, int j, int k)
{ fprintf(fp, " %d %d %d.\n", i, j, k);
}

void p4e(int i, int j, int k, int l)
{ fprintf(fp, " %d %d %d %d.\n", i, j, k, l);
}

void pr(int a, int b)
{ int i;
  if (b >= a) for (i=a; i<=b; i++) fprintf(fp, " %d", i);
         else for (i=a; i>=b; i--) fprintf(fp, " %d", i);
}
```

*PART C*

# Graphics Programming Details

# CHAPTER 4

## *Programs D3D and PLOTHP*

### 4.1 INTRODUCTION

This chapter is mainly about program D3D, which is much larger than all other programs discussed so far. Its executable version, D3D.EXE, is obtained by linking together the four object modules D3D.OBJ, GRPACK.OBJ, HLPFUN.OBJ, and TRAFO.OBJ, which are produced by the Turbo C compiler when compiling the corresponding four source files. The places where you can find a brief discussion of each of these four modules and the program listings themselves are as follows:

| Module | Discussion | Listing |
|--------|------------|---------|
| D3D | Section 4.2 | Appendix A |
| GRPACK | Section 4.3 | Section 4.3 |
| HLPFUN | Section 4.4 | Appendix B |
| TRAFO | Section 3.7 | Section 3.7 |

Recall that in Section 3.7 we have discussed 3D rotations in the context of curve fitting and cables; the very functions (*initrotate* and *rotate*, in module TRAFO) that we have been using there will now be useful again.

Program D3D is too large to be explained in detail in this book, so we will discuss only some aspects of it. If you want to know more about it than explained in the text of Section 4.2, please refer to the program text itself, listed in Appendix A.

Section 4.3 will be about GRPACK, a package of graphics routines that is useful not only in connection with D3D but also for many other purposes. It is similar to a graphics package with the same name, listed and discussed in my book *Computer Graphics for the IBM PC*. That book was based on both the IBM Color Graphics Adapter (CGA) and the Hercules Graphics Adapter (HGA), whereas the present version of GRPACK also supports the Enhanced Graphics Adapter (EGA). Besides, the new version of GRPACK is based on Turbo C, which was not yet available when I wrote my previous book. Another new aspect is the possibility of obtaining graphics output in a file that can be read later by another program to produce a hard copy, using, for example, a plotter. An example of such a program is given in Section 4.5.

In Section 4.4 we will discuss HLPFUN, a function for *hidden-line elimination*. It is based on a method that has also been used in HIDLINPIX, a program that plays a central role in my book *Programming Principles in Computer Graphics*. As an extension to that program, HLPFUN offers facilities for curved surfaces; it also differs from the original program in other respects. For example, it uses computer memory in a more flexible way, and it is nonrecursive, so that any danger of stack overflow is avoided.

So much for the modules which, when compiled and linked, comprise program D3D. In contrast to this, Section 4.5 is about a stand-alone program, PLOTHP. It can produce drawings on a Hewlett-Packard plotter; with this program many illustrations in this book have been made. In case you do not have such a plotter, this program may still be useful to you because you can also use it to send graphics output both to the video display and to a matrix printer. Besides, the files written by means of the option $O$ (in connection with the commands $H$ and $E$) can be read by programs written by yourself to obtain output on other graphics devices, such as, for example, laser printers; in other words, you may regard program PLOTHP as just an example of a program for deferred graphics output.

## 4.2   D3D MAIN MODULE

Before dealing with program D3D itself, let us briefly discuss how perspective images of three-dimensional objects can be obtained by computation. We will be using a *central object point* O, lying more or less central in the object that we want to display in perspective. Another important point is viewpoint E, given by its spherical coordinates $\rho$, $\theta$, $\varphi$, as discussed in Section 1.2. These spherical coordinates are related to the axes of a right-handed coordinate system, obtained by translating the user's *world-coordinate system* in such a way that point O becomes its origin. Thus $\rho$ is equal to EO. For each vertex of the object, we are given its world coordinates $x_w$, $y_w$, $z_w$, expressed in the user's coordinate system (the origin of which may be different from O).

As you will remember, the $z$-axis of each of these two coordinate systems points upward, and normally the $x$-axis points towards us. We use the world coordinates $x_w$, $y_w$, $z_w$ to compute the *eye coordinates* $x_e$, $y_e$, $z_e$. The eye-coordinate system is left-handed; its origin lies in viewpoint E, its positive $z$-axis points to the central object point O, its $x$-axis points horizontally to the right, and its $y$-axis (perpendicular to the $x$- and the $z$-axes) points upward. The eye coordinates are the result of the so-called *viewing transformation*

$$[x_e \ \ y_e \ \ z_e \ \ 1] \ = \ [x_w - x_O \ \ y_w - y_O \ \ z_w - z_O \ \ 1] \ V$$

In this matrix multiplication we use the $4 \times 4$ matrix

$$V \ = \ \begin{bmatrix} -\sin\theta & -\cos\varphi\cos\theta & -\sin\varphi\cos\theta & 0 \\ \cos\theta & -\cos\varphi\sin\theta & -\sin\varphi\sin\theta & 0 \\ 0 & \sin\varphi & -\cos\varphi & 0 \\ 0 & 0 & \rho & 1 \end{bmatrix}$$

Note that in the above matrix product we could have omitted the terms $-x_O$, $-y_O$, $-z_O$ if these had been equal to zero, that is, if the world coordinates $x_w$, $y_w$, $z_w$ had referred to the translated coordinate system (with origin O) instead of to the user's coordinate system.

The viewing transformation is only the first of two steps we have to take. We use the eye coordinates to compute the two-dimensional *screen coordinates* $x_s$, $y_s$, which we need for the desired perspective image. They are found in the second step, the *perspective transformation*:

$$x_s \ = \ d \times x_e + c_1$$
$$y_s \ = \ d \times y_e + c_2$$

It will be clear that $d$ is a scaling factor and that $c_1$, $c_2$ are used to shift the image horizontally and vertically, respectively, to its proper position. My previous graphics book *Programming Principles in Computer Graphics* (*PPCG*) shows how matrix $V$ can be found as the product of some other matrices. It also contains a section about automatically adjusting the size and position to a given *viewport* (that is, the portion of the screen to be used). This, too, is relevant for our present purposes. Remember that, when using D3D, we may enter new points whose images do not lie inside the viewport. In that case we have to find new values of the above constants $c_1$, $c_2$, and $d$. They should be chosen such that the entire image again falls inside the boundaries of the screen. Not only the world coordinates $x_w$, $y_w$, $z_w$ but also the eye-coordinates $x_e$, $y_e$, $z_e$ will be stored internally. This reduces the amount of work in adjusting the image size considerably, since with new values of $c_1$, $c_2$, and $d$ we only have to perform the perspective transformation. After all, this work is to be applied to all vertices, so it would be a waste of time to perform the more time-consuming viewing transformation unnecessarily.

In *PPCG* (mentioned above) the format of input files is such that the coordinates $x_O$, $y_O$, $z_O$ of the central object point O precede the coordinates of all vertices. We are now in a different situation in that we are dealing with an interactive program, which accepts new points at any moment and which does not require the user to specify a central object point in advance. Therefore, with a given set of points, either given in an object file or entered by hand, the central object point is computed as

$$x_O = (xwmin + xwmax)/2$$
$$y_O = (ywmin + ywmax)/2$$
$$z_O = (zwmin + zwmax)/2$$

where *xwmin* and *xwmax* are the smallest and the greatest $x$-world-coordinates, and so on. Thus, point O lies precisely in the middle of the smallest right prism (with bounding faces parallel to the axes of the world-coordinate system) in which all given points lie. Let us call such prisms *bounding prisms*. If a new point is entered which lies outside the bounding prism, then, strictly speaking, we would have to compute a new central object point. But then the eye coordinates $x_e$, $y_e$, $z_e$ would also have to be updated, since point O influences the eye-coordinate system. However, we know that the position of point O is not very critical as long as it lies somewhere near the center of the object. We therefore leave point O unchanged as long as it lies within some reasonable distance from the center of the bounding prism. When this distance, to be regarded as a 'tolerance', is exceeded, we really have to update point O, accepting the possibly time-consuming task of computing new eye coordinates for all vertices. In program D3D, the following tolerance values for the $x$-, $y$-, and $z$-directions are used:

$$xtol = 0.4(xwmax - xwmin)$$
$$ytol = 0.4(ywmax - ywmin)$$
$$ztol = 0.4(zwmax - zwmin)$$

Thus, inside the bounding prism, we can imagine a similar concentric prism, obtained by scaling the bounding prism by a factor 0.8. As long as point O lies inside the smaller prism, we regard it as acceptable.

The heart of program D3D is a while-loop, in which repeatedly the first character of a command is read from the keyboard and the corresponding action is performed. Normally, the latter is done by means of a function call. For example, if the user enters command $F$ (or $f$), then the function *faces* is called. Functions, such as *faces*, occur in alphabetic order so that we can quickly find them. All vertices are stored in a table; instead of a normal array, a pointer variable $p$ is used, which enables us to use a table length that depends on the amount of memory available. For each vertex, both the *world coordinates* $(x_w, y_w, z_w)$ and the *eye coordinates* $(x_e, y_e, z_e)$ are stored, as we have discussed. The position of the current central object point O is checked in function *reposition*. If that position is unacceptable, the center of the bounding prism is used as the new point O, and new eye coordinates $x_e, y_e, z_e$ are computed for all vertices by calling function *storepoint*, which in turn calls function *viewing*. Returning to *reposition*, we also call function *screencoor*, which, if necessary, updates the variables *xmin*, *xmax*, *ymin*, and *ymax* (not to be confused with *xwmin* etc.). They are the minimum and maximum values of the expressions $x_e/z_e$ and $y_e/z_e$, which occur in the perspective transformation, and they enable us to compute the important 'constants' $c_1$, $c_2$ and $d$, also occurring in the perspective transformation. With

$$Xrange = xmax - xmin$$
$$Yrange = ymax - ymin$$
$$Xcenter = (xmin + xmax)/2$$
$$Ycenter = (ymin + ymax)/2$$

and using also both the center $(Xvp\_center, Yvp\_center)$ and the dimensions $Xvp\_range$ and $Yvp\_range$ of the given viewport, we have

$$f_x = \frac{Xvp\_range}{Xrange}$$
$$f_y = \frac{Yvp\_range}{Yrange}$$

$$d = \text{the smaller of the two values } f_x \text{ and } f_y$$
$$c_1 = Xvp\_center - d \times Xcenter$$
$$c_2 = Yvp\_center - d \times Ycenter$$

as explained in my previous book *PPCG*, Section 2.6.

It follows from the above that we are dealing with 3D as well as 2D boundaries. As for the 3D boundaries, we have to take care that the bounding prism (determined by *xwmin*, *xwmax*, *ywmin*, *ywmax*, *zwmin*, *zwmax*) is updated whenever a point is entered that lies outside it. The 2D boundaries are given by *xmin*, *xmax*, *ymin*, *ymax*, which determine the viewport. For every new point, we have to check that its 2D image lies within these 2D boundaries. In function *plotpoint*, the function *screencoor* is called, which may set the global variable *inside* to 0 as a signal that the 2D check has failed. The function *reposition* is then called, and a 3D check is performed first: if the current 'central object point' O lies too far from the exact center of the bounding prism, it is updated and, for all vertices, function *storepoint* is called to compute new eye coordinates $x_e, y_e, z_e$. Regardless of the outcome of the 3D test, function *reposition* computes new values $c_1$, $c_2$, and $d$. Then a subsequent call of the function *display* will use these new values to refresh the screen, and the images of all points will now lie inside the viewport. Thus, refreshing the screen may or may not be combined with computing new eye coordinates. When it is not, the image will appear much quicker on the screen than when it is. Yet, a screen refreshment that computes only new screen coordinates (leaving the eye coordinates unchanged) will take some time. Now suppose that we are moving the cursor in a fixed direction, using only very small steps, and that we continue to do so after we have reached the boundary of the viewport. It would then be annoying if the screen were refreshed in each such small step. Therefore, while using the working screen, each new value of $d$ is reduced by some 'tolerance' factor, for which I have used 0.85. This means that, immediately after refreshing the screen, the size of the image is only 0.85 times the maximum size permitted by the viewport. In this way, the cursor can again take some steps in the same direction before it reaches the viewport boundary again. The value 0.85 of this 'tolerance factor' is rather arbitrary, and you can change it (in function *reposition*) if you like. The larger it is (not greater than 1), the more often the screen will be refreshed as a consequence of cursor movements, so you can reduce it if screen refreshment takes place too frequently in your opinion. However, the price to be paid for this is that immediately after screen refreshment the unused margins along the four sides of the viewport will be larger; in other words, the image will be smaller.

You may wonder if it is really necessary to perform the 2D check for all individual points; after all, if we take care that all eight vertices of the bounding prism have images that lie inside the viewport, then the images of all points inside the bounding prism will also lie inside the viewport. This method is indeed safe, but, unfortunately, it is too safe. In many objects it may produce images that are considerably smaller than what would be possible. Take, for example, a sphere; its bounding prism is a cube in which it fits. With most viewpoints, the cube would require more space on the screen than the sphere, so it is no good basing the perspective transformation of the sphere on the dimensions of the cube. Besides, this method would often cause the screen to be refreshed for points (or cursor positions) that, though lying outside the current bounding prism, still lie within the viewport. With our method, on the other hand, the position of a point is compared with the viewport instead of with the bounding prism. The bounding prism is allowed to have an image that does not fit in the viewport; we need it only in order that we may be able to compute a new central object point O, when necessary.

The above remarks are by no means a complete explanation of program D3D, but they are about some of the most essential elements of it. Some other essential ingredients are 3D rotations, low-level graphics, and hidden-line elimination, which are the subjects of Sections 3.7, 4.3, and 4.4, respectively. The module D3D itself is listed in Appendix A. As it consists of a great many functions of moderate size, listed in alphabetic order, the program text itself may also be helpful if you want to know how it works.

### 4.3  LOW-LEVEL GRAPHICS FUNCTION

Five of the six chapters of my previous book *Computer Graphics for the IBM PC* (from now on abbreviated *CGIP*) are about the development of a package, GRPACK, of low-level graphics C functions. The nature of that kind of software differs from most programs in the present book in that it is closely related to specific hardware and compiler versions, and when I wrote *CGIP*, I was aware that some of the low-level graphics functions in it were not particularly elegant, which is a consequence of the fact that the IBM PC and its basic software is not elegant in all respects. However, we cannot always avoid machine- and compiler-dependent aspects if we want to discuss real-life programs. The low-level graphics functions are the basic building blocks for high-level graphics: both the main program D3D and the hidden-line module HLPFUN use the low-level functions discussed in this section.

We will now use and discuss an updated version of GRPACK, mentioned above. In contrast to the version published in *CGIP*, it will not include any functions for filling closed regions and for drawing circles, because we do not need these facilities in D3D. More importantly, the present version is accepted by Turbo C (whereas the original was based on Lattice C). Another new point is that GRPACK now gives better results on machines that work with an Enhanced Graphics Adapter (EGA). The original version distinguished between the Hercules Graphics Adapter (HGA), resolution 720 × 348, and the Color Graphics Adapter (CGA), resolution 640 × 200, and chose the latter resolution if EGA was being used. Instead, GRPACK can now choose among three possibilities, namely HGA, CGA (both with the resolutions just mentioned), and EGA with resolution 640 × 350.

Finally, there is now also the possibility of obtaining a hard copy on a Hewlett-Packard plotter. This is done by writing data to a file that can be read by another program, PLOTHP, to be discussed in Section 4.5. As this file is a normal ASCII file containing user's coordinates, we can use it for other purposes as well. For example, program PLOTHP can also be used for deferred graphics output on the video display and on a matrix printer. Another possibility is to write a program yourself which reads that file and converts it to commands for some other graphics output device.

Besides GRPACK, there is an alternative, GRPACK1; the latter is based on the Turbo C Version 1.5, which has built-in graphics facilities; we will discuss GRPACK1 later in this section.

As I do not presume you to be familiar with my book *CGIP*, let us first discuss how my low-level graphics functions can be used. We distinguish between real screen coordinates in inches, denoted by lower-case letters $x$ and $y$, and integer pixel coordinates, denoted by capital letters $X$ and $Y$. The origin of the real coordinate system lies in the bottom-left corner of the screen:

$$0 \leq x \leq x\_max$$
$$0 \leq y \leq y\_max$$

Unless *setprdim* is called, see below, we have

$$x\_max = 10.0$$
$$y\_max = 7.0$$

(Thus we assume the actual dimensions of the video screen to be 10 × 7 inches; since this is only an approximation, the term *inch* is not to be taken too literally, as far as the video screen is concerned.)

The origin ($X = 0$, $Y = 0$) of the pixel-coordinate system lies in the top-left corner of the screen, and we have

$$0 \leq X \leq X\_\_max$$
$$0 \leq Y \leq Y\_\_max$$

where the maximum values of $X$ and $Y$ depend on the adapter type that is being used:

|        | X__max | Y__max |
|--------|--------|--------|
| CGA:   | 639    | 199    |
| HGA:   | 719    | 347    |
| EGA:   | 639    | 349    |

Like the functions that we will be using, the variables $x\_max$, $y\_max$, $X\_\_max$, $Y\_\_max$, and some others mentioned below, are defined in GRPACK.C and declared in the header file GRPACK.H. It is strongly recommended to use this file, writing

```
#include "grpack.h"
```

in any program that uses GRPACK (or GRPACK1).

The following summary shows the functions that are available in GRPACK. (They are also available in GRPACK1, but there some will have a slightly different effect, as we will see.) Arguments $x$ and $y$, written in lower case, have type *float*, and those that begin with capital letters $X$ and $Y$ have type *int*.

| | |
|---|---|
| *initgr*( ) | Initialize graphics; the video display switches to graphics mode. To be used in text mode. |
| *endgr*( ) | Wait until a key is pressed. After this, the video display returns to text mode. Don't forget to call this function (or *to_text*) before program termination. To be used in graphics mode. |
| *to_text*( ) | Return to text mode immediately. To be used in graphics mode. |
| *move*(x, y) | Move a fictitious pen to point $(x, y)$ ($x$ and $y$ are nonnegative real coordinates, not greater than $x\_max$ and $y\_max$, respectively). To be used in graphics mode. |
| *draw*(x, y) | Draw line segment from current pen position to new pen position $(x, y)$. To be used in graphics mode. |
| *imove*(X, Y) | Move pen to point $(X, Y)$ ($X$ and $Y$ are nonnegative integer pixel coordinates, not greater than $X\_\_max$ and $Y\_\_max$, respectively). To be used in graphics mode. |
| *idraw*(X, Y) | Draw line segment from old pen position to new pen position $(X, Y)$. To be used in graphics mode. |
| *draw_line*(X1, Y1, X2, Y2) | Draw line segment from $(X1, Y1)$ to $(X2, Y2)$ (without changing the 'current pen position'). To be used in graphics mode. |
| *dot*(X, Y) | Place a dot in point $(X, Y)$. To be used in graphics mode. |
| *clearpage*( ) | Clear the graphics screen. (The term *page* has to do with the fact that the HGA has two pages, 0 and 1; incidentally, only page 1 is used.) To be used in graphics mode. |
| *text*(str) | Display string *str*, starting at the current pen position (probably obtained by *imove* or *move*). The 'current pen position' is updated. To be used in graphics mode. |
| *textXY*(X, Y, str) | The same as *text*(str), except for the starting point, which is now given explicitly. Does not change the 'current pen position'. To be used in graphics mode. |
| *printgr*(Xlo, Xhi, Ylo, Yhi) | Print the (graphics) contents of the 'viewport' $Xlo \le X \le Xhi$, $Ylo \le Y \le Yhi$, using a matrix printer. See also *setprdim*( ). To be used in graphics mode. |

*setprdim( )*                       'Set print dimensions'. If we call this function prior to *initgr*, the variables *x_max* and *y_max* will be assigned values that correspond to the aspect ratio of the matrix printer. As a result, function *printgr* will produce output on the printer with correct dimensions both in the horizontal and vertical directions. Thus, a circle (approximated by a regular polygon) will be printed as a circle, not as an ellipse. Unfortunately, a circle will then be displayed on the screen as an ellipse, so this function should not be used if optimal results on the video display are required. To be used in text mode.

The following four functions return integer values:

*IX(x)*                             The integer pixel coordinate *X* that corresponds to the real screen coordinate *x*. To be used in graphics mode.
*IY(y)*                             The integer pixel coordinate *Y* that corresponds to the real screen coordinate *y*. To be used in graphics mode.
*pixlit(X, Y)*                      Returns 1 if pixel *(X, Y)* is lit and 0 if it is dark. To be used in graphics mode.
*iscolor( )*                        Returns a code for the graphics adapter that is being used:

                                    2 = EGA (new in this version of GRPACK)
                                    1 = CGA
                                    0 = HGA
                                    −1 = adapter that is unsuitable for graphics

                                    Can be used both in text mode and in graphics mode.

There are three functions in GRPACK that are not really graphics functions (although they deal with the video display). They can be used only in text mode, not in graphics mode:

*wrscr(row, column, str)*           Write the (null-terminated) string *str* on the screen, starting at position *row, column*. The row numbers range from 0 to 24 and the column numbers from 0 to 79. The position in the upper-left corner of the screen has (0, 0) as its row and column numbers. To be used in text mode.
*settxtcursor(row, column)*         Set the text cursor (a blinking underscore) at position *row, column*. To be used in text mode.
*clearscr( )*                       Clear the screen. To be used in text mode.

(The three last functions, *wrscr*, *settxtcursor*, *clearscr*, were not included in the original version of GRPACK, so they are not discussed in my previous book *CGIP*.)

In graphics mode, we can erase objects on the screen by assigning −1 to the variable *drawmode*, declared in the header file GRPACK.H and normally having the value 1. With *drawmode* = −1, the functions *draw*, *idraw*, *draw_line*, *dot* of GRPACK will then turn pixels dark. As a third option, we can set *drawmode* to 0, which will cause pixels to be 'inverted': if they are dark they will be lit, and if they are lit they will turn dark by calls of the four functions just mentioned.

As mentioned above, there is a header file, which should be used as follows:

```
#include "grpack.h"
```

I strongly recommend this in any program that uses GRPACK (or GRPACK1). The text of this header file is listed below.

```
/* GRPACK.H: Header file for graphics functions.
*/
extern int in_textmode, adaptype, X__max, Y__max, drawmode;
extern float x_max, y_max, horfact, vertfact;
extern FILE *fplot;
/* File for deferred graphics output. For example, program
   PLOTHP can read this file and convert it to output on
   the video screen, a matrix printer, or an HP plotter.
   The identifier FILE is defined in 'stdio.h', which
   must therefore be included prior to the present file.
*/
#ifndef __HUGE__
#error Use Turbo C huge mem. model.
#endif
void initgr(void);
void endgr(void);
void to_text(void);
void move(float x, float y);
void draw(float x, float y);
void imove(int X, int Y);
void idraw(int X, int Y);
void draw_line(int X1, int Y1, int X2, int Y2);
void dot(int X, int Y);
void clearpage(void);
void text(char *str);
void textXY(int X, int Y, char *str);
void printgr(int Xlo, int Xhi, int Ylo, int Yhi);
void setprdim(void);
int IX(float x);
int IY(float y);
int pixlit(int X, int Y);
int iscolor(void);
void wrscr(int line, int col, char *str);
void settxtcursor(int line, int col);
void clearscr(void);
```

Besides $X\_\_max$, $Y\_\_max$, and *drawmode*, mentioned above, there are two other useful global variables of type *int*:

$in\_textmode$ = 1 if the system is in text mode
= 0 if the system is in graphics mode
*adaptype* = the value returned by *iscolor*( ), as defined above; it has this value after *initgr*( ) has been called

Besides the *float* global variables $x\_max$, and $y\_max$, we have:

*horfact* = number of pixels in one inch in the horizontal direction

*vertfact* = number of pixels in one inch in the vertical direction

The values of *x_max*, *y_max*, *horfact*, *vertfact* apply to the video display, unless, prior to calling *initgr*( ), the function *setprdim*( ) is called; in that case they apply to the matrix printer.

Finally, GRPACK defines the file pointer *fplot*, which is also a global variable. It normally has the (default) value *NULL*, and is then ignored. If, on the other hand, we have given it some other value, normally obtained by a call of the standard function *fopen*, then all calls of the graphics functions *move* and *draw*, in addition to their normal effects, will write text lines to the file given by *fplot*. Each of these text lines contains three numbers, namely the two arguments (*x* and *y*) of *move* and *draw*, and either 0 or 1, as a code for *move* and *draw*, respectively. In this way, the line drawing that we are producing not only appears on the video display but it becomes available in machine-readable form as well. In Section 4.5 we shall see that this can be very useful, in particular if a Hewlett-Packard plotter is available.

The text of GRPACK is listed below; most of the functions in it are explained in my book *CGIP*. Remember, if you find elements in it that you cannot use because of your specific hardware or software, you have an alternative, namely GRPACK1, to be discussed after this listing of GRPACK.

```
/* GRPACK: A graphics package.
        Turbo C version, to be used in the huge memory model.
        ('Huge' should be used for ALL modules involved!)
        For: Enhanced Graphics Adapter (EGA, 640 x 350)
             Color Graphics Adapter (CGA, 640 x 200)
             Hercules Graphics Adapter (HGA, 720 x 348)
        See also:
        L. Ammeraal (1987). Computer Graphics for the
             IBM PC, Chichester: John Wiley & Sons.
*/
#include <stdio.h>
#include <dos.h>
#include <conio.h>
#include <process.h>
#include <string.h>
#ifndef __HUGE__
#error Use Turbo C huge mem. model.
#endif

union REGS regs;

int in_textmode=1, X__max, Y__max, drawmode=1, adaptype;

FILE *fplot=NULL;

float x_max=10.0, y_max=7.0, horfact, vertfact;

static int old_vid_state, X1, Y1, offset,
    Ystart[350]; /*  350 >=  Ymax + 1 */

static long int startaddress;

static char
    lastchar,
    gtable[12] =
        {53, 45, 46,  7, 91, 2, 87, 87, 2,  3,  0,  0},
```

```
    ttable[12] =
      {97, 80, 82, 15, 25, 6, 25, 25, 2, 13, 11, 12},
    zeros[128]; /* implicitly initialized to zero */

void to_text(void);
void textXY(int X, int Y, char *str);


int IX(float x) { return (int)(x*horfact+0.5); }
int IY(float y) { return Y__max-(int)(y*vertfact+0.5); }


static void error(char *str)
/* Display a message and terminate program execution */
{ if (!in_textmode) to_text();
  printf("%s\n", str); exit(1);
}


void clearpage(void)  /* Clear the graphics screen */
{ int i, n;
  unsigned segsrc, offsrc, segdest;
  n = (adaptype == 1 ? 128 :
      adaptype == 0 ? 256 : 219);
                              /* EGA: 219 x 128 = 28032 */
  segsrc = FP_SEG(zeros); offsrc = FP_OFF(zeros);
  segdest = (adaptype == 2 ? 0xA000 : 0xB800);
  for (i=0; i<n; i++)
  movedata(segsrc, offsrc, segdest, i << 7, 128);
}


int iscolor(void)      /* Find out which adapter is used */
{ char ch0, ch1, x;
  if (peekb(0x40, 0x87)) return 2;                .
  /* EGA, see Dr. Dobbs Journal, November 1987, p.34 */
  int86(0x11, &regs, &regs);
  if ((regs.x.ax & 0x30) != 0x30) return 1; /* CGA */
    /* Color graphics                         */
  outport(0x3BF, 3);
    /* Configuration switch                   */
  ch0 = *(char *)0xB8000000;
    /* Try to read ch0 from screen memory    */
  ch1 = ch0 ^ 0xFF;
    /* Find some value different from  ch0    */
  *(char *)0xB8000000 = ch1;
    /* Try to write this into screen memory  */
  x = *(char *)0xB8000000;
    /* Try to read the latter value           */
  *(char *)0xB8000000 = ch0;
    /* Restore the old value  ch0             */
  return ( x == ch1 ? 0 : -1);
    /* Has written value been read?           */
}

static void setgrcon(int adaptype)
/* Set graphics constants */
```

```
{ int Y, c1, c2, c3;
  startaddress = (adaptype == 2 ? 0xA0000000 : 0xB8000000);
  if (adaptype == 2)
  { X__max = 639; Y__max = 349;
     for (Y=0; Y<=Y__max; Y++) Ystart[Y] = 80 * Y;
     return;
  }
  if (adaptype == 1)
  { X__max = 639; Y__max = 199;
     c1 = 1; c2 = 80; c3 = 1;
  } else
  { X__max = 719; Y__max = 347;
     c1 = 3; c2 = 90; c3 = 2;
  }
  for (Y=0; Y<=Y__max; Y++)
  Ystart[Y] = 0x2000*(Y&c1) + c2*(Y>>c3);
}


static int grbrfun(void)
/* Used by  ctrlbrk, to specify what to do with a console
   break
*/
{ to_text(); return 0;
}


static void initcgaorega(int mode)
    /* Switch to graphics mode (CGA or EGA)       */
{ regs.h.ah = 15; /* Inquire current video state */
  int86(0x10, &regs, &regs);
  old_vid_state = regs.h.al;
  regs.h.ah = 0;  /* Set graphics mode           */
  regs.h.al = mode;
  /* mode = 6:  CGA, 640 x 200, black/white      */
  /* mode = 16: EGA, 640 x 350, black/white      */
  int86(0x10, &regs, &regs);
}


static void initmongr(void)
/* Switch to graphics mode (monochrome graphics) */
{ static int firstcall=1;
  int i;
  outport(0x3B8, 0x82);
  for (i=0; i<12; i++)
  { outport(0x3B4, i);
    outport(0x3B5, gtable[i]);
  }
  if (firstcall) { firstcall=0; clearpage(); }
  outport(0x3B8, 0x8A);
}


void initgr(void)   /* Initialize graphics */
{ if (!in_textmode)
    error("initgr is called in graphics mode");
```

```
  adaptype = iscolor();
  if (adaptype < 0) error("Wrong display adapter");
  ctrlbrk(grbrfun);     /* Set break trap, Turbo C    */
  if (adaptype == 2) initcgaorega(16); /* EGA */ else
  if (adaptype == 1) initcgaorega(6);  /* CGA */ else
  /* adaptype == 0 */ initmongr();     /* HGA */
  setgrcon(adaptype);
  in_textmode=0;
  horfact = X__max/x_max; vertfact = Y__max/y_max;
}


static void endcolgr(void)
/* Revert to text mode (color graphics or EGA): */
{ regs.h.ah = 0; regs.h.al = old_vid_state;
  int86(0x10, &regs, &regs);
}


static void endmongr(void)
/* Revert to text mode (monochrome graphics): */
{ int i;
  char *source;
  unsigned segsrc, offsrc;
  outport(0x3B8, 0);
  for (i=0; i<12; i++)
  { outport(0x3B4, i);
    outport(0x3B5, ttable[i]);
  }
  source =
  "\40\7\40\7\40\7\40\7\40\7\40\7\40\7\40\7";
  segsrc = FP_SEG(source); offsrc = FP_OFF(source); .
  for (i=0; i<256; i++)
    movedata(segsrc, offsrc, 0xB000, i << 4, 16);
  outport(0x3B8, 0x08);
}


static int txtbrfun(void)
{ return 0;
}


void to_text(void)
/* Revert to text mode */
{ if (in_textmode)
    error("endgr or to_text is called in text mode");
  if (adaptype) endcolgr(); /* CGA or EGA */
          else endmongr(); /* HGA        */
  in_textmode = 1;
  ctrlbrk(txtbrfun);
  /* Restore default break interrupt handler */
}


void endgr(void)
/* Wait until any key is hit and revert to text mode   */
```

```
{ getch();
  to_text();
}


void dot(int X, int Y)   /* Light or darken a pixel */
{ int pattern;
  offset = Ystart[Y] + (X>>3);
  lastchar = *(char *)(startaddress + offset);
                                              /* Turbo C   */
  pattern = 0x80 >> (X&7);
  if (drawmode == 1) lastchar |= pattern; else
  if (drawmode == -1) lastchar &= (~pattern);
                    else lastchar ^=pattern;
  *(char *)(startaddress + offset) = lastchar;
}


static void checkbreak(void)
{ char ch;
  if (kbhit()) { ch = getch(); kbhit(); ungetch(ch); }
}


void draw_line(int X1, int Y1, int X2, int Y2)
/* Draw the line segment from (X1, Y1) to (X2, Y2);
   X1, Y1, X2, Y2 are pixel coordinates   */
{ int X, Y, T, E, dX, dY, denom, Xinc = 1, Yinc = 1,
  vertlonger = 0, aux;
  checkbreak(); /* To make DOS check for console break */
  if (in_textmode)
    error("Not in graphics mode (call initgr)");
  dX = X2 - X1; dY = Y2 - Y1;
  if (dX < 0) {Xinc = -1; dX = -dX;}
  if (dY < 0) {Yinc = -1; dY = -dY;}
  if (dY > dX)
  { vertlonger = 1; aux = dX; dX = dY; dY = aux;
  }
  denom = dX << 1;
  T = dY << 1;
  E = -dX; X = X1;
  Y = Y1;
  if (vertlonger)
  while (dX-- >= 0)
  { dot(X, Y);
    if ((E += T) > 0)
    { X += Xinc; E -= denom;
    }
    Y += Yinc;
  } else
  while (dX-- >= 0)
  { dot(X, Y);
    if ((E += T) > 0)
    { Y += Yinc; E -= denom;
    }
    X += Xinc;
  }
```

```
      if (drawmode == 0) dot(X1, Y1);
}

static void fatal(void)
/* Draw a diagonal, then wait until a key is pressed, and
   finally revert to text mode
*/
{ draw_line(0, Y__max,  X__max, 0); endgr();
}


static void check(int X, int Y)
/* If point (X, Y) lies outside the screen boundaries, then
   call  fatal, display the incorrect coordinates, and stop
*/
{ if (X < 0 || X > X__max || Y < 0 || Y > Y__max)
   { fatal();
     printf(
"Point outside screen (X and Y are pixel coordinates):\n");
      printf("X = %d        Y = %d\n", X, Y);
      printf("x = %10.3f    y = %10.3f\n",
      X/horfact, (Y__max-Y)/vertfact);
      printf(
      "X__max = %d  Y__max = %d  x_max = %f y_max = %f\n",
       X__max, Y__max, x_max, y_max);
      printf("horfact = %f  vertfact = % f\n",
              horfact, vertfact);
      exit(1);
   }
}


void move(float x, float y)
/* Move the current point to (x, y);
   x and y are screen coordinates  */
{ int XX, YY;
   XX = IX(x); YY = IY(y); check(XX, YY);
   if (fplot != NULL && (XX != X1 || YY != Y1))
      fprintf(fplot, "%6.3f %6.3f 0\n", x, y);
   X1 = XX; Y1 = YY;
}


void draw(float x, float y)
/* Draw a line segment from the current point to  (x, y) */
{ int X2, Y2;
   X2 = IX(x); Y2 = IY(y); check(X2, Y2);
   draw_line(X1, Y1, X2, Y2);
   if (fplot != NULL)
      fprintf(fplot, "%6.3f %6.3f 1\n", x, y);
   X1 = X2; Y1 = Y2;
}


int pixlit(int X, int Y)
/* Inquire if pixel (X, Y) is lit */
{ int pattern;
   offset= Ystart[Y] + (X>>3);
```

```
      pattern = 0x80 >> (X&7);
      lastchar = *(char *)(startaddress + offset);
                                                  /* Turbo C   */
      return ((lastchar & pattern) != 0);
  }

  static void prchar(char ch)
  /* Send byte ch to parallel printer port */
  { regs.x.dx=0;              /* Printer selection         */
    regs.h.ah=0;             /* Send byte from AL to printer  */
    regs.h.al=ch;           /* Byte to be sent to printer     */
    int86(0x17, &regs, &regs);
  }

  void printgr(int Xlo, int Xhi, int Ylo, int Yhi)
  /* Print contents of rectangle on matrix printer */
  { int n1, n2, ncols, i, X, Y, val, Xhi1;
    char line[720];                              /* 720 >= X__max */
    regs.x.dx = 0;                               /* LPT1           */
    regs.h.ah = 2;   /* Service 2: Get Printer Status    */
    int86(0x17, &regs, &regs);   /* Printer services       */
    if ((regs.h.ah & 8) == 8)      /* Printer status in AH */
    { if (in_textmode) printf("In textmode"); else
      textXY(0, Y__max - 15, "Printer not ready");
      return;

    }
    prchar(27); prchar('1'); /* Line spacing 7/72 inch */
    for (i=Ylo; i<=Yhi; i+=7)
    { checkbreak();
      /* To make DOS check for console break  */
      Xhi1 = Xlo-1;
      for (X=Xlo; X<=Xhi; X++)
      { val=0;
        for (Y=i; Y<i+7; Y++)
        { val <<= 1; val |= (Y>Yhi ? 0 : pixlit(X, Y));
        }
        line[X] = val;
        if (val) Xhi1 = X;
      }
      ncols = Xhi1-Xlo+1;
      if (ncols)
      { n1=ncols%256; n2=ncols/256;
        prchar(27); prchar('L'); prchar(n1); prchar(n2);
        for (X=Xlo; X<=Xhi1; X++) prchar(line[X]);
      }
      prchar('\n');
    }
    prchar(27); prchar('@');
  }

  void setprdim(void)
  /* This function sets x_max and y_max such that graphics
     results will eventually be printed with correct
     dimensions, both horizontally and vertically */
  { extern float x_max, y_max;
    extern int X__max, Y__max;
```

```
    setgrcon(iscolor());
    x_max = (X__max + 1)/120.0; y_max=(Y__max + 1)/72.0;
}


#define NASCII 128
static char chlist[NASCII][11]=
{
  {0}, {0}, {0}, {0}, {0}, {0}, {0}, {0}, {0}, {0}, {0},
  {0}, {0}, {0}, {0}, {0}, {0}, {0}, {0}, {0}, {0}, {0},
  {0}, {0}, {0}, {0}, {0}, {0}, {0}, {0}, {0}, {0},
/* */ {0},
/*!*/ {0x10, 0x38, 0x38, 0x38, 0x10, 0x10, 0x10, 0, 0x10},
/*"*/ {0x48, 0x48, 0x48},
/*#*/ {0x24, 0x24, 0x64, 0xFE, 0x44, 0xFE, 0x4C, 0x48,
       0x48},
/*$*/ {0x10, 0x7C, 0xD0, 0xD0, 0x7C, 0x16, 0x16, 0x7C,
       0x10},
/*%*/ {0xC2, 0x02, 0x04, 0x08, 0x10, 0x20, 0x40, 0x80,
       0x86},
/*&*/ {0x30, 0x48, 0x48, 0x30, 0x50, 0x92, 0x8A, 0x8C,
       0x72},
/*'*/ {0x18, 0x18, 0x18, 0x10},
/*(*/ {0x08, 0x10, 0x20, 0x20, 0x20, 0x20, 0x20, 0x10,
       0x08},
/*)*/ {0x40, 0x20, 0x10, 0x10, 0x10, 0x10, 0x10, 0x20,
       0x40},
/***/ {0, 0x82, 0x44, 0x28, 0xFE, 0x28, 0x44, 0x82},
/*+*/ {0, 0x10, 0x10, 0x10, 0xFE, 0x10, 0x10, 0x10},
/*,*/ {0, 0, 0, 0, 0, 0, 0, 0x30, 0x30, 0x10, 0x20},
/*-*/ {0, 0, 0, 0, 0xFE},
/*.*/ {0, 0, 0, 0, 0, 0, 0, 0x30, 0x30},
/*/*/ {0, 0x02, 0x04, 0x08, 0x10, 0x20, 0x40, 0x80},
/*0*/ {0x38, 0x6C, 0x44, 0x44, 0x44, 0x44, 0x44, 0x6C,
       0x38},
/*1*/ {0x10, 0x30, 0x50, 0x10, 0x10, 0x10, 0x10, 0x10,
       0x38},
/*2*/ {0x7C, 0xC6, 0x02, 0x06, 0x0C, 0x18, 0x30, 0x60,
       0xFE},
/*3*/ {0x7C, 0xC6, 0x02, 0x06, 0x0C, 0x06, 0x02, 0xC6,
       0x7C},
/*4*/ {0x04, 0x0C, 0x1C, 0x34, 0x64, 0xC4, 0xFE, 0x04,
       0x04},
/*5*/ {0xFE, 0x80, 0x80, 0xFC, 0x06, 0x02, 0x02, 0xC6,
       0x7C},
/*6*/ {0x7C, 0xC6, 0x80, 0xFC, 0xC6, 0x82, 0x82, 0xC6,
       0x7C},
/*7*/ {0xFE, 0x02, 0x06, 0x0C, 0x18, 0x30, 0x60, 0xC0,
       0x80},
/*8*/ {0x7C, 0xC6, 0x82, 0xC6, 0x7C, 0xC6, 0x82, 0xC6,
       0x7C},
/*9*/ {0x7C, 0xC6, 0x82, 0xC2, 0x7E, 0x02, 0x02, 0x06,
       0x7C},
/*:*/ {0, 0x30, 0x30, 0, 0, 0, 0, 0x30, 0x30},
/*;*/ {0, 0, 0x30, 0x30, 0, 0, 0, 0x30, 0x30, 0x10, 0x20},
/*<*/ {0x04, 0x08, 0x10, 0x20, 0x40, 0x20, 0x10, 0x08,
       0x04},
```

```
/*=*/ {0, 0, 0, 0, 0xFC, 0, 0, 0xFC},
/*>*/ {0x40, 0x20, 0x10, 0x08, 0x04, 0x08, 0x10, 0x20,
       0x40},
/*?*/ {0x78, 0xCC, 0x84, 0x0C, 0x18, 0x10, 0x10, 0, 0x10},
/*@*/ {0x7C, 0xC6, 0x8E, 0x92, 0x92, 0x92, 0x8C, 0xC0,
       0x7C},
/*A*/ {0x10, 0x38, 0x6C, 0xC6, 0x82, 0x82, 0xFE, 0x82,
       0x82},
/*B*/ {0xFC, 0x86, 0x82, 0x86, 0xFC, 0x86, 0x82, 0x86,
       0xFC},
/*C*/ {0x7C, 0xC6, 0x80, 0x80, 0x80, 0x80, 0x80, 0xC6,
       0x7C},
/*D*/ {0xFC, 0x86, 0x82, 0x82, 0x82, 0x82, 0x82, 0x86,
       0xFC},
/*E*/ {0xFE, 0x80, 0x80, 0x80, 0xF8, 0x80, 0x80, 0x80,
       0xFE},
/*F*/ {0xFE, 0x80, 0x80, 0x80, 0xFC, 0x80, 0x80, 0x80,
       0x80},
/*G*/ {0x7C, 0xC6, 0x82, 0x80, 0x80, 0x8E, 0x82, 0xC6,
       0x7C},
/*H*/ {0x82, 0x82, 0x82, 0x82, 0xFE, 0x82, 0x82, 0x82,
       0x82},
/*I*/ {0x38, 0x10, 0x10, 0x10, 0x10, 0x10, 0x10, 0x10,
       0x38},
/*J*/ {0x02, 0x02, 0x02, 0x02, 0x02, 0x02, 0x02, 0xC6,
       0x7C},
/*K*/ {0x86, 0x8C, 0x98, 0xB0, 0xE0, 0xB0, 0x98, 0x8C,
       0x86},
/*L*/ {0x80, 0x80, 0x80, 0x80, 0x80, 0x80, 0x80, 0x80,
       0xFE},
/*M*/ {0x82, 0xC6, 0xEE, 0xBA, 0x92, 0x82, 0x82, 0x82,
       0x82},
/*N*/ {0x82, 0xC2, 0xE2, 0xA2, 0xB2, 0x9A, 0x8E, 0x86,
       0x82},
/*O*/ {0x7C, 0xC6, 0x82, 0x82, 0x82, 0x82, 0x82, 0xC6,
       0x7C},
/*P*/ {0xFC, 0x86, 0x82, 0x86, 0xFC, 0x80, 0x80, 0x80,
       0x80},
/*Q*/ {0x7C, 0xC6, 0x82, 0x82, 0x82, 0x82, 0x92, 0xD6, 0x7C,
       0x08, 0x08},
/*R*/ {0xFC, 0x86, 0x82, 0x86, 0xFC, 0x90, 0x98, 0x8C,
       0x86},
/*S*/ {0x7C, 0xC6, 0x80, 0xC0, 0x7C, 0x06, 0x02, 0xC6,
       0x7C},
/*T*/ {0xFE, 0x10, 0x10, 0x10, 0x10, 0x10, 0x10, 0x10,
       0x10},
/*U*/ {0x82, 0x82, 0x82, 0x82, 0x82, 0x82, 0x82, 0xC6,
       0x7C},
/*V*/ {0x82, 0x82, 0x82, 0xC6, 0x44, 0x6C, 0x28, 0x38,
       0x10},
/*W*/ {0x82, 0x82, 0x82, 0x92, 0x92, 0xBA, 0xEE, 0x6C,
       0x44},
/*X*/ {0xC6, 0x44, 0x6C, 0x28, 0x38, 0x28, 0x6C, 0x44,
       0xC6},
/*Y*/ {0x82, 0x82, 0xC6, 0x6C, 0x38, 0x10, 0x10, 0x10,
       0x10},
```

```
/*Z*/ {0xFE, 0x04, 0x0C, 0x18, 0x10, 0x30, 0x60, 0x40,
       0xFE},
/*[*/ {0x7C, 0x40, 0x40, 0x40, 0x40, 0x40, 0x40, 0x40,
       0x7C},
/*\*/ {0, 0x80, 0x40, 0x20, 0x10, 0x08, 0x04, 0x02},
/*]*/ {0x78, 0x08, 0x08, 0x08, 0x08, 0x08, 0x08, 0x08,
       0x78},
/*^*/ {0x10, 0x28, 0x44, 0x82},
/*_*/ {0, 0, 0, 0, 0, 0, 0, 0, 0xFE},
/*`*/ {0x40, 0x20, 0x10, 0x08},
/*a*/ {0, 0, 0, 0x7C, 0x06, 0x7E, 0xC2, 0xC2, 0x7E},
/*b*/ {0x80, 0x80, 0x80, 0xFC, 0x86, 0x82, 0x82, 0x86,
       0xFC},
/*c*/ {0, 0, 0, 0x7C, 0xC6, 0x80, 0x80, 0xC6, 0x7C},
/*d*/ {0x04, 0x04, 0x04, 0x7C, 0xC4, 0x84, 0x84, 0xC4,
       0x7C},
/*e*/ {0, 0, 0, 0x7C, 0xC6, 0xFE, 0x80, 0xC0, 0x7C},
/*f*/ {0x1C, 0x30, 0x20, 0xFC, 0x20, 0x20, 0x20, 0x20,
       0x20},
/*g*/ {0, 0, 0, 0x7A, 0xCE, 0x82, 0x82, 0xC2, 0x7E, 0x06,
       0x7C},
/*h*/ {0x80, 0x80, 0x80, 0xFC, 0xC6, 0x82, 0x82, 0x82,
       0x82},
/*i*/ {0, 0x30, 0, 0x30, 0x10, 0x10, 0x10, 0x10, 0x38},
/*j*/ {0, 0x0C, 0, 0x0C, 0x04, 0x04, 0x04, 0x04, 0x04, 0xCC,
       0x78},
/*k*/ {0x40, 0x40, 0x40, 0x46, 0x4C, 0x78, 0x58, 0x4C,
       0x46},
/*l*/ {0x30, 0x10, 0x10, 0x10, 0x10, 0x10, 0x10, 0x10,
       0x38},
/*m*/ {0, 0, 0, 0xEC, 0x92, 0x92, 0x92, 0x92, 0x92},
/*n*/ {0, 0, 0, 0xBC, 0xC6, 0x82, 0x82, 0x82, 0x82},
/*o*/ {0, 0, 0, 0x7C, 0xC6, 0x82, 0x82, 0xC6, 0x7C},
/*p*/ {0, 0, 0, 0xFC, 0x86, 0x82, 0x82, 0x86, 0xFC, 0x80,
       0x80},
/*q*/ {0, 0, 0, 0x7C, 0xC4, 0x84, 0x84, 0xC4, 0x7C, 0x04,
       0x06},
/*r*/ {0, 0, 0, 0xBC, 0xE6, 0x80, 0x80, 0x80, 0x80},
/*s*/ {0, 0, 0, 0x7C, 0xC0, 0x7C, 0x06, 0x06, 0x7C},
/*t*/ {0, 0x40, 0x40, 0xF0, 0x40, 0x40, 0x40, 0x66, 0x3C},
/*u*/ {0, 0, 0, 0x84, 0x84, 0x84, 0x84, 0xC4, 0x7E},
/*v*/ {0, 0, 0, 0x82, 0x82, 0xC6, 0x6C, 0x38, 0x10},
/*w*/ {0, 0, 0, 0x82, 0x82, 0x92, 0xBA, 0xEE, 0x44},
/*x*/ {0, 0, 0, 0xC6, 0x6C, 0x28, 0x38, 0x6C, 0xC6},
/*y*/ {0, 0, 0, 0x82, 0x82, 0x82, 0x82, 0xC6, 0x7E, 0x06,
       0x7C},
/*z*/ {0, 0, 0, 0xFE, 0x0C, 0x18, 0x30, 0x60, 0xFE},
/*{*/ {0x10, 0x20, 0x20, 0x20, 0x40, 0x20, 0x20, 0x20,
       0x10},
/*|*/ {0x10, 0x10, 0x10, 0x10, 0x10, 0x10, 0x10, 0x10,
       0x10},
/*}*/ {0x20, 0x10, 0x10, 0x10, 0x08, 0x10, 0x10, 0x10,
       0x20},
/*~*/ {0, 0, 0, 0x60, 0x92, 0x0C},
  {0}};
```

```
void textXY(int X, int Y, char *str)
/* Display string  str in graphics mode, starting at
   point (X, Y).
*/
{ char *p;
  int offset, i, j, len, hpos, vpos;
  len=strlen(str);
  hpos = X>>3;
  check(8*(hpos+len)-1, Y+10);
  for (i=0; i<len; i++)
  { p=chlist[str[i]];
    for (j=0; j<11; j++)
    { vpos=Y+j;
      offset= Ystart[vpos] + hpos + i;
      *(char *)(startaddress + offset) = p[j];
    }
  }
}

void text(char *str)
/* Display string  str, starting at
   the current point (X1, Y1).
*/
{ textXY(X1, Y1, str);
  X1 += strlen(str) * 8;
  check(X1, Y1);
}

void imove(int X, int Y)
/* Let (X, Y) be the new current point */
{ check(X, Y); X1=X; Y1=Y;
}

void idraw(int X, int Y)
/* Draw a line segment from the current point to (X, Y)   */
{ check(X, Y);
  draw_line(X1, Y1, X, Y);
  X1=X; Y1=Y;
}

#define B000 (char *)0xB0000000
#define B800 (char *)0xB8000000

void wrscr(int row, int col, char *str)   /* In textmode */
/*  Writes characters into video display memory while in
    text mode.
    row = 0, 1, ..., 24;   col = 0, 1, ..., 79
*/
{ static char *displayptr;
  static int first=1;
  int i, offset;
  char *p;
  if (first)
  { displayptr = (iscolor() ? B800 : B000);
    first=0;
  }
```

```
   offset = row*160+col*2;
   p = displayptr+offset;
   for (i=0; str[i]; i++) p[i << 1] = str[i];
}

void clearscr(void)
/* To be used in textmode.
   Don't confuse this with clearpage, to be used in
   graphics mode
*/
{ static unsigned segdst;
  static first=1;
  int i;
  char *source;
  unsigned segsrc, offsrc;
  if (first)
  { segdst = (iscolor() ? 0xB800 : 0xB000);
    first = 0;
  }
  source =
  "\40\7\40\7\40\7\40\7\40\7\40\7\40\7\40\7";
  segsrc = FP_SEG(source); offsrc = FP_OFF(source);
  for (i=0; i<256; i++)
    movedata(segsrc, offsrc, segdst, i << 4, 16);
}

void settxtcursor(int row, int col)
/* Set cursor in textmode */
{ regs.h.dh = row;
  regs.h.dl = col;
  regs.h.ah = 2;
  regs.h.bh = 0;
  int86(0x10, &regs, &regs);
}
```

Recall that in C the keyword *static* written at the beginning of a function definition means that the function in question is local to the module in which it is defined. Such functions are only for internal use, and they are not available to the user. In GRPACK all functions not discussed before are made *static*; in this way we can easily distinguish them from the other functions, which can be called in user's programs. If we (possibly unintentionally) use the same names for functions of our own, then there will be no confusion, because the 'static' functions are not published to the linker.

Just when I had completed the first draft of this book, I received Version 1.5 of the Turbo C compiler from Borland International (probably as a very generous reaction to my reporting two minor compiler errors to them). This new version offers superb low-level graphics facilities, which could be used instead of GRPACK. Although GRPACK works satisfactorily for the machines that are available to me, I realize that I cannot compete with Borland in testing graphics routines on all present and future machine types; nor can I promote my work in the way they do, so I considered the possibility of abolishing my GRPACK routines and make a radical shift to the new Turbo C graphics functions. Users of older Turbo C versions will sooner or later update their compilers, so requiring Version 1.5 or higher would not be a serious drawback. However, it seemed to me that there are some aspects of Turbo C which perhaps not all users may appreciate. Due to their generality the Turbo graphics routines use considerably more memory space, and some of them are slower than those of GRPACK; the latter may be called *tiny*, and if a tiny package does all we need satisfactorily then some users may prefer it to a more extensive package. With GRPACK, everything is expressed in very low-level functions, such as *int86* (for software interrupts) and *outport* (for addressing I/O ports), which at least are well-known facilities for anyone who is familiar with IBM-PC programming. Consequently, these facilities are also available to users of other C compilers. The latter is important, since there are many other good C compilers around, and it is not likely that all IBM-PC users who program in C will switch to Turbo C. In short, the graphics routines of GRPACK are transparent, while those of Turbo C are to be used as *black boxes*.

Perhaps the most important reason for not abolishing GRPACK altogether is that it leads to executable programs (*xxx.EXE* files) that run on machines with various graphics adapters, without requiring an 'installation' procedure or a set of 'driver files'. In contrast to this, the new Turbo C function *initgraph* (used to switch from text mode to graphics mode) normally loads the driver for the installed graphics adapter at execution time. This means that a general executable program, which should work on any machine regardless of the adapter type, is to be accompanied by various driver files. Instead, we can use a utility (*BGIOBJ*) to convert such driver files to object files and then link these together with our programs; but in that case we have to link in all drivers that may possibly be needed. All this is somewhat complicated, and, considering also some other drawbacks, some of which are mentioned above, I think that there will be readers who appreciate my suggestion to use GRPACK, as long as this works satisfactorily.

As said at the beginning of this section, low-level graphics functions are very essential, since without them our high-level graphics applications won't work. It should therefore not be considered a waste of time to provide a second solution to the very crucial problem of how to display lines and characters on the screen of our computer. A chain is as strong as its weakest link, and if this link should happen to be GRPACK (which is not unlikely because of its hardware-dependent aspects), then it will be nice if you can replace it. Besides, there will be readers of this book who are enthusiastic about the graphics functions of Turbo C Version 1.5 (or higher) and who want to use it in connection with D3D anyway. I was just using the term 'superb' for these graphics functions, and I think that is what they are, in spite of some drawbacks compared with GRPACK. To mention just some possibilities, there are various text fonts and styles available, we can manipulate viewports, fill closed regions with various patterns, use colors, and display text in windows. I therefore realized that it would be unwise not to use the new Turbo C graphics facilities in this book.

Since the modules D3D and HLPFUN are rather large and complex, it would not be a good idea to give two versions of these, one for GRPACK and one for Turbo C Version 1.5. Instead, we can express the functions of GRPACK in terms of the new Turbo C functions. In this way we obtain GRPACK1, a package that for the user is almost similar to GRPACK, but which uses the new Turbo C functions. It can be compiled separately to obtain the object module GRPACK1.OBJ, which can replace GRPACK.OBJ. The other modules (D3D, HLPFUN, TRAFO) can be left unchanged, and so can the header file GRPACK.H. This Turbo C (Version 1.5) alternative, GRPACK1, is listed below.

```
/* GRPACK1: A graphics package, using Turbo C
           graphics functions, available in
           Version 1.5.
           Memory model: Huge (for ALL modules involved)
```

```
          For: Enhanced Graphics Adapter (EGA, 640 x 350)
               Color Graphics Adapter (CGA, 640 x 200)
               Hercules Graphics Adapter (HGA, 720 x 348)
*/
#include <stdio.h>
#include <dos.h>
#include <conio.h>
#include <process.h>
#include <string.h>
#include <alloc.h>
#include <graphics.h>

union REGS regs;

int in_textmode=1, X__max, Y__max, drawmode=1, adaptype;

FILE *fplot=NULL;

float x_max=10.0, y_max=7.0, horfact, vertfact;

static int X1, Y1, foregroundcol, backgroundcol,
   g_driver, g_mode;

static long int startaddress;

void to_text(void);
void textXY(int X, int Y, char *str);


int IX(float x) { return (int)(x*horfact+0.5); }
int IY(float y) { return Y__max-(int)(y*vertfact+0.5); }


static void error(char *str)
/* Display a message and terminate program execution */
{ if (!in_textmode) to_text();
  printf("%s\n", str); exit(1);
}

void clearpage(void)  /* Clear the screen */
{ clearviewport();
}


int iscolor(void)     /* Find out which adapter is used */
{ detectgraph(&g_driver, &g_mode);
  if (g_mode == MCGAHI) g_mode = MCGAMED;
  if (g_mode == ATT400HI) g_mode = ATT400MED;
  if (g_mode == VGAHI) g_mode = VGAMED;
  return g_driver == CGA || g_driver == MCGA ||
         g_driver == ATT400 ?
         1 /* 640 x 200 */ :
         g_driver == EGA || g_driver == EGA64 ||
         g_driver == EGAMONO || g_driver == VGA ?
         2 /* 640 x 350 */ :
         g_driver == HERCMONO ? 0 /* 720 x 348 */ : -1;
}
```

```c
static void setgrcon(int adaptype)
/* Set graphics constants */
{ startaddress = (adaptype == 2 ? 0xA0000000 : 0xB8000000);
  if (adaptype == 2)
  { X__max = 639; Y__max = 349;    /* EGA */
  } else
  if (adaptype == 1)
  { X__max = 639; Y__max = 199;    /* CGA */
  } else
  { X__max = 719; Y__max = 347;    /* HGA */
  }
}

static int grbrfun(void)
/* Used by  ctrlbrk, to specify what to do with a console
   break
*/
{ to_text(); return 0;
  /* Before exit, return to text mode!
  */
}


void initgr(void)   /* Initialize graphics */
{ static int again=0;
  int errcode;
  if (again) setgraphmode(g_mode); else
  { adaptype = iscolor(); /* Detects driver and mode */
    if (adaptype < 0) error("Wrong display adapter");
    ctrlbrk(grbrfun);    /* Set break trap, Turbo C   */
    initgraph(&g_driver, &g_mode, "\\turboc");
    errcode = graphresult();
    if (errcode < 0)
    { printf("Graphics error code: %d", errcode); exit(1);
    }
    again = 1;
    setgrcon(adaptype);
  }
  horfact = X__max/x_max; vertfact = Y__max/y_max;
  if (adaptype == 0) /* HCG */
  { setvisualpage(1); setactivepage(1);
  }
  in_textmode=0;
  foregroundcol=getcolor();
  backgroundcol=getbkcolor();
}


static int txtbrfun(void)
{ return 0;
}


void to_text(void)
/* Revert to text mode */
{ if (!in_textmode) restorecrtmode();
  in_textmode = 1;
```

```
   ctrlbrk(txtbrfun);
   /* Restore default break interrupt handler */
}


void endgr(void)
/* Wait until any key is hit and revert to text mode  */
{ getch();
  to_text();
}


void dot(int X, int Y)  /* Light or darken a pixel */
{ putpixel
   (X, Y,
     (drawmode == 0 ?
       ( getpixel(X, Y) == foregroundcol ?
         backgroundcol : foregroundcol
       ) :
       ( drawmode == 1 ? foregroundcol : backgroundcol
       )
     )     /* drawmode =  1: draw positively */
   );      /* drawmode = -1: draw negatively */
}         /* drawmode =  0: toggle          */


void checkbreak(void)
{ char ch;
  if (kbhit()) { ch = getch(); kbhit(); ungetch(ch); }
}


void draw_line(int X1, int Y1, int X2, int Y2)
/* Draw the line segment from (X1, Y1) to (X2, Y2);
   X1, Y1, X2, Y2 are pixel coordinates  */
{ if (drawmode == 1) line(X1, Y1, X2, Y2);
  /* 'drawmode' values 0 and -1 not implemented for
     this function. See also dot()
  */
}


static void fatal(void)
/* Draw a diagonal, then wait until a key is pressed, and
   finally revert to text mode
*/
{ draw_line(0, Y__max,  X__max, 0); endgr();
}

static void check(int X, int Y)
/* If point (X, Y) lies outside the screen boundaries, then
   call  fatal, display the incorrect coordinates, and stop
*/
{ if (X < 0 || X > X__max || Y < 0 || Y > Y__max)
  { fatal();
    printf(
```

```
      "Point outside screen (X and Y are pixel coordinates):\n");
      printf("X = %d          Y = %d\n", X, Y);
      printf("x = %10.3f    y = %10.3f\n",
             X/horfact, (Y__max-Y)/vertfact);
      printf(
      "X__max = %d   Y__max = %d   x_max = %f y_max = %f\n",
             X__max, Y__max, x_max, y_max);
      printf("horfact = %f   vertfact = % f\n",
             horfact, vertfact);
      exit(1);
   }
}


void move(float x, float y)
/* Move the current point to (x, y);
   x and y are screen coordinates  */
{ int XX, YY;
  XX = IX(x); YY = IY(y); check(XX, YY);
  if (fplot != NULL && (XX != X1 || YY != Y1))
     fprintf(fplot, "%6.3f %6.3f 0\n", x, y);
  X1 = XX; Y1 = YY;
}


void draw(float x, float y)
/* Draw a line segment from the current point to  (x, y) */
{ int X2, Y2;
  X2 = IX(x); Y2 = IY(y); check(X2, Y2);
  draw_line(X1, Y1, X2, Y2);
  if (fplot != NULL)
  fprintf(fplot, "%6.3f %6.3f 1\n", x, y);
  X1 = X2; Y1 = Y2;
}


int pixlit(int X, int Y)
/* Inquire if pixel (X, Y) is lit */
{ return (getpixel(X, Y) == foregroundcol);
}


static void prchar(char ch)
/* Send byte ch to parallel printer port */
{ regs.x.dx=0;            /* Printer selection          */
  regs.h.ah=0;            /* Send byte from AL to printer */
  regs.h.al=ch;           /* Byte to be sent to printer  */
  int86(0x17, &regs, &regs);
}


void printgr(int Xlo, int Xhi, int Ylo, int Yhi)
/* Print contents of rectangle on matrix printer */
{ int n1, n2, ncols, i, X, Y, val, Xhi1;
  char line[720];                   /* 720 >= X__max */
  regs.x.dx = 0;                    /* LPT1          */
  regs.h.ah = 2;   /* Service 2: Get Printer Status */
```

```
    int86(0x17, &regs, &regs);   /* Printer services  */
    if ((regs.h.ah & 8) == 8)      /* Printer status in AH */
    { if (in_textmode) printf("In textmode"); else
      textXY(0, Y__max - 15, "Printer not ready");
      return;
    }
    prchar(27); prchar('1'); /* Line spacing 7/72 inch */
    for (i=Ylo; i<=Yhi; i+=7)
    { checkbreak(); /* To make DOS check for console break  */
      Xhil = Xlo-1;
      for (X=Xlo; X<=Xhi; X++)
      { val=0;
        for (Y=i; Y<i+7; Y++)
        { val <<= 1; val |= (Y>Yhi ? 0 : pixlit(X, Y));
        }
        line[X] = val;
        if (val) Xhil = X;
      }
      ncols = Xhil-Xlo+1;
      if (ncols)
      { n1=ncols%256; n2=ncols/256;
        prchar(27); prchar('L'); prchar(n1); prchar(n2);
        for (X=Xlo; X<=Xhil; X++) prchar(line[X]);
      }
      prchar('\n');
    }
    prchar(27); prchar('@');
}


void setprdim(void)
/* This function sets x_max and y_max such that graphics
   results will eventually be printed with correct
   dimensions, both horizontally and vertically */
{ extern float x_max, y_max;
  extern int X__max, Y__max;
  setgrcon(iscolor());
  x_max = (X__max + 1)/120.0; y_max=(Y__max + 1)/72.0;
}


void textXY(int X, int Y, char *str)
/* Display string  str in graphics mode, starting at
   point (X, Y).
*/
{ int height, width;
  height = textheight(str); width = textwidth(str);
  setviewport(X, Y, X+width, Y+height, 0);
  clearviewport();   /* To erase old text, if any */
  outtext(str);
  setviewport(0, 0, X__max, Y__max, 0);
}


void text(char *str)
/* Display string  str, starting at
   the current point (X1, Y1).           */
```

```
{ textXY(X1, Y1, str);
  X1 += strlen(str) * 8;
  check(X1, Y1);
}


void imove(int X, int Y)
/* Let (X, Y) be the new current point */
{ check(X, Y); X1=X; Y1=Y;
}


void idraw(int X, int Y)
/* Draw a line segment from the current point to (X, Y)  */
{ check(X, Y);
  draw_line(X1, Y1, X, Y);
  X1=X; Y1=Y;
}


void wrscr(int row, int col, char *str)  /* In textmode */
/*  Writes characters into video display memory while in
    text mode.
    row = 0, 1, ..., 24;  col = 0, 1, ..., 79
*/
{ gotoxy(col+1, row+1);
  cputs(str);
}

void clearscr(void)
/* To be used in textmode.
   Don't confuse this with clearpage, to be used in.
   graphics mode
*/
{ clrscr();
}

void settxtcursor(int row, int col)
/* Set cursor in textmode */
{ gotoxy(col+1, row+1);
}

void far * far _graphgetmem(unsigned size)
{ char *p;
  p = farmalloc((long)size);
  if (p == NULL) error("Mem. space in _graphgetmem");
  return p;
}

void far _graphfreemem(void far *ptr, unsigned size)
{ farfree(ptr);
}
```

If you want to use GRPACK1, it is important to pay attention to the third argument of the function *initgraph*, which is called in *initgr*. This argument, called *pathtodriver* in the manual, must tell where in your system the graphics driver can be found. These graphics drivers are files with names ending in *.BGI*. For example, this file name is *HERC.BGI* for the Hercules Graphics Adapter. These drivers are supplied on the disks that contain the Turbo C Version 1.5 compiler, libraries, and so on. If on your system they are placed in the directory \\*turboc* of the current drive, then you can write "\\\\*turboc*", as was done in the above program text. The double backslash is needed here because only one character pair \\*t* would denote a 'horizontal tab' (as the C language requires!). If the graphics driver in question is not in the directory specified, then *initgraph* looks in the current directory for it. You can also use the empty string "" instead of a real directory; then the graphics driver must then be in the current directory.

The last two functions, *graphgetmem* and *graphfreemem*, replace the default functions used by the Turbo C function *initgraph* (which in turn is called in by function *initgr*) in order to allocate memory for the graphics driver. The peculiar first lines in these functions (with several occurrences of *far*) have been copied from the Turbo C Version 1.5 Additions & Enhancements manual. In connection with a main program such as D3D, which dynamically allocates large amounts of memory itself, it is really necessary to supply these two functions. This is due to the fact that the corresponding default functions use *malloc* instead of *farmalloc*, as I discovered only after a great many unsuccessful program runs, usually resulting in system crashes.

GRPACK1 is not completely equivalent to GRPACK. With GRPACK, the effect of the functions *draw*, *idraw*, *draw_line*, and *dot* depends on the value of the variable *drawmode*. As we have discussed, the default value of this variable is 1. If we make it equal to $-1$, the functions mentioned turn pixels dark, and with *drawmode* = 0 the state of each pixel is inverted by them. With GRPACK1 this applies only to the function *dot*, not to the line-drawing functions. This is because in *draw line* the Turbo C function *line* is used, which does not offer the possibility to invert the state of the pixels on the line in question. Inverting pixels (with *drawmode* = 0) is done in D3D both for the cursor and for perpendiculars dropped from the cursor to the *xy*-plane in cursor operations. Note that we must not simply light the pixels that comprise the cursor and darken these pixels later, for then we would erase other lines when we moved the cursor through them. By inverting the pixel state twice (once when the cursor arrives at a point and once when it leaves that point) the original state of all pixels is preserved. Fortunately, for the cursor itself the function *dot* is used, and, as we can inquire into the pixel state (using the Turbo C function *getpixel*), we can change the foreground color (light) into the background color (dark) and vice versa. With the 'black box' function *line*, we cannot do this, but, as far as program D3D is concerned, this is not a serious problem. After all, the vertical lines that connect the cursor with the *xy*-plane are not essential, so instead of finding a more complex solution we can simply omit these lines. This is why in GRPACK1 the function *draw_line* draws a line segment only if *drawmode* is equal to 1. With the same version of the module D3D, the vertical lines just mentioned are then omitted if we use GRPACK1 and drawn (and erased later) if we use GRPACK.

The source text of GRPACK is larger than that of GRPACK1, but this should not mislead us. I used both GRPACK and GRPACK1 for program D3D, resulting in the executable files D3D.EXE and D3D1.EXE, respectively. The latter file was 11 630 bytes larger than the former, and even this figure may be misleading. We must not forget that D3D1.EXE loads

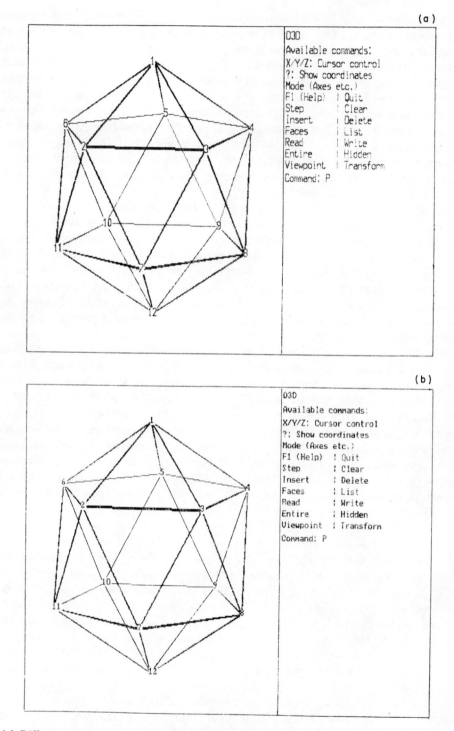

Fig. 4.1 Difference in text fonts (a) Font defined in GRPACK, (b) Turbo C graphics font (default), obtained by using GRPACK1

the graphics driver at execution time and D3D.EXE does not. For the Hercules Graphics Adapter, this means that the Turbo C graphics functions use another 10 046 bytes during execution time. Thus, in total, with GRPACK1, we need about 21 KB more than with GRPACK. This is the price we have to pay for the extra facilities offered by Turbo C graphics. To avoid any misunderstanding, let me add that, as there are so many such facilities, that price seems very reasonable to me.

If we compare D3D.EXE and D3D1.EXE experimentally, using a machine with the relatively slow 8088 processor, then we find that in general the former is faster than the latter. Another difference is the text font in graphics mode. In the Turbo C graphics routines the default character size is $8 \times 8$, whereas in GRPACK, it is $11 \times 8$, as explained in my book *CGIP*. Figures 4.1(a) and (b) show the difference between the two fonts.

## 4.4   HIDDEN-LINE ELIMINATION

Perhaps the most interesting command of D3D is $H$, which enables us to remove the hidden lines of an object. A very substantial portion of my book *Programming Principles in Computer Graphics (PPCG)* is devoted to hidden-line elimination, and I will not repeat such a detailed discussion here. Instead, let us deal with some essential aspects of the hidden-line algorithm and the data structures that are used. The algorithm is essentially the same as that used in program HIDLINPIX, which can be found in *PPCG*. (That program has really proved to be useful, as was demonstrated, for example, by W.D. May in his article '3-D Images from Contour Maps', published in *Dr. Dobb's Journal of Software Tools*, November 1987.) Instead, we will now use a function (in module HLPFUN), that in D3D is invoked whenever we enter command $H$. Compared with its predecessor, mentioned above, HLPFUN offers some improvements and new features:

1 It can deal with curved surfaces, as we have discussed near the end of Section 1.5.
2 It allocates memory in a more sophisticated way in the sense that takes into account how much memory is available.
3 In order to avoid any problems with the stack size, recursion has been eliminated.
4 The method of decomposing polygons into triangles has been improved; it can now be used for any polygon.

In the following discussion, I will often mention the names of program variables. This will enable you to look them up, but, as program module HLPFUN is rather complex, you had perhaps better do this only after reading the present text.

The polygons entered by the user by means of command $F$ provide us with both the line segments that are candidates for being drawn and the faces that may (entirely or partially) hide them. The vertex numbers of each polygon are stored in a consecutive area which we can access through a pointer stored in 'array' *pface*. Actually, *pface* itself is also a pointer variable, to which we assign the begin address of a dynamically allocated memory area. This is shown in Fig. 4.2; we can use *pface* as an array whose elements are pointers to integers. (In C a pointer to an integer can in fact be a pointer to a sequence of integers.)

We can write either *pface*[j] or pface[j][0] for the integer pointed to by array element pface[j]. It is equal to the number of vertex numbers that follow. Thus, if pface[j][0] = n, then pface[j][1] through pface[j][n] are the vertex numbers of the jth polygon. If we know the number $i$ of a vertex, we can find its eye-coordinates $x_e$, $y_e$, $z_e$ in the structure

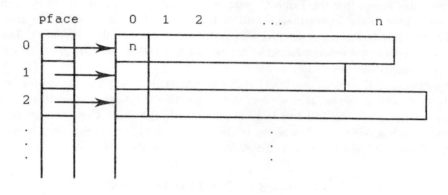

*Fig. 4.2 Data structure for faces*

*VERTEX*[$i$]. (Actually, *VERTEX* is a pointer variable to which we assign the value of variable
$p$ in module D3D.)

The sides of the polygons are the line segments that we have to draw as far as they are
visible. For simplicity, we decompose all polygons into triangles, and we use the latter to
find out what is visible and what is not. Then, for a given line segment, we could combine
it with all triangles and determine if certain portions of it are not hidden by any triangle;
those portions (which may vary from nothing to the entire line segment) are then to be
drawn. However, this leads to enormous computing times. For example, if we have 1000
line segments and 1000 triangles, then there would be 1 000 000 distinct pairs consisting
of a line segment and a triangle. My book *PPCG* gives a method to reduce such numbers
of pairs, and we will use this method again. When dealing with a given line segment we
need a means to build a reasonably limited subset of the set of all triangles, and we want
to do this even *without inspecting all triangles* at this stage. The clue lies in the screen
onto which both line segments and triangles are projected. To explain the method in simple
terms, let us regard the smallest viewport in which the entire image fits as a chessboard
with 64 squares. The idea is that in each square we store information about the triangles
whose perspective images contain points lying in that square. To make the usefulness of
this absolutely clear, let us use the letters $A$ through $H$, for the eight columns (counting
from left to right) and the numbers 1 through 8 for the rows (from bottom to top). Now if,
for example, some image triangle near the lower-left corner lies (only) in the squares $A1$,
$B1$, $B2$, then in some way or other we store that information in these squares. Then later,
when dealing with a line segment, we again determine in which squares its image lies. If,
for example, $E5$, $D6$, $C7$, $B8$ are the squares associated with line segment PQ, then only
the triangles of which information is stored in these squares are selected, which means that
the triangle just mentioned, lying in the lower-left corner of our chessboard, is ignored. In
this way we can form a rather small set of triangles that may hide line segment PQ and,
while dealing with PQ, ignore all others.

Actually, we need to consider even fewer triangles than suggested in the above discussion.
If, for a given square, there are several triangles which cover that square *completely* (which

means that the entire square lies within the images of these triangles), then we can ignore all those triangles except the one that is nearest to the viewpoint.

What we now have been calling a *square* was called a (device-independent) *pixel* in PPCG, hence the program name HIDLINPIX and the name HLPFUN for the function module discussed in this section. As in this book we have been using the word *pixel* in the usual (device-dependent) sense, it might be confusing to use it also for some larger portion of the screen. Since such a screen portion is actually not a square but a *rectangle*, we will now use the latter term rather than 'square'. Not the entire screen but only the smallest rectangle (with horizontal and vertical sides) in which the two-dimensional image fits will be divided into $N \times N$ rectangles of equal size; in the program version listed in Appendix B we have $N = 15$. The value of $N$ does not influence the final result, so it should not be mistaken for some kind of 'resolution'. It affects computing time though. I have found that, for the IBM PC, computing time usually increases if the value 15 is replaced with either a much smaller or a much larger value (such as, for example, 4 or 30).

We will associate the rectangles just mentioned with elements of array *SCREEN*; array element $SCREEN[i][j]$ (where $i$ and $j$ are nonnegative integers less than $N$) corresponds to a rectangle in the $i$th column and the $j$th row; in other words, we compute $i$ from $X$ and $j$ from $Y$. For the sake of simplicity, let us also use the word *rectangle* for the elements of array *SCREEN* themselves, so we will say that we want to store (information about) triangles in rectangles.

As our rectangles are all of the same size and each rectangle is to be associated with a variable number of triangles, we will actually store the triangles outside the rectangles, in such a way that the rectangles can tell us where to find them. We will use the table *TRIANGLE* with a structure $TRIANGLE[i]$ for each triangle. In this structure we find the vertex numbers $A$, $B$, $C$ of triangle $i$ as well as the coefficients $a$, $b$, $c$, $h$ of

$$ax + by + cz = h$$

which is the equation of the plane in which the triangle lies. We can then use a single integer $i$ to identify a triangle; we would therefore store some set of triangle numbers in each rectangle if that were possible. However, there is a variable number of triangles to be associated with each rectangle. We therefore store a starting pointer of a linear list in each rectangle, and, instead of storing a triangle number in some rectangle, we store it in the linear list that starts in that rectangle. At first, I did this in the most natural way, using real pointers and memory allocated for every individual list element. However, this turned out to have a serious drawback. As we have to implement this method in function *hlpfun*, which in program D3D may be called more than once, we must not forget to release all memory dynamically allocated in this function before we return to the main program, so that the same memory space can be reused later. If the displayed object is complex, the linear lists containing triangle numbers may be quite long and there will be a great many of them. Consequently, it turned out that releasing the memory occupied by the list elements took an enormous amount of time in such cases. The average user of D3D will understand that the generation of a hidden-line image will take some computing time, but he (or she) would be astonished if disposing of such an image took almost as much time. As this was really the case, I modified the program and implemented the linear list as a table, called *TRLIST*. In this way, disposing of all the linear lists is achieved by disposing of this table, which is done in a single action. Each entry in the table *TRLIST* can be used as an element of a linear list; it is a structure with the following two fields:

*ptria* An integer 'pointing' to an entry in the table *TRIANGLE*. Thus, if this integer is equal to $i$, then *TRIANGLE*[$i$] is the triangle in question.

*next* An integer 'pointing' to the next element of the linear list. (If this integer is equal to $k \geq 0$, then *TRLIST*[$k$] is that next element. If $k$ is equal to $-1$, there is no next element.) The first element of each list is pointed to by an integer stored in array *SCREEN*, see below.

Each 'rectangle' *SCREEN*[$i$][$j$] of the screen is a structure with the following three fields:

*tr_cov* An integer $i$ pointing to a triangle: *TRIANGLE*[$i$] is the nearest triangle that covers the entire rectangle.

*tr_dist* A floating-point number, which is the distance between the nearest triangle, pointed to by *tr_cov*, and the viewpoint.

*start* An integer $k$ pointing to the first list element *TRLIST*[$k$].

In Fig. 4.3 we have *tr_cov* = 3, *tr_ start* = 2, and *tr_dist* = 8.0. The latter means that there is a distance 8.0 between the viewpoint and a point P of triangle 3 such that the projection P' of this point P is the center of the rectangle we are considering. Here we have 8 × 8 rectangles (whereas there are 15 × 15 of them in the program). Figure 4.3 shows a situation that can occur while the screen lists are being built on the basis of the given triangles. After this 'first scan' is completed, any triangle pointed to by *SCREEN*[$i$][$j$]. *tr_cov* is inserted at the beginning of the linear list starting at *SCREEN*[$i$][$j$].*start*. In our example, this means that triangle 3 will be inserted in the linear list of the rectangle under consideration (unless, for that rectangle, a triangle with a distance to the viewpoint less than 8.0 follows).

When we are dealing with polygons, not only triangles but also line segments become available. They must be stored somewhere so that we can use them later to draw them as far as they are visible. However, we must not do this unconditionally. First, it will be remembered from Section 1.7 (see Fig. 1.17) that vertex numbers may have been stored with a minus sign, as a coding technique for artificial edges in polygons with holes. It is obvious that we will simply ignore such edges. As this is a very simple matter, we shall not mention this any further and consider only positive vertex numbers. Second, we should be aware that each edge is the intersection of two bounding faces, which means that it will appear twice, and, as it needs to be drawn at most once, we had better ignore each second occurrence. These two aspects are not new; they are also discussed in *PPCG*. There is a third condition for each line segment to be drawn, which is new in the present book. Recall that D3D has a provision for curved surfaces: if the angle between the normal vectors of two intersecting bounding faces is less than some threshold, given by the user, then the line of intersection of these two faces is not to be drawn. This means that for every edge that becomes available as a side of a polygon and that we want to store, we must store not only the vertex numbers P and Q of its endpoints but also the three components $a$, $b$, $c$ of a normal vector. Note that these are the coefficients of $x$, $y$, $z$ occurring in the equation of the plane in which the polygon lies. In this way, we can use the normal vector [$a$ $b$ $c$] later, when the same line segment turns up as a side of another polygon, of which a normal vector is given as well.

There are some lines of intersection, which, if visible, must be drawn, even though the angle between the two normal vectors mentioned above is less than the given threshold value. These are the *contours* of the object. To make this clear, consider the cylinder of Fig. 2.6. The vertical contour lines at the extreme left and right must be drawn, even though they

SCREEN

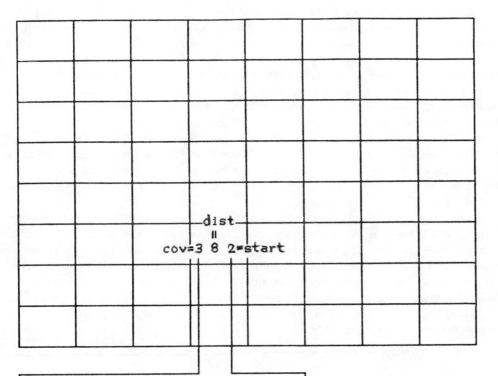

TRIANGLE                                          TRLIST

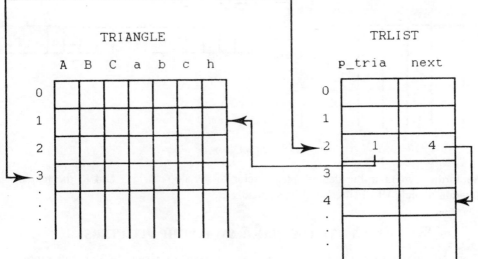

*Fig 4.3 Screen, screen lists and triangle table*

are edges similar to others which are omitted. Fortunately, no special measures are necessary to draw them because each contour edge is the line where a visible face and a backface meet, and will therefore turn up only once. Although not mentioned in the above discussion, we ignore polygons that are backfaces: first, if they hide certain points then these points are also hidden by visible faces, and, second, their edges are either hidden or will turn up as edges of visible faces. Recall that the user has to specify the vertices of each polygon in counter-clockwise order and that the second vertex must be convex. Then we can tell a backface from a visible face by the orientation of the first three vertices after projection. If these are no longer counter-clockwise, then the face in question is a backface. It is now very nice that each contour edge becomes available only once because the backface in which it lies does not contribute to the supply of line segments.

It will now be clear that each edge PQ that is a candidate to be stored has to be looked up first, to see if a copy of it has been stored previously. If so, we will certainly not store the new copy, but apart from this, we may even have to dispose of the old copy (so that the number of stored edges decreases by one). Of course, the latter will never happen if the user has given a zero threshold value.

In order that edges may be looked up efficiently, we store them in linear lists, as shown in Fig. 4.4. For any edge PQ, we exchange P and Q, if necessary, so that the vertex number P is less than Q. Then vertex number Q is stored in an element of the linear list whose starting point lies in *VERTEX*[*P*]. (Recall that *VERTEX* is a table where the coordinates of all vertices can be found.) Besides vertex number Q, we also store the coefficients $a$, $b$, $c$ belonging to the plane in which we have just found edge PQ, so that we can perform the 'threshold test' when a copy of PQ becomes available later. Figure 4.4 shows how the line segments (1, 5) and (1, 6) are stored.

VERTEX

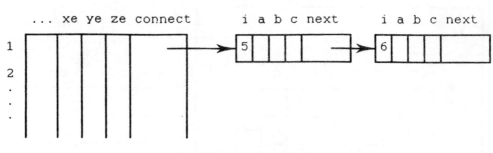

*Fig. 4.4 Linear lists for edges*

For further programming details, please refer to my book *PPCG* and to the text of the program module HLPFUN, listed in Appendix B.

## 4.5   A UTILITY PROGRAM FOR HP PLOTTERS

There are two reasons why the hard copy of our graphics results on the matrix printer is not of high quality. First, the printer does not give a very good contrast between black and white, and, second, we have been using the resolution of the video display for the printer, and that resolution will sometimes produce ragged lines, especially if CGA with a resolution of only 640 × 200 is being used. Our rather complex three-dimensional computations, and, in particular, our hidden-line algorithm, supply us with the exact endpoints of every line segment in the two-dimensional result. As we may have graphics output devices that can use this data, D3D has a facility to write these two-dimensional results to a file. Recall that this is done by typing $O$ (short for *Output file*) after command $H$ or command $E$. This type of file should clearly be distinguished from what we have called *object files*. Let us consistently use names ending in *.DAT* for object files (which are input files for D3D); the output files obtained by command $O$ always have names ending in *.PLT*. For example, if D3D has been reading the object file *CUBE.DAT* (or has been writing this file as a result of command $W$), then our command $O$ will create the output file *CUBE.PLT*. The latter name will also be assigned if your object-file name begins with *CUBE*, but, against my advice, has been given an extension other than *.DAT*, or no extension at all. If you have not mentioned a file name because you have not used any input file nor command $W$, then command $O$ will create the output file *NONAME.PLT*.

Let us refer to the output files of D3D (that are obtained by command $O$ and have names ending in *.PLT*) as *plotfiles*. Plotfiles have a quite simple format: they are ASCII files with only lines of the form

```
x   y    code
```

where $x$ and $y$ are two-dimensional coordinates ranging from 0 to 10 and 0 to 7, respectively. The third element, *code*, is either 0, meaning *pen up*, or 1, as a code for *pen down*. The origin of the coordinate system lies in the lower-left corner of some virtual sheet of paper. For example, we can draw a right angle as follows:

```
2.000   6.000   0
2.000   1.000   1
5.500   1.000   1
```

We imagine a pen, which first moves to the point with coordinates $x = 2$, $y = 6$. Then it draws a line downward to point $x = 2$, $y = 1$, and, finally, it draws a line to the point with $x = 5.5$, $y = 1$. The two pen positions ('up' = 0 or 'down' = 1) during pen movements can be distinguished by using the words *move* and *draw*, as in the above description of what happens. Thus, we may denote the above three lines of text symbolically as

```
move(2.0, 6.0);
draw(2.0, 1.0);
draw(5.5, 1.0);
```

As *move* and *draw* are real C functions, discussed in Section 4.3, it will be clear that converting a plotfile into a real drawing is a rather simple task. This task is performed by program PLOTHP. Originally, I wrote this program only to obtain graphics output on a Hewlett-Packard plotter, but later it seemed a good idea to me to let it also produce graphics output on the video display and on the matrix printer, if desired. You start the program by typing

```
PLOTHP
```

Then the line

```
Name of input file:
```

appears on the screen, which means that we have to enter the name of a plotfile, such as, for example, *CUBE.PLT*. If this file really exists, the following three messages are successively displayed:

```
Output on video display? (Y/N)
Output on matrix printer? (Y/N)
Output on HP plotter? (Y/N)
```

Thus, even if no HP plotter is available, program PLOTHP will be useful. Although we have already been able to have graphics output on the video display and on the matrix printer when we were using program D3D, it may be desired to repeat this later, for example, when new ribbon has been placed in the printer, and, if the displayed object is complex, program PLOTHP will display it much faster than program D3D does, because it does not have to perform any three-dimensional computations. If our answer to the first question is *Y*, we are asked to enter a scaling factor. If, for example, we want the image to be displayed in half its normal size then we should enter 0.5; in most cases we will use the scaling factor 1. (This is in sharp contrast to scaling factors for plotters, as is discussed below.) Scaled with the given factor the picture will appear on the video display and, if desired, on the matrix printer.

If you are fortunate enough to have an HP plotter, then you can use the most interesting option of PLOTHP by replying *Y* to the last of the three above questions. The plotter should be connected to a serial I/O port, called either *COM1* or *COM2* in MS-DOS terminology. There are a number of serial port parameters, which are requested as follows the first time you use the plot option:

```
Enter serial port number (1 for com1, 2 for com2):
Baud rate
(110, 150, 300, 600, 1200, 2400, 4800, 9600):
If not sure, try the following options in the given order:
Parity (0 = none, 1 = odd, 2 = even):
Number of stop bits? (1 or 2):
Character size (8 or 7):
```

After each of the six above colons you have to enter one of the suggested answers. The best thing to do is to look these data up in the technical documentation of your computer and your plotter. You may find a reference to DIP switches on the plotter, which, for example, set the baud rate. On the various plotters that I have been using, I had to enter 0, 1, 8 as answers to the last three questions, so you may try these first if you find it difficult to find the correct settings in your manuals. It would be very annoying if we had to answer these six questions each time we run PLOTHP; I therefore thought it a good idea that PLOTHP should write the answers to these questions to a 'configuration file', and I implemented this idea as follows. Program PLOTHP looks to see if there is a file called PLCONFIG.TXT in the current directory. As this will not be the case the first time you run the program, it will ask for the above six parameters; it then creates the file PLCONFIG.TXT and the parameters that you have been entering are written to it. Thus, if you run the program later, it will find that file; then it reads the parameters from it, and, in order that you may change them, it displays them on the video display and inquires if they are correct. If not, you can (and must) enter new values for them.

After entering the serial port parameters, you have to enter a scaling factor to be applied to the coordinates read from the file. Recall that in the file the $x$-coordinate ranges from 0 to 10 and the y-coordinates from 0 to 7. Instead, the plotter needs quite large integer values, ranging, for example, from 0 to 11 420. The latter number is the greatest $x$ value that is possible on an HP 7225A/B plotter. It is expressed in plotter units, where one plotter unit is 0.025 mm. The plotter itself offers facilities for scaling, but, as this is an extremely simple operation, program PLOTHP does the scaling internally, using the factor entered by the user. We need not base our drawing on the mechanical limits of the plotter; instead of 11 420, we may, for example, want 8000 to be the greatest $x$-coordinate, which means that we have to enter a scaling factor of 800. As a result, the drawing will then have a length of 800 × 10 = 8000 plotter units, which is 8000 × 0.025 = 200 mm. Similarly, the size in the y-direction is then 800 × 7 × 0.025 = 140 mm. You will soon find out what is the best scaling factor to use. The most important thing to remember is that it should be a quite large value (such as 800).

Finally, we can change the default speed (or velocity) of the pen when drawing lines. Instead of the default maximum speed which for my plotter is 25 cm/s, a lower value (between 1 and 25) gives better results because the ink will then have more time to flow down to the paper. If you answer the question

```
Default velocity? (Y/N):
```

in the negative you will be asked to enter the desired velocity, and, immediately after this, the plotter will start plotting on the basis of the given plotfile. Many drawings in this book have been made in this way, and, as can be expected, their quality is much better than that of some other illustrations, produced by a matrix printer.

The above discussion of PLOTHP is intended for the user, who need not necessarily be familiar with programming. We will now deal with some rather technical programming details. In the manual of your HP plotter you will find an explanation of about 40 Hewlett-Packard Graphic Language (HP-GL) instructions, only five of which we will use, namely:

```
IN          Initialize
VS          Velocity Select
PU          Pen Up
PD          Pen Down
PA          Plot Absolute
```

Consider, for example, the following character string:

```
IN;VS4;PU;PA4000,3000;PD;PA4000,5000;PU;
```

When sent to the plotter, the following steps will be taken:

1 IN initializes the plotter.
2 VS selects a velocity of 4 cm/s.
3 PU raises the pen.
4 PA moves the pen to the point with plotter coordinates $X = 4000$, $Y = 3000$.
5 PD puts the pen down.
6 PA draws a line from the point mentioned in step 4 to point $X = 4000$, $Y = 5000$.
7 PU raises the pen.

Program PLOTHP reads lines of text from the given plotfile and converts them to HP-GL instructions, each of which is placed in a string *str* and then sent to the serial output port by the function call

```
ser_str(str);
```

This function, *ser_str*, sends all characters *ch* that precede the terminating null character of the string *str* to the serial output port by means of

```
ser_char(ch);
```

These are two functions of our own; the former will not present any difficulties for an experienced C programmer, but the second will require some knowledge of data communications, as we will see below.

There is a ROM-BIOS call for serial (RS232) communication services; these services are available through interrupt 20 (hexadecimal 0x14), as explained in great detail in *The Peter Norton Programmer's Guide to the IBM PC*. There are four services, numbered 0 through 3; prior to the software interrupt, an assembly-language programmer will place the service number in register AH, and, in the case of service 1, place the character to be sent in register AL. Also, a code (0 for COM1 and 1 for COM2) for the serial port must be placed in register DX. Although we are using C rather than assembly language, we can use all this by calling the function *int86*, which we have been using in GRPACK for other purposes as well (see Section 1.2.6 of my previous book *CGIP*, or Section 4.3 of the current book). This function is available in many C implementations for the IBM PC, including Turbo C, Lattice C, and Microsoft C. Although I have used *int86* in the first version of PLOTHP quite satisfactorily, I have replaced it with the function *bioscom*, which I found later in the Turbo C manual. The latter function is easier to use than *int86* because it is less general, and it makes program PLOTHP more readable. The name *bioscom* will probably mean 'communications through BIOS', and this function can only be used for serial communications. Instead of using registers in assembly-language style, we can simply express what we want by means of function arguments, as the function prototype suggests:

```
int bioscom(int cmd, char byte, int port);
```

This line occurs in the header file *bios.h*, which we will therefore include in our program. Please refer to the Turbo C manual for a full explanation of *bioscom*. Here we shall discuss it only as far as we need it. Its first argument, *cmd*, is the service number mentioned above; it can be one of the following:

0 Sets the communication parameters to the value in *byte*.
1 Sends the character in *byte* to the serial port.
2 Receives a character from the serial port; it can be found in the lower eight bits of the returned integer value.
3 Returns the current status of the serial port.

If *cmd* = 0, the second argument shows how to set the communication parameters. This argument, *byte*, should be interpreted as a sequence of eight bits, numbered 7, 6, ..., 0, from left to right. There are four groups of bits in *byte*:

7, 6, 5: The baud rate, coded as 000, 001, ..., 111 for 110, 150, 300, 600, 1200, 2400, 4800, 9600 baud, respectively.

4, 3: 00, 01, 11 as codes for *No parity*, *Odd parity*, and *Even parity*.

2: 0 = *One stop bit*, 1 = *Two stop bits*.

1, 0: 10 = *7 data bits*, 11 = *8 data bits*.

The third argument, *port*, is a code for the port number: it is 0 for *COM1* and 1 for *COM2*.

Although all this may sound very technical, it is not difficult to implement, provided that the baud rate, parity, and the numbers of stop and data bits are known. When I did this, it worked well for some simple test cases, but it went wrong with more complex drawings, because of *buffer overflow*. In the plotter manual I had seen a chapter about handshake protocols, which I thought had been written for electrical engineers rather than for programmers. In the section 'Hardwire Handshake Mode' I found a flowchart which shows a wait loop, and although some technical terms in it were not clear to me, it was sufficient for me to find the following solution, which works correctly:

```
void ser_char(char ch)
{ int retval;
  do
  { retval = bioscom(3, byte, port);
  } while ((retval & 0x0030) != 0x0030);
  bioscom(1, ch, port);
}
```

Before sending character *ch* to the serial port (using service number 1), the processor waits in a do-while loop until it may do so. Within the loop, we enquire about the status of the serial port (using service number 3). Function *bioscom*, when called with service number 3, gives the current port status as its returned value. Each bit of this integer value has some meaning, which will probably be fully understood by data-communication experts. As follows from the hexadecimal constant $0x0030$ in the above program text, only the bits 5 and 4 are selected; their meaning is *Data set ready* and *Clear to send*, respectively. Only when these two bits in the returned value are equal to 1 does the loop terminate. In this way, we can prevent overflow of the data buffer in the plotter. Further details will be clear from the source text of program PLOTHP. If you want to use this source text you should not forget that the header file GRPACK.H should be available so that it can be included, and that GRPACK.OBJ should be supplied to the linker.

```
/* PLOTHP: The main purpose of this program is to transform
           an input file xxx.PLT to a drawing on a
           Hewlett-Packard plotter.
           Besides, it can display the same drawing on the
           video display and print it on a matrix printer.
           The input file must consist of lines of the form

               x   y   c

           The coordinates x and y are nonnegative
           real numbers, typically not greater than 10.0 and
           7.0, respectively, and the code c is either 0
           (pen up) or 1 (pen down).
*/
#include <stdio.h>
#include <conio.h>
```

```c
#include <bios.h>
#include <ctype.h>
#include <process.h>
#include "grpack.h"

void display(int printer);
void plotter(void);
void initplotter(void);
float scalingfactor(void);
void ser_str(char *p);
void ser_char(char ch);
void initialize(void);
char getcapital(void);

FILE *fp;
char filnam[40];
unsigned char byte;
int penposition, port;


main()
{ char ch;
  printf("Name of input file: "); scanf("%s", filnam);
  fp = fopen(filnam, "r");
  if (fp == NULL) {printf("File problem"); exit(1);}
  printf("Output on video display? (Y/N): ");
  ch = getcapital();
  if (ch == 'Y')
  { printf("\nOutput on matrix printer? (Y/N): ");
    ch = getcapital();
    display(ch == 'Y');
    fclose(fp); fp = NULL;
  }
  printf("\nOutput on HP plotter? (Y/N): ");
  ch = getcapital();
  if (ch == 'Y')
  { if (fp == NULL)
    { fp = fopen(filnam, "r");
      if (fp == NULL){printf("File problem"); exit(1);}
    }
    plotter();
  }
  exit(0); /* Close file fp, if open */
}

void display(int printer)
{ float f, x, y, xfact, yfact, fact;
  char ch, code;
  f = scalingfactor();
  if (printer) setprdim();
     /* Change x_max and y_max (float)    */
  initgr();          /* Set X__max and Y__max (int)       */
  xfact = f*x_max/10.0; yfact = f*y_max/7.0;
  fact = (xfact < yfact ? xfact : yfact);
  while (fscanf(fp, "%f %f %d", &x, &y, &code) == 3)
  { ch = getc(fp);
    if (code < 0 || code > 1 || ch != '\n')
```

```
    { textXY(40, 40, "Incorrect file format"); endgr();
      exit(1);
    }
    x *= fact; y *= fact;
    if (x > x_max || y > y_max)
    { to_text();
      printf("Outside boundaries: x = %6.3f  y = %6.3f\n",
               x, y);
      return;
    }
    if (code) draw(x, y); else move(x, y);
  }
  if (printer) printgr(0, X__max, 0, Y__max);
  endgr();
}

void plotter(void)
{ float f, x, y;
  int ix, iy, code, count=0, velo;
  char str[50], ch;
  initplotter();
  printf(
  "\nThe scaling factor f for a plotter is\n");
  printf("normally quite large. For example, if x or y\n");
  printf("ranges from 0 to 10 in the input file, and\n");
  printf(
  "is to range from 0 to 8000 in plotter coordinates,\n");
  printf(
  "then the scaling factor f should be 800.\n");
  f = scalingfactor();
  printf("\nDefault velocity? (Y/N): "); ch = getcapital();
  if (ch == 'N')
  { printf("\nEnter an integer, the velocity in cm/s,\n");
    printf("(not less than 1 or greater than 127): ");
    scanf("%d", &velo);
    sprintf(str, "VS%d;", velo);
    ser_str(str);
  }


  while (fscanf(fp, "%f %f %d", &x, &y, &code) == 3)
  { ch = getc(fp);
    if (code < 0 || code > 1 || ch != '\n')
    { printf("Incorrect file format"); exit(1);
    }
    count++;
    ix = (int)(f * x + 0.5);
    iy = (int)(f * y + 0.5);
    if (code != penposition)
    { ser_str(code ? "PD;" : "PU;");
      penposition = code;
    }
    sprintf(str, "PA%04d,%04d;", ix, iy);
    ser_str(str);
  }
  printf("\n%d points\n", count); ser_str("PU;");
}
```

```c
void initplotter(void)
{ FILE *fplconfg;
  int code, comnr, baud, parity, stopbits, charsize,
      oldvalues=0, retval;
  char answer='Y';
  fplconfg = fopen("plconfig.txt", "r");
  if (fplconfg != NULL)
    oldvalues = (fscanf(fplconfg, "%d %d %d %d %d",
      &comnr, &baud, &parity, &stopbits, &charsize) == 5);
  if (oldvalues)
  { printf("\nDefault serial port parameters:\n\n");
    printf("Serial port number: %4d\n", comnr);
    printf("Baud rate:          %4d\n", baud);
    printf("Parity:             %4s\n",
    (parity == 2 ? "even" : parity ? "odd" : "none"));
    printf("Number of stop bits:%4d\n", stopbits);
    printf("Character size:     %4d bits\n", charsize);
    printf("Are these correct? (Y/N): ");
    answer = getcapital();
    printf("\n");

  }
  if (oldvalues == 0 || answer == 'N')
  { printf(
    "\nEnter serial port number (1 for com1, 2 for com2): ");
    scanf("%d", &comnr);
    printf("Baud rate\n");
    printf("(110, 150, 300, 600, 1200, 2400, 4800, 9600):");
    scanf("%d", &baud);
    printf(
    "\n\nIf not sure, try the following options in the"
    " given order:\n");
    printf("Parity (0 = none, 1 = odd, 2 = even): ");
    scanf("%d", &parity);
    printf("Number of stop bits? (1 or 2): ");
    scanf("%d", &stopbits);
    printf("Character size (8 or 7): ");
    scanf("%d", &charsize);
    if (fplconfg != NULL) fclose(fplconfg);
    fplconfg = fopen("plconfig.txt", "w");
    fprintf(fplconfg, "%d %d %d %d %d\n",
        comnr, baud, parity, stopbits, charsize);
    fclose(fplconfg);
  }


  code = (baud == 110 ? 0 :
          baud == 150 ? 1 :
          baud == 300 ? 2 :
          baud == 600 ? 3 :
          baud == 1200 ? 4 :
          baud == 2400 ? 5 :
          baud == 4800 ? 6 :
          baud == 9600 ? 7 : -1);
  if (code == -1) {printf("Baud rate incorrect"); exit(1);}
  if (parity == 2) parity = 3;
  /* Internal code for 'even' is 3 */
```

```
  port = comnr-1;   /* 0 for com1, 1 for com2 */
  byte = (code << 5) | (parity << 3) |
                 ((stopbits-1) << 2) | (charsize - 5);
  retval = bioscom(0, byte, port);
  /* Test on: transfer shift register empty,
     transfer holding register empty,
     data ready.
  */
  if ((retval & 0x6100) != 0x6100)
  { printf("Initialization error;\n");
    printf("AH = %02XH\n", retval >> 8);
    exit(1);
  }
  ser_str("IN;PU;"); /* Initialize */
  penposition = 0;
}

float scalingfactor(void)
{ float f;
  printf("\nEnter scaling factor f\n");
  printf("(f = 1: true length\n");
  printf(" f > 1: magnify\n");
  printf(" f < 1: reduce): "); scanf("%f", &f);
  getchar();            /* Newline character skipped */
  return f;
}

void ser_str(char *p)
{ while (*p) ser_char(*(p++));
}

void ser_char(char ch)
{ int retval;
  /* Test on: Data set ready, Clear to send.
  */
  do
  { retval = bioscom(3, byte, port);
  } while ((retval & 0x0030) != 0x0030);
  bioscom(1, ch, port);
}

char getcapital(void)
{ char ch;
  ch = getche();
  return toupper(ch);
}
```

# Appendix A

```c
/* D3D: Designing in Three Dimensions.
   After compilation, this module (D3D) is to be linked
   together with the modules
   GRPACK (or GRPACK1) (see Section 4.3),
   HLPFUN  (see Section 4.4), and
   TRAFO   (see Section 3.7).
   The compiler to be used is Turbo C of Borland.
   Memory model: Huge.
*/
#include <stdio.h>
#include <math.h>
#include <ctype.h>
#include <alloc.h>
#include <conio.h>
#include <string.h>
#include <process.h>
#include "grpack.h"

#include <dos.h>

#define BIG 1e10
#define IBIG 30000
#define EPS 1e-6
#define MAXFACES 2500
#define LIN1 156
#define LIN2 168
#define LIN3 180

void
   initrotate(double a1, double a2, double a3,
            double v1, double v2, double v3, double alpha),
   rotate(double x, double y, double z,
        double *px1, double *py1, double *pz1),
   /* initrotate and rotate are defined in TRAFO */

   init_viewport(void),
   hlpfun(
     float rho, float theta, float phi, float surflimit),

   coeff(float rho, float theta, float phi),
```

```
   ermes(char *s);
   /* init_viewport, hlpfun and coeff are defined in HLPFUN
   */

int abs(int x);

static void
   aspect(void),
   getstr(int X, int Y, char *str),
   mv(float x, float y, float z),
   dw(float x, float y, float z),
   screencoor(int mode, int i, int *pX, int *pY),
   viewing(float x, float y, float z,
                        double *pxe, double *pye, double *pze),

   display(void),
   plotpoint(int i, int Bold),
   grmes(int meslin, char *s),
   rdfile(int normal),
   wrfile(void),
   cursorcontrol(char direc),
   cursor(float x, float y, float z, int new),
   show(char c),
   faces(void),
   eyepos(void),
   plotsph(float rho, float theta, float phi, int down),
   enquire(int vpos, char *str, float *px),
   textcursor(int col, int line),
   checkfaces(int i),
   infopage(int i),
   helpinfo(void),
   myungetch(char ch),
   line3(int P, int Q),
   checkall(void),
   clear(void),
   zoom(int large),
   reposition(void),
   plotaxes(int checksize),
   fresh(void),
   list_faces(void),
   points(void),
   transform(void),
   check_alloc(int i),
   asksave(void),
   entire(void),
   open_plotfile(void),
   close_plotfile(void),
   pressanykey(char *str);
static int
   storepoint(int i, float x, float y, float z),
   rdnumber(int *p),
   rdoldnr(int *p),
   getch1(void);
static char
   query(int line, char *s),
   mygetch(void);


struct linsegface
```

```
{int i; double a, b, c; struct linsegface *next;};
                            /* See module HLPFUN */
struct vertex
{ int inuse;
  float xw, yw, zw;
  double xe, ye, ze;
  struct linsegface *connect; /* See module HLPFUN */
} *p;

float xO, yO, zO;

double v11, v12, v13, v21, v22, v23, v32, v33, v43,
  PI, PIdiv180;
float xmin, ymin, xmax, ymax;

static float c1, c2, d, c1first, c2first, dfirst,
  rho, theta, phi, xxx, yyy,
  Xvp_range, Yvp_range, Xvp_center, Yvp_center,
  Xvp_min, Xvp_max, Yvp_min, Yvp_max,
  xwmin, ywmin, zwmin, xwmax, ywmax, zwmax,
  xcur, ycur, zcur, step=0.2, zemin, zemax;
static int margin, modified, faces_present, inside, newcentralpoint,
  zoomin, pridim, bufposition, inside, newcentralpoint,
  numbers=1, numO, axes, axesO, auxlines=1, auxO,
  bold=1, boldO, plength, psize, faces_entering,
  points_entering, X__max1, progr_arg;
int nmax, **pface, nface, object_present;
static char buffer[50], s2[2], char_avail, filnam[40],
  spaces[60];

main(int argc, char *argv[])
{ int i, lowest, highest;
  long lbytes;
  float threshold, surflimit, xlowest, xhighest;
  char str[30], ch, chO, ch1;
  if (argc > 1)
  { strcpy(filnam, argv[1]); progr_arg = 1;
  }
  PI = 4 * atan(1.0);
  PIdiv180 = PI/180;
  pface = (int **)farcalloc(MAXFACES, sizeof(int *));
  psize = sizeof(struct vertex);
  lbytes = farcoreleft(); plength = lbytes/(3L * psize);
  /* About one third of free memory space is allocated for
     vertices
  */
  p = (struct vertex *)farcalloc(plength+7, psize);
  if (p == NULL) ermes("Memory problem");
  s2[1] = '\0';
  margin = 456;
  rho = 1000; theta = 20; phi = 75;
  coeff(rho, theta, phi);
  clearscr();
  wrscr(1, 0, "D3D: Designing in Three Dimensions");
  wrscr(2, 0, "=================================");
  wrscr(4, 0, "This program is the main subject of:");
  wrscr(6, 4,
  "Ammeraal, L. (1988), INTERACTIVE 3D COMPUTER GRAPHICS,");

  wrscr(7, 4, "  Chichester: John Wiley & Sons.");
```

```
wrscr(9, 0,
"Related books from the same author and publisher:");
wrscr(11, 4,
"PROGRAMMING PRINCIPLES IN COMPUTER GRAPHICS (1986),");
wrscr(12, 4, "COMPUTER GRAPHICS FOR THE IBM PC  (1987),");
wrscr(13, 4, "C FOR PROGRAMMERS (1986),");
wrscr(14, 4, "PROGRAMS AND DATA STRUCTURES IN C (1987).");

if (progr_arg)
{ wrscr(16, 0,
  "Do you want difference in line thicknesses? (Y/N): ");
  settxtcursor(17, 0); ch = mygetch(); s2[0] = ch;
  if (isalpha(ch)) wrscr(17, 0, s2);
  bold = (ch == 'Y' || ch == 'y');
}
wrscr(19, 0,
"If you want help, press function key F1; otherwise,");
wrscr(20, 0,
"press any other key. (You may also press F1 for help"
" later");
settxtcursor(21, 0);
ch = mygetch();
if (ch == 0 && getch() == 59 /* F1 */) helpinfo();
initgr(); X__max1 = X__max+1;
for (i=(X__max1 - margin - 16)/8; i>=0; i--)
  spaces[i]=' '; /* String of spaces; '\0' at the end   */
zoom(0); /* Set viewport constants; 0 = small viewport */
clear(); display();
if (progr_arg) rdfile(0);

/* Main loop: */
while
(grmes(LIN1, "Command:"), textcursor(margin+72, LIN1),
    ch0=mygetch(), ch=toupper(ch0), ch != 'Q')
{ grmes(LIN2, "  ");
  grmes(LIN3, "  ");
  if (ch0==0)
  { ch1=mygetch();
    if (ch1 == 59) /* Function key 1 */ helpinfo();
    continue;
  }
  show(ch);
  if (isdigit(ch))
  { if (points_entering) {myungetch(ch); points();} else
    if (faces_entering) {myungetch(ch); faces();} else
    grmes(LIN2,"Don't begin with digit");
    continue;
  }

  if (ch == 'I')
  { points_entering = 1; points(); continue;
  }
  points_entering = 0;

  if (ch == 'F')
  { faces_entering = 1; faces(); modified = 1; continue;
  }
  faces_entering = 0;

  if (ch=='X' || ch=='Y' || ch=='Z')
```

```
{ cursorcontrol(ch); continue;
}
if (ch == 'R') rdfile(1); else
if (ch == 'W') {wrfile(); modified = 0;} else
if (ch == 'V') eyepos(); else
if (ch == 'L') list_faces(); else
if (ch == 'C')
{ *filnam='\0'; asksave(); clear(); display();
} else
if (ch == '?')
{ if (kbhit()) getch();
  grmes(LIN2, "Point number:");
  getstr(margin, LIN3, str);
  if (sscanf(str, "%d", &i) != 1 || i >= nmax ||
                                    p[i].inuse == 0)
  { grmes(LIN2, "Number or format wrong"); continue;
  }
  sprintf(str, "%4.2f %4.2f %4.2f",
                p[i].xw, p[i].yw, p[i].zw);
  grmes(LIN3, str);
} else
if (ch == 'D')
{ if (kbhit()) getch();
  while (nmax > 0 && p[nmax-1].inuse == 0) nmax--;
  xlowest = nmax;
  enquire(LIN2, "Lower bound: ", &xlowest);
  lowest = (int)(xlowest + 0.1);
  if (lowest < 1) lowest = 1;
  xhighest = xlowest;
  enquire(LIN3, "Upper bound: ", &xhighest);
  highest = (int)(xhighest + 0.1);
  if (highest >= nmax) highest = nmax - 1;
  if (lowest <= highest)
  { for (i=lowest; i<=highest; i++)
    { p[i].inuse = 0; checkfaces(i);
    }
    checkall(); modified = 1;
    display();
  }
} else
if (ch == 'M')
{ numbers =
  (query(LIN1, "Point numbers? (Y/N):") == 'Y');
  axes0 = axes; aux0 = auxlines;
  axes = (query(LIN1, "Axes? (Y/N): ") == 'Y');
  if (axes)
    auxlines =
    (query(LIN1, "Aux. lines? (Y/N): ") == 'Y');
  else auxlines = 0;
  bold = (query(LIN1, "Bold lines? (Y/N):") == 'Y');
  if (axes0 && !axes || aux0 && !auxlines) checkall();
  /* Adapt image size now that axes have been removed
     and more room may have become available for the
     image.
  */
  if (query(LIN1, "Entire screen? (Y/N):") == 'Y')
    entire(); else
  if (numbers != num0 || axes != axes0 ||
      auxlines != aux0 || bold != bold0) display();
} else
```

```
        if (ch == 'E') entire(); else
        if (ch == 'P') printgr(0.0, X__max, 0.0, Y__max); else
        if (ch == 'S') enquire(LIN2, "Step size:", &step); else
        if (ch == 'T') transform(); else
        if (ch == 'H')
        { clearpage();
          to_text();
          if (kbhit()) getch();
          wrscr(0, 0,
          "Do you want the object faces to approximate curved"
          " surfaces? (Y/N): ");
          settxtcursor(0, 68);
          ch = mygetch(); s2[0]=ch;
          if (ch>32) wrscr(0, 68, s2);
          if (ch == 'Y' || ch == 'y')
          { wrscr(2, 0, "Enter 'threshold', in degrees. The"
            " line of intersection of any");
            wrscr(3, 0, "two adjacent faces, if visible, will"
            " be drawn only if the angle");
            wrscr(4, 0, "between the normal vectors of these"
            " two faces is greater than");
            wrscr(5, 0, "'threshold'. The default value 35 will"
            " be used if you press only");
            wrscr(6, 0, "the Enter key.");
            settxtcursor(6, 15); ch = getchar();
            if (ch == '\n' ||
            (ungetc(ch, stdin), scanf("%f", &threshold) != 1))
                threshold = 35;
            surflimit = cos(threshold*PIdiv180);
          } else surflimit = 1.0;
          aspect();
          initgr();
          hlpfun(rho, theta, phi, surflimit);
          close_plotfile();
          ch = mygetch();
          if (ch == 'P' || ch == 'p')
            printgr(0, X__max, 0, Y__max);
          if (pridim)
          { clearpage(); to_text();
            x_max = 10.0; y_max = 7.0; pridim = 0;
            initgr();
          }
          display();
        } else grmes(LIN2, "Invalid command");
    }
    asksave();
    to_text();
}

static void asksave(void)
{ char ch;
  if (modified && nmax + nface > 7)
  { ch = query(LIN2, "Save object (Y/N): ");
    if (ch == 'Y' || ch == 'y') wrfile();
    grmes(LIN2, " ");
  }
}

static void aspect()
{ char ch;
```

```
  wrscr(7, 0, "After displaying the result on the screen,"
  " you can print");
  wrscr(8, 0, "it on a matrix printer by giving command P."
  " (If, instead,");
  wrscr(9, 0, "you press any other key, the previous"
  " graphics screen will be");
  wrscr(10, 0, "restored.) As for printing, please note the"

  " following:");
  wrscr(11, 0, "We say that we are using a 'correct aspect"
  " ratio' if a");
  wrscr(12, 0, "circle is displayed as a real circle, not"
  " as an ellipse.");
  wrscr(13, 0, "Normally the aspect ratio will be correct"
  " on the screen.");
  wrscr(14, 0, "If you want a correct aspect"
  " ratio on the printer");
  wrscr(15, 0, "(accepting an incorrect aspect ratio on the"

  " screen), then");
  wrscr(16, 0, "please enter A. Instead, you can enter the"
  " letter O if you");
  wrscr(17, 0, "want an output file (xxx.PLT), which, for"
  " example, can be");
  wrscr(18, 0, "read by program PLOTHP to produce output on"

  " a HP plotter.");
  wrscr(19, 0, "If neither is desired, press"
  " any other key...");
  settxtcursor(20, 0);
  ch = mygetch(); s2[0]=ch;
  if (ch > ' ') wrscr(20, 0, s2);
  if (ch == 'A' || ch == 'a')
  { setprdim(); pridim = 1;
  } else
  if (ch == 'O' || ch =='o') open_plotfile();
}


static void checkall(void)
/* Shrink, if required, after point deletion. */
{ int i, count=0;
  float xw, yw, zw, ze;
  xwmin = ywmin = zwmin = zemin = BIG;
  xwmax = ywmax = zwmax = zemax = -BIG;
  for (i=1; i<nmax; i++)
  if (p[i].inuse)
  { count++;
    xw = p[i].xw;
    yw = p[i].yw;
    zw = p[i].zw;
    ze = p[i].ze;
    if (xw < xwmin) xwmin = xw;
    if (xw > xwmax) xwmax = xw;
    if (yw < ywmin) ywmin = yw;
    if (yw > ywmax) ywmax = yw;
    if (zw < zwmin) zwmin = zw;
    if (zw > zwmax) zwmax = zw;
    if (ze < zemin) zemin = ze;
    if (ze > zemax) zemax = ze;
```

```
    }
    if (count == 0) clear(); else
    { if (xwmax < 0.5) xwmax = 0.5;
      /* To avoid axes of length 0 */
      if (ywmax < 0.5) ywmax = 0.5;
      if (zwmax < 0.5) zwmax = 0.5;
      xO = BIG;
      /* Forces 'reposition' to compute new central object
         point
      */
      reposition();
    }
}


static void check_alloc(int i)
{ if (i >= plength) ermes("Vertex number too high");
}


static void checkfaces(int i)
{ /* Point i has just been deleted. If any faces have i as
     a vertex, then these faces are deleted.
  */
  int j, n, k;
  if (nface == 0) return;
  grmes(LIN3, "Please wait ...");
  for (j=0; j<nface; j++)
  { if (pface[j] == NULL) continue;
    n = pface[j][0];
    if (n<0) ermes("n<0 in checkfaces");
    for (k=1; k<=n; k++)
    if (abs(pface[j][k]) == i)
    { farfree(pface[j]); pface[j] = NULL; break;
    }
  }
  grmes(LIN3, " ");
}


static void clear(void)
{ static int first=1;
  int i, j;
  axes = auxlines = numbers = 1;
  for (i=0; i<nmax; i++) p[i].inuse = 0;
  p[0].xw = p[0].yw = p[0].zw = 0.0;
  nmax = 1;
  for (j=0; j<nface; j++)
    if (pface[j] != NULL)
    { farfree(pface[j]); pface[j] = NULL;
    }
  nface = 0;
  xwmin = ywmin = zwmin = 0.0;
  xwmax = ywmax = zwmax = 1.0;
  xO = yO = zO = 0.5;
  fresh();
  reposition();
  if (first)
  { c1first = c1; c2first = c2; dfirst = d; first = 0;
  }
```

```
   modified = 0; object_present = 0;
}

static void close_plotfile(void)
{ if (fplot != NULL)
  { fclose(fplot);
    fplot = NULL;
  }
}


static void cursor(float xw, float yw, float zw, int new)
{ extern int drawmode;
  int i, j, dm, cnt;
  static int X, Y, X0, Y0;
  if (new)
  { inside = 1;
    for (cnt=0; cnt<2; cnt++)
    { storepoint(nmax+4, xw, yw, zw);
      storepoint(nmax+5, xw, yw, 0.0);
      screencoor(1, nmax+4, &X, &Y);
      screencoor(1, nmax+5, &X0, &Y0);
      if (inside) break; else
      { reposition(); display();
      }
    }
    if (cnt == 2) ermes("cnt = 2 in cursor");
    p[nmax+4].inuse = 0;
    p[nmax+5].inuse = 0;
  }
  dm = drawmode; drawmode = 0;
  for (j=-2; j<=2; j+=4)
  for (i=-4; i<=4; i++) dot(X+i, Y+j);
  dot(X-4, Y-1); dot(X-3, Y-1);
  dot(X+3, Y-1); dot(X+4, Y-1);
  dot(X-4, Y); dot(X-3, Y); dot(X+3, Y);
  dot(X+4, Y);   dot(X, Y);
  dot(X-4, Y+1); dot(X-3, Y+1);
  dot(X+3, Y+1); dot(X+4, Y+1);
  draw_line(X, Y, X0, Y0);
  drawmode = dm;
}


static void cursorcontrol(char direc)
{ char c, c0, str[30];
  float *axis, x0, y0, z0, dx, dy, dz, dist2, d2;
  int i, j, jumped=0;
  if (!auxlines)
  { axes = auxlines = 1; display();
  }
  xcur = ycur = zcur = 0.0;
  cursor(xcur, ycur, zcur, 1);
  axis =
  (direc == 'X' ? &xcur : direc == 'Y' ? &ycur : &zcur);
  grmes(LIN2, "Press +, -, I, J, or D");
  grmes(LIN3, "(or press Enter)");
  while (c0 = mygetch(), c = toupper(c0),
    c == '+' || c == '-' || c == 'X' || c == 'Y' || c == 'Z'
```

```
    || c == 'I' || c == 'J' || c == 'D' || c == 0)
{ if (c != 'D') jumped = 0;
  if (c == '+' || c == '-')
  { x0 = xcur; y0 = ycur; z0 = zcur;
    if (c == '-') *axis -= step; else *axis += step;
    cursor(x0, y0, z0, 0);
    cursor(xcur, ycur, zcur, 1);
    sprintf(str, "%5.2f %5.2f %5.2f    ",
                      xcur, ycur, zcur);
    grmes(LIN3, str);
    continue;
  }
  show(c);
  if (c == 'X') {axis = &xcur; direc = c;} else
  if (c == 'Y') {axis = &ycur; direc = c;} else
  if (c == 'Z') {axis = &zcur; direc = c;} else
  if (c == 'I')
  { for (i=1; i<plength; i++) if (p[i].inuse == 0) break;
    check_alloc(i);
    if (i >= nmax) nmax = i+1;
    cursor(xcur, ycur, zcur, 0); /* Delete */
    storepoint(i, xcur, ycur, zcur); modified = 1;
    plotpoint(i, 1);
    cursor(xcur, ycur, zcur, 0); /* Draw again */
  } else
  if (c == 'J')
  { if (nmax == 0)
    { grmes(LIN2, "No points present");
      cursor(xcur, ycur, zcur, 0);
      grmes(LIN3, " "); return;
    }
    dist2 = BIG;
    for (i=1; i<nmax; i++)
    if (p[i].inuse)
    { dx = p[i].xw - xcur;
      dy = p[i].yw - ycur;
      dz = p[i].zw - zcur;
      d2 = dx*dx + dy*dy + dz*dz;
      if (d2 < dist2) {dist2 = d2; j=i;}
    }
    jumped = 1;
    cursor(xcur, ycur, zcur, 0); /* Delete old cursor */
    xcur = p[j].xw; ycur = p[j].yw; zcur = p[j].zw;
    cursor(xcur, ycur, zcur, 1);
    sprintf(str, "%4d %4.2f %4.2f %4.2f",
                      j, xcur, ycur, zcur);
    grmes(LIN3, str);
  } else
  if (c == 'D')
  { if (!jumped) grmes(LIN3, "Use J first"); else
    { p[j].inuse = 0; cursor(xcur, ycur, zcur, 0);
      checkfaces(j);
      checkall(); modified = 1; jumped = 0;
      display(); cursor(xcur, ycur, zcur, 1);
      grmes(LIN2, "Press +, -, I, J, ?, D");
      grmes(LIN3, "(or press Enter)");
    }
  } else  /* c == 0: Probably arrow key pressed */
  { if (getch() == 59) helpinfo(); else
    { grmes(LIN3, "Wrong key pressed");
```

```
      }
    }
    show(direc);
  }
  cursor(xcur, ycur, zcur, 0); /* Delete cursor */
  if (c0 != '\n' && c0 != '\r') myungetch(c0);
  show(' ');
  grmes(LIN2, " ");
  grmes(LIN3, " ");
}


static void display(void)
{ int i, j, k, n, drawn, i_old;
  faces_present = 0;
  clearpage();
  if (axes) plotaxes(1);
  if (zoomin) init_viewport();
  /* Defined in module HLPFUN */
  else
  { imove(0, 0); idraw(X__max, 0); idraw(X__max, Y__max);
    idraw(0, Y__max); idraw(0, 0);
    imove(margin-4, 0); idraw(margin-4, Y__max);
    textXY(margin, 5,   "D3D");
    textXY(margin, 20,  "Available commands:");
    textXY(margin, 34,  "X/Y/Z: Cursor control");
    textXY(margin, 46,  "?: Show coordinates");
    textXY(margin, 58,  "Mode (Axes etc.)");
    textXY(margin, 70,  "F1 (Help)  | Quit");
    textXY(margin, 82,  "Step         Clear");
    textXY(margin, 94,  "Insert       Delete");
    textXY(margin, 106, "Faces        List");
    textXY(margin, 118, "Read         Write");
    textXY(margin, 130, "Entire       Hidden");
    textXY(margin, 142, "Viewpoint  | Transform");
    grmes(LIN3, "Please wait ...");
  }
  for (j=0; j<nface; j++)
  { if (pface[j] == NULL) continue;
    faces_present = 1; /* See 'list_faces' */
    i_old = abs(pface[j][1]);
    n = pface[j][0];
    if (n<0) ermes("n<0 in display");
    for (k=2; k<=n; k++)
    { i = pface[j][k]; drawn = i >= 0; i = abs(i);
      if (drawn) line3(i_old, i);
      i_old = i;
    }
    i = pface[j][1]; drawn = i >= 0; i = abs(i);
    if (drawn) line3(i_old, i);
  }
  for (i=1; i<nmax; i++)
  if (p[i].inuse)
    plotpoint(i, 0);
  if (!zoomin)
  { grmes(LIN1, "Command:");
    grmes(LIN3, " ");
    num0 = numbers; axes0 = axes; aux0 = auxlines;
    bold0 = bold;
  }
```

```c
  if (axes) plotaxes(0);
  /* Only to make letters x, y, z legible */
}

static void dw(float x, float y, float z)
{ int X, Y;
  double xe, ye, ze;
  viewing(x-0.5, y-0.5, z-0.5, &xe, &ye, &ze);
  /* xO = yO = zO = 0.5 */
  X = IX(d*xe/ze+c1);
  Y = IY(d*ye/ze+c2);
  idraw(X, Y);
}


static void enquire(int vpos, char *str, float *px)
{ char snum[40], dum[40];
  int len, slen, j;
  char ch;
  if (kbhit()) getch();
  len = 8*strlen(str);
  if (margin+len > X__max1)
    ermes("String too long in 'enquire'");
  textXY(margin, vpos, str);
  sprintf(snum, "%3.1f", *px);
  slen = strlen(snum);
  if (snum[slen-1] == '0' && snum[slen-2] == '.')
    snum[slen-2] = '\0';
  if (margin+len+8*strlen(snum) > X__max1)
    ermes("String plus number too long in 'enquire'");
  slen = (X__max - margin - len)/8;
  for (j=0; j<slen; j++) dum[j] = ' ';

  dum[slen] = '\0';
  do
  { j = 100;
    do textXY(margin+len, vpos, dum);
      while (--j && !kbhit());
    j = 200;
    do textXY(margin+len, vpos, snum);
      while (--j && !kbhit());
  } while (!kbhit());
  ch = mygetch();
  if (ch == 0)
  { ch = mygetch();
    if (ch == 59) /* key F1 */
    { helpinfo();
      textXY(margin+len, vpos, dum);
    } else
    if (ch == 3) /* break */
    { to_text(); exit(1);
    }
  } else
  if (ch == '\n' || ch == '\r') return; else myungetch(ch);
  while (1)
  { getstr(margin+len, vpos, snum);
    if (sscanf(snum, "%f", px) == 1) break;
    textXY(margin+len, vpos, dum);
  }
}
```

```
static void entire(void)   /* Use entire screen */
{ float c1save, c2save, dsave;
  char ch;
  c1save = c1; c2save = c2; dsave = d;
  clearpage();
  to_text();
  if (kbhit()) getch();
  aspect(); /* May cause x_max and y_max to be changed   */
  initgr(); /* Computes horfact and vertfact              */
  zoom(1);   /* Changes Xvp_max etc.                      */
  newcentralpoint = 0; /* May be changed in reposition    */
  reposition();   /* Compute new c1, c2, d                */
                  /* May also change central point        */
  display();       /* Show large picture                  */
  close_plotfile();
  ch = mygetch();
  if (ch == 'P' || ch == 'p') printgr(0, X__max, 0, Y__max);

  clearpage(); to_text();
  if (pridim)
  { x_max = 10.0; y_max = 7.0; pridim = 0;
  }
  initgr();
  zoom(0);
  if (newcentralpoint) reposition();
          /* Compute new c1, c2, and d   */
  else
  { c1 = c1save; c2 = c2save; d = dsave;
  }
  display();
}


void ermes(char *s)
{ char ch;
  if (in_textmode) {printf(s); exit(1);}
  /* 'in_textmode' is an external variable */
  to_text();
  printf(s);
  if (!modified || nmax + nface <= 7) exit(1);
  printf("\n\nD3D will stop execution.\n");
  printf("Do you want to save the object? (Y/N): ");
  ch = getche();
  if (ch == 'Y' || ch == 'y')
  { initgr(); wrfile(); to_text();
  }
  exit(1);
}


static void eyepos(void)
{ float rho_1, theta_1, phi_1, rho1, theta1, phi1,
     dtheta, dphi, rho2;
  int i, n = 5;
  rho_1 = rho; theta_1 = theta; phi_1 = phi;
  rho = 1000; theta = 20; phi = 75;
  coeff(rho, theta, phi);
  clearpage();
```

```
    c1 = c1first; c2 = c2first; d = dfirst;
    mv(0.0, 0.0, 0.0); dw(1.0, 0.0, 0.0); text("x");
    mv(0.0, 0.0, 0.0); dw(0.0, 1.0, 0.0); text("y");
    mv(0.0, 0.0, 0.0); dw(0.0, 0.0, 1.0); text("z");
    mv(0.0, 0.0, 0.0);
    rho1 = 1.0; theta1 = 40; phi1 = 40;
    rho2 = rho1*sin(theta1*PIdiv180);
    plotsph(rho2, theta1, 90.0, 1);
    plotsph(rho1, theta1, phi1, 1);
    dw(0.0, 0.0, 0.0);
    rho1 = 0.9;
    dtheta = theta1/n;
    rho2 = 0.9 * rho2;
    mv(rho2, 0.0, 0.0);
    for (i=1; i<=n; i++) plotsph(rho2, i*dtheta, 90.0, 1);
    dphi = phi1/n;
    plotsph(rho1, 0.0, 0.0, 0);
    for (i=1; i<=n; i++) plotsph(rho1, theta1, i*dphi, 1);
    plotsph(0.5*rho1, theta1, phi1, 0); text("rho");
    plotsph(rho2, 0.4*theta1, 90.0, 0); text("theta");
    plotsph(rho1, theta1, 0.4*phi1, 0); text("phi");
    plotsph(1.2*rho1, theta1, phi1, 0); text("Eye");
    textXY(margin, 15, "Enter rho, theta, phi");
    textXY(margin, 30, "(theta, rho in degr.)");
    textXY(margin, 45, "If you press Enter,  ");
    textXY(margin, 60, "the values displayed ");
    textXY(margin, 75, "will be used.");
    enquire(90,  "rho   = ", &rho_1);
    enquire(105, "theta = ", &theta_1);
    enquire(120, "phi   = ", &phi_1);
    rho = rho_1; theta = theta_1; phi = phi_1;
    coeff(rho, theta, phi);
    xO = BIG;
    /* Forces 'reposition' to compute new central object point
    */
    reposition(); display();
}


static void faces(void)
{ int i, n=0, draw, i_old=0;
  char str[30];
  double xA, yA, zA, xB, yB, zB, xC, yC, zC, a, b, c, h;
  if ((pface[nface] = (int *)farcalloc(5, sizeof(int)))
     == NULL)
    ermes("Not enough memory");
  grmes(LIN2, "Nrs. closed by period:");
  textcursor(margin, LIN3);
  bufposition = -1;
  while (1)
  { if (rdnumber(&i) == 0) break;
    draw = i >= 0; i = abs(i);
    n++;
    if (p[i].inuse == 0)
    { sprintf(str, "Undef. point: %6d", i);
      pressanykey(str); display();
      faces_entering = 0; return;
    }
    if (n == 1)
    { xA = p[i].xw; yA = p[i].yw; zA = p[i].zw;
```

```
    } else
    if (n == 2)
    { xB = p[i].xw; yB = p[i].yw; zB = p[i].zw;
    } else
    if (n == 3)
    { xC = p[i].xw; yC = p[i].yw; zC = p[i].zw;
      h = xA * (yB*zC - yC*zB) -
          xB * (yA*zC - yC*zA) +
          xC * (yA*zB - yB*zA);
        a = yA * (zB-zC) - yB * (zA-zC) + yC * (zA-zB);
        b = -(xA * (zB-zC) - xB * (zA-zC) + xC * (zA-zB));
        c = xA * (yB-yC) - xB * (yA-yC) + xC * (yA-yB);
    } else
    if (fabs(a*p[i].xw + b*p[i].yw + c*p[i].zw - h) >
                          0.001 * fabs(h) + EPS)
      { pressanykey("Not in the same plane");
        display(); /* Remove any wrong lines */
        faces_entering = 0; return;
      }
      if (n > 1 && draw) line3(i_old, i);
      i_old = i;
      if (n > 4)
      { if ((pface[nface] = (int *)farrealloc(
                  pface[nface], (n+1) * sizeof(int))) == NULL)
        ermes("Not enough memory");
      }
      pface[nface][n] = (draw ? i : -i);
  }
  if (n == 0)
  { grmes(LIN2, "Invalid integer");
    farfree(pface[nface]); faces_entering = 0; return;
  }
  i = pface[nface][1];
  if (i >= 0)
  line3(i_old, i);
  pface[nface][0] = n; nface++;
  if (nface == MAXFACES)
  { grmes(LIN2, "Too many faces"); nface--;
  }
}


static void fresh(void)
{ int i, X, Y;
  xmin = ymin = zemin = BIG;
  xmax = ymax = zemax = -BIG; /* to be updated */
  /* Compute xmin, xmax, ymin, ymax:   */
  storepoint(nmax, 0.0, 0.0, 0.0);
  storepoint(nmax+1, xwmax, 0.0, 0.0);
  storepoint(nmax+2, 0.0, ywmax, 0.0);
  storepoint(nmax+3, 0.0, 0.0, zwmax);
  screencoor(0, nmax, &X, &Y);
  screencoor(0, nmax+1, &X, &Y);
  screencoor(0, nmax+2, &X, &Y);
  screencoor(0, nmax+3, &X, &Y);
  for (i=nmax; i<nmax+4; i++) p[i].inuse = 0;
}


static int getch1(void)  /* Called only in 'rdnumber' */
```

```c
{ char ch;
  if (bufposition < 0)
  { getstr(margin, LIN3, buffer); bufposition = 0;
  }
  ch = buffer[bufposition++];
  if (8*bufposition >= X__max1 - margin)
  { getstr(margin, LIN3, buffer);
    ch = buffer[0]; bufposition = 1;
  } else
  if (ch == '\0')
  { bufposition = -1; ch = '\n';
  }
  return ch;
}


static void getstr(int X, int Y, char *str)
{ char ch;
  int i=0, first=1, j, k;
  while (1)
  { j=X+8*i;
    if (j >= X__max1-8) break;
    if (first)
    { for (k=X; k<X__max1-8; k+=8) textXY(k, Y, " ");
      first=0;
    }
    textcursor(j, Y);
    ch=mygetch();
    if (ch == '\n' || ch == '\r') break;
    if (ch==8) /* backspace */
    { if (--i<0) i=0;
    } else
    { str[i] = s2[0] = ch;
      textXY(j, Y, s2);
      i++;
    }
  }
  str[i] = '\0';
}


static void grmes(int meslin, char *s)
{ int len;
  len = 8*strlen(s);
  if (!in_textmode) /* external variable */
  { textXY(margin, meslin, spaces);
    if (margin+len > X__max1)
    { to_text(); printf("In grmes:\n");
      printf("s='%s' len=%d margin=%d", s, len, margin);
      exit(1);
    }
    textXY(margin, meslin, s);
  } else
  printf("%s\n", s);
}


static void helpinfo(void)
{ int i=1, was_in_grmode;
```

```
  was_in_grmode = !in_textmode; /* external variable */
  settxtcursor(24, 37);
  if (was_in_grmode)  { clearpage(); to_text();}
  do
  { infopage(i);
    if (i == 1)
    wrscr(24, 0, "Press any key to continue ..."); else
    { wrscr(23, 0,
      "Press 'arrow up' for the previous info page,");
      wrscr(24, 0, "or any other key to continue  ...");
    }
    if (mygetch() == 0 && mygetch() == 72)
    { if (--i == 0) i = 1;
    } else i++;
  } while (i < 4);
  if (was_in_grmode)
  { initgr(); display();
  }
}


static void infopage(int i)
{ if (i == 1)
  {
  clearscr();
  wrscr(0, 68, "Info page 1");
  wrscr(1, 68, "(of 3 pages)");
  wrscr(2, 0,  "D3D: Designing in Three Dimensions,");
  wrscr(3, 0, "by L. Ammeraal");
  wrscr(5, 0, "Program D3D enables you to produce"
    " realistic images of 3D objects.");
  wrscr(6, 0, "The easiest way to do this is using a file"
    " prepared by this very");
  wrscr(7, 0, "program or by any other means. Instead, you"
    " can begin without");
  wrscr(8, 0, "any input file, and define points yourself"
    " by using command I,");
  wrscr(9, 0, "either immediately or under cursor control."
    " In the former case,");
  wrscr(10, 0, "command I is followed by entering a"
    " nonnegative integer n and the");
  wrscr(11, 0, "3D coordinates x, y, z of a new point. In"
    " the latter case, a cursor");
  wrscr(12, 0, "is used to define the position of a point."
    " You can simply press one");
  wrscr(13, 0, "one of the keys X, Y, Z, followed by + or"
    " - to move the cursor. Under");
  wrscr(14, 0, "cursor control, command I inserts a new"
    " point, and command J causes the");
  wrscr(15, 0, "cursor to jump to the nearest existing"
    " point. You can give command S");
  wrscr(16, 0, "to change the step size for cursor"
    " movements. To display the coordinates");
  wrscr(17, 0, "of a point, enter its number preceded"
    " by a question mark. With");
  wrscr(18, 0, "command D you can delete all points"
    " with numbers lying in a given");
  wrscr(19, 0, "range; in cursor-control mode, D deletes"
    " only one point, selected by J.");
```

```
wrscr(20, 0, "Mode command M is used to display or omit"
             " point numbers, axes, vertical");
wrscr(21, 0, "projection lines, and to control line"
             " thicknesses and screen size.");

} else
if (i == 2)
{
clearscr();
wrscr(0, 68, "Info page 2");
wrscr(1, 68, "(of 3 pages)");
wrscr(2, 0, "After having entered some points, you can"
            " define faces and draw");
wrscr(3, 0, "lines by using command F, followed by point"
            " numbers and then");
wrscr(4, 0, "followed by a period (.), as, for"
            " example, in:");
wrscr(5, 0, "    F");
wrscr(6, 0, "    1 2 3 4 5.");
wrscr(7, 0, "If F is followed by more than two point"
            " numbers, then these must");
wrscr(8, 0, "be the vertices of a polygon, all lying in"
            " the same plane, see");
wrscr(9, 0, "also command R. After command H, see below,"
            " these polygons will");
wrscr(10, 0, "act as bounding faces of a"
             " three-dimensional object; the vertices");
wrscr(11, 0, "must be given in counter-clockwise order"
             " (viewed from outside");
wrscr(12, 0, "the object). Any mistakes with command F"
             " can be corrected by");
wrscr(13, 0, "command L. Command R reads an object from"
             " a file, and command W");
wrscr(14, 0, "writes it onto a file. To change the"
             " viewpoint, use command V.");
wrscr(15, 0, "Automatic hidden-line elimination is"
             " performed by command H.");
wrscr(16, 0, "By choosing the requested value 'threshold'"
             " greater than 0, you");
wrscr(17, 0, "can make two adjacent faces (with a"
             " dihedral angle of almost 180");
wrscr(18, 0, "degrees) approximate a curved surface."
             " The intersecting edge");
wrscr(19, 0, "of two such faces is drawn only if"
             " the angle between their");
wrscr(20, 0, "normal vectors is greater than the"
             " given 'threshold'. Command E");
wrscr(21, 0, "causes the entire screen to be used for"
             " the image. Commands E and");
wrscr(22, 0, "H can also give printer"
             " and plotter output.");
} else
if (i == 3)
{
clearscr();
wrscr(0, 68, "Info page 3");
wrscr(1, 68, "(of 3 pages)");
wrscr(2, 0, "There are some accompanying files, called"
            " EXAMPLE1.DAT, etc., which");
wrscr(3, 0, "show the structure of 'object files',"
```

```
                        " written by command W and read");
    wrscr(4, 0, "by command R. First, all relevant points"
                        " are given in the form");
    wrscr(5, 0, "n x y z, where n is a point number. Then"
                        " the keyword 'Faces:' may");
    wrscr(6, 0, "follow, to introduce sequences of point"
                        " numbers, see also command F.");
    wrscr(7, 0, "Each sequence is followed by a period (.),"
                        " or by character #. The");
    wrscr(8, 0, "points given in each sequence are the"
                        " vertices of a polygon, which,");
    wrscr(9, 0, "after command H, acts as a bounding face."
                        " The sides of such polygons");
    wrscr(10, 0, "are line segments to be drawn, if visible,"
                        " except for negative point");
    wrscr(11, 0, "numbers. For example, in '8 3 -5 2 7.',"
                        " side 3 5, even if visible, is not");
    wrscr(12, 0, "to be drawn. A sequence of only two"
                        " points denotes a loose line segment.");
    wrscr(13, 0, "Command T offers four types of"
                        " transformations, namely rotation,");
    wrscr(14, 0, "translation, scaling and reflection.");
    wrscr(16, 0, "The simplest way to begin is using command"
                        " R to read a given");
    wrscr(17, 0, "file, such as EXAMPLE1.DAT; then you can"
                        " try the commands");
    wrscr(18, 0, "V to change the viewpoint and E to display"
                        " your results on");
    wrscr(19, 0, "the entire screen. Command H for hidden-"
                        " line removal is recommended");
    wrscr(20, 0, "next. If, after this, you want to draw a"
                        " new picture yourself,");
    wrscr(21, 0, "then you should use command C first"
                        " to clear the screen.");
  }
}

static void line3(int P, int Q)
{ float ze1, ze2, zrange=zemax-zemin+1e-15;
  int X1, Y1, X2, Y2, i1, i2, j1, j2;
  char str[10];
  static int dx[]={0, 1, -1, 0, 0},
             dy[]={0, 0, 0, 1, -1},
             n[]={5, 4, 3, 2, 1};
  screencoor(1, P, &X1, &Y1); /* Computes xxx and yyy */
  if (zoom && fplot != NULL) move(xxx, yyy);
  screencoor(1, Q, &X2, &Y2);
  if (zoom && fplot != NULL) draw(xxx, yyy);
  if (!zoom || bold)
  { ze1 = p[P].ze; ze2 = p[Q].ze;
    i1 = (int)((ze1-zemin)/zrange * 4.999);
    i2 = (int)((ze2-zemin)/zrange * 4.999);
    if (i1<0 || i2<0 || i1>4 || i2>4)
    { to_text(); printf("i1=%d i2=%d\n", i1, i2);
      printf("P = %d\n", P);
      printf("Q = %d\n", Q);
      printf("ze1=%f ze2=%f zemin=%f zrange=%f\n",
              ze1, ze2, zemin, zrange);
      exit(1);
    }
```

```
      for (j1=0; j1<n[i1]; j1++)
      for (j2=0; j2<n[i2]; j2++)
      draw_line(X1+dx[j1], Y1+dy[j1], X2+dx[j2], Y2+dy[j2]);
   ) else draw_line(X1, Y1, X2, Y2);
   if (numbers)
   ( sprintf(str, "%d", P); imove(X1-2, Y1-5); text(str);
      sprintf(str, "%d", Q); imove(X2-2, Y2-5); text(str);
   )
}


static void list_faces(void)
( int j, i, nch, nch0, count=0, n, nchmax;
   char str[50], ch;
   nchmax = (X__max-margin)/8;
   for (j=0; j<nface; j++)
   ( if (pface[j] == NULL) continue;
      count++;
      n = pface[j][0]; nch = 0;
      if (n<0) ermes("n<0 in list_faces");
      for (i=1; i<=n; i++)
      ( nch0=nch;
        nch += sprintf(str+nch, " %d", pface[j][i]);
        if (nch > nchmax) { str[nch0] = '\0'; break; }
      )
      s2[0] = '.';
      grmes(LIN2, str);
      textXY(margin + 8*strlen(str), LIN2, s2);
      ch = query(LIN3, "OK? (Y/N): ");
      if (ch == 'N')
      ( farfree(pface[j]); pface[j] = NULL; display();
        if (!faces_present &&
            (! axes || !auxlines || !numbers))
        ( axes = auxlines = numbers = 1; display();
        )
      ) else
      if (ch != 'Y') break;
   )
   if (count == 0) grmes(LIN2, "No faces");
                else grmes(LIN2, " ");
   grmes(LIN3, " ");
}


int matherr(struct exception *a)
( if (a->type == DOMAIN)
   ( if (strcmp(a->name, "sqrt") == 0)
      ermes("sqrt domain error");
   )
   ermes("Floating point error");
   return(0); /* will not be executed due to ermes */
)


static void mv(float x, float y, float z)
( int X, Y;
   double xe, ye, ze;
   viewing(x-0.5, y-0.5, z-0.5, &xe, &ye, &ze);
   /* x0 = y0 = z0 = 0.5 */
   X = IX(d*xe/ze+c1);
```

```
    Y = IY(d*ye/ze+c2);
    imove(X, Y);
}


static char mygetch(void)
{ char ch;
  ch = getch();
  if (ch == 3)     /* Ctrl-C  or Ctrl-Break */
  { if (!in_textmode) to_text();
    exit(1);
  }
  char_avail = 0;
  return ch;
}

static void myungetch(char ch)
{ ungetch(ch); char_avail = 1;
}


static void open_plotfile(void)
{ char *p, *q, plfilnam[40];
  if (*filnam)
  { p=filnam; q=plfilnam;
    while (*p && *p != '.') *q++ = *p++;
    strcpy(q, ".plt");
  } else strcpy(plfilnam, "noname.plt");
  fplot = fopen(plfilnam, "w");
  if (fplot == NULL) ermes("Can't open plotfile");
}


static void plotaxes(int checksize)
{ int X0, Y0, X1, Y1, X2, Y2, X3, Y3, cnt, i;
  if (checksize)
  { storepoint(nmax, 0.0, 0.0, 0.0);
    storepoint(nmax+1, xwmax, 0.0, 0.0);
    storepoint(nmax+2, 0.0, ywmax, 0.0);
    storepoint(nmax+3, 0.0, 0.0, zwmax);
    screencoor(0, nmax, &X0, &Y0);
    screencoor(0, nmax+1, &X1, &Y1);
    screencoor(0, nmax+2, &X2, &Y2);
    screencoor(0, nmax+3, &X3, &Y3);
    reposition();
    inside = 1;
  }
  storepoint(nmax, 0.0, 0.0, 0.0);
  storepoint(nmax+1, xwmax, 0.0, 0.0);
  storepoint(nmax+2, 0.0, ywmax, 0.0);
  storepoint(nmax+3, 0.0, 0.0, zwmax);
  screencoor(1, nmax, &X0, &Y0);
  screencoor(1, nmax+1, &X1, &Y1);
  screencoor(1, nmax+2, &X2, &Y2);
  screencoor(1, nmax+3, &X3, &Y3);
  for (i=nmax; i<nmax+4; i++) p[i].inuse = 0;
  if (checksize && !inside)
  { to_text();
    printf("not inside in plotaxes\n");
    printf("d=%f c1=%f c2=%f\n", d, c1, c2);
```

```
      printf("Xvp_min=%f Xvp_max=%f  Yvp_min=%f Yvp_max=%f\n",

             Xvp_min, Xvp_max, Yvp_min, Yvp_max);
      for (cnt=nmax; cnt<nmax+4; cnt++)
      { printf("cnt=%d xe=%f ye=%f ze=%f X=%d Y=%d\n",
               cnt, p[cnt].xe, p[cnt].ye, p[cnt].ze,
               IX(d*p[cnt].xe/p[cnt].ze+c1),
               IY(d*p[cnt].ye/p[cnt].ze+c2));
      }
      exit(0);
   }
   imove(X0, Y0); idraw(X1, Y1); text("x");
   imove(X0, Y0); idraw(X2, Y2); text("y");
   imove(X0, Y0); idraw(X3, Y3); text("z");
}


static void plotpoint(int i, int Bold)
{ char str[30];
  int X, Y, Xxy0, Yxy0, cnt;
  inside = 1;
  for (cnt=0; cnt<2; cnt++)
  { screencoor(1, i, &X, &Y);
    if (auxlines)
    { storepoint(nmax+6, p[i].xw, p[i].yw, 0.0);
      screencoor(1, nmax+6, &Xxy0, &Yxy0);
      p[nmax+6].inuse = 0;
    }
    if (inside) break; else
    { reposition(); display();
    }
  }
  if (cnt == 2) ermes("cnt = 2 in plotpoint");
  if (auxlines) draw_line(Xxy0, Yxy0, X, Y);
  dot(X, Y);
  if (numbers)
  { sprintf(str, "%d", i); imove(X-2, Y-5); text(str);
  } else
  if (nface == 0 || Bold)
  { dot(X-1, Y-1); dot(X, Y-1); dot(X+1, Y-1);
    dot(X-1, Y);                dot(X+1, Y);
    dot(X-1, Y+1); dot(X, Y+1); dot(X+1, Y+1);
  }
}


static void
plotsph(float rho, float theta, float phi, int down)
{ float x, y, z, rcosphi, rsinphi,
    costh, sinth;
  theta = theta * PIdiv180; phi = phi * PIdiv180;
  rcosphi = rho * cos(phi); rsinphi = rho * sin(phi);
  costh = cos(theta); sinth = sin(theta);
  x = rsinphi * costh; y = rsinphi * sinth; z = rcosphi;
  if (down) dw(x, y, z); else mv(x, y, z);
}

static void points(void)
{ char str[50];
  int i;
```

```
   float x, y, z;
   grmes(LIN2, "n   x   y   z:");
   getstr(margin, LIN3, str);
   if
   (sscanf(str, "%d %f %f %f", &i, &x, &y, &z) != 4 ||
      i <= 0)
   { grmes(LIN2, "Invalid number format");
     points_entering = 0;
     return;
   }
   check_alloc(i);
   if (i >= nmax) nmax = i+1;
   if (storepoint(i, x, y, z)) {checkall(); display();}
   plotpoint(i, 1); modified = 1;
}

static void pressanykey(char *str)
{ grmes(LIN2, str);
  grmes(LIN3, "Press any key ...");
  mygetch();
}

static char query(int line, char *s)
{ int pos;
  char ch;
  grmes(line, s);
  pos = margin + 8 * strlen(s);
  textcursor(pos, line); ch = mygetch();
  s2[0] = ch; ch = toupper(ch);
  textXY(pos, line, s2);
  return ch;
}


static void rdfile(int normal)
{ FILE *fp;
  int ch, i_old=0, base, lowlimit,
      i, n, drawn, X, Y;
  float x, y, z, i_float;
  char str[40];
  modified = 0; /* File and data structure identical! */
  if (normal)
  { if (object_present)
    { ch = query(LIN2, "Clear screen? (Y/N) ");
      if (ch == 'Y' || ch == 'y') clear();
      else modified = 1;
    }
    if (kbhit()) getch();
    grmes(LIN2, "Input file: ");
    getstr(margin, LIN3, filnam);
  }
  fp = fopen(filnam, "r");
  if (fp == NULL) {grmes(LIN2, "Can't open file"); return;}
  grmes(LIN3, "Please wait ...");

  base = nmax - 1; inside = 1; lowlimit = 32767;
  while
  (fscanf(fp, "%f %f %f %f", &i_float, &x, &y, &z) == 4)
  { if (getc(fp) != '\n')
    { grmes(LIN2, "Wrong file format.");
```

```
      grmes(LIN3, "Use: n x y z");
      fclose(fp); return;
   }
   i = (int)(i_float + 0.001);
   if (i <= 0)
   { grmes(LIN3, "Point nr. not positive");
     fclose(fp); return;
   }
   i += base;
   if (i < lowlimit) lowlimit = i;
   check_alloc(i);
   if (i >= nmax) nmax = i+1;
   storepoint(i, x, y, z);
   screencoor(0, i, &X, &Y);
}
if (base && lowlimit < 32767)
{ grmes(LIN1, "Range of new points:");
  sprintf(str, "%d-%d", lowlimit, nmax - 1);
  pressanykey(str);
}
inside = 1;
for (i=base; i<nmax; i++)
  if (p[i].inuse) screencoor(1, i, &X, &Y);

if (!inside) reposition();
do ch = getc(fp); while (isspace(ch));
axes = numbers = (ch != 'F' && ch != 'f');
if (!axes) auxlines = 0;
display();
if (!axes) /* That is, if there are faces */
{ do ch = getc(fp); while (ch != '\n' && ch != EOF);
  /* Skip input line with keyword "Faces" */
  while (fscanf(fp, "%d", &i) == 1)
  { if ((pface[nface] = (int *)farcalloc(5, sizeof(int)))
       == NULL)
      ermes("Not enough memory");
    n = 0;
    while (1)
    { if (n > 0) {if (fscanf(fp, "%d", &i) <= 0) break;}
      n++;
      drawn = i >= 0; i = abs(i) + base;
      if (p[i].inuse == 0)
      { sprintf(str, "Undef. point: %6d", i);
        grmes(LIN3, str); fclose(fp); return;
      }
      if (n > 1 && drawn) line3(i_old, i);
      i_old = i;
      if (n > 4)
      { if ((pface[nface] = (int *)
          farrealloc(pface[nface], (n+1) * sizeof(int)))
          == NULL)
          ermes("Not enough memory");
      }
      pface[nface][n] = (drawn ? i : -i);
    }
    ch = getc(fp);
    if (ch != '#' && ch != '.')
    { grmes(LIN3, "Period or # expected"); fclose(fp);
      return;
    }
```

```
      if (n > 2)
      { i = pface[nface][1];
         if (i >= 0) line3(i_old, i);
      }
      pface[nface][0] = n; nface++;
      if (nface == MAXFACES) ermes("Too many faces");
    }
    ch = getc(fp);
  } else numbers = 1;
  if (ch != EOF) grmes(LIN2, "Incorrect file format"); else
     grmes(LIN2, " ");
  grmes(LIN3, " ");
  fclose(fp);
}


static int rdnumber(int *p)
/* Called only in 'faces' and in 'transform' */
{ int i, neg, d, i0;
  char ch;
  *p = 0;
  do ch = getch1(); while (isspace(ch));
  neg = ch == '-';
  if (neg || ch == '+') ch = getch1();
  if (!isdigit(ch)) return 0;
  i = ch - '0';
  while (ch = getch1(), isdigit(ch))
  { d = ch - '0';
     i0 = i; i = 10 * i + d;
     if (i < i0) {grmes(LIN3, "Too many digits"); return 0;}
  }
  *p = (neg ? -i : i);
  if (bufposition > 0) bufposition--;
  /* i.e. myungetch1(ch) */
  return 1;
}


static int rdoldnr(int *q)
{ int code, i, pnr;
  code = rdnumber(&i); pnr = abs(i); *q = i;
  if
  (code == 0 || pnr >= nmax ||   pnr  && p[pnr].inuse == 0)
  { grmes(LIN2, "Incorrect point nr."); mygetch(); return 0;

  } else return 1;
}


static void reposition(void)
/* Requires xwmin etc. to be correct */
{ float Xrange, Yrange, fx, fy, Xcenter, Ycenter,
     x1, y1, z1, q=0.4, xtol, ytol, ztol;
  int i, X, Y;
  x1 = 0.5 * (xwmin + xwmax);
  y1 = 0.5 * (ywmin + ywmax);
  z1 = 0.5 * (zwmin + zwmax);
  xtol = q * (xwmax - xwmin);
  ytol = q * (ywmax - ywmin);
  ztol = q * (zwmax - zwmin);
```

```
    if (fabs(x0-x1) > xtol ||
        fabs(y0-y1) > ytol ||
        fabs(z0-z1) > ztol)
    { grmes(LIN3, "Please wait ...");
      x0 = x1; y0 = y1; z0 = z1;
      newcentralpoint = 1; /* See command 'E' */
      fresh();
      for (i=0; i<nmax+6; i++)   /* See 'clear' and 'cursor' */

      { if (p[i].inuse)
        { storepoint(i, p[i].xw, p[i].yw, p[i].zw);
          screencoor(0, i, &X, &Y);
          /* Compute new xmin etc. */
          if (axes)
          { storepoint(nmax+6, p[i].xw, 0.0, 0.0);
            screencoor(0, nmax+6, &X, &Y);
            storepoint(nmax+6, 0.0, p[i].yw, 0.0);
            screencoor(0, nmax+6, &X, &Y);
            storepoint(nmax+6, 0.0, 0.0, p[i].zw);
            screencoor(0, nmax+6, &X, &Y);
          }
          if (auxlines)
          { storepoint(nmax+6, p[i].xw, p[i].yw, 0.0);
            screencoor(0, nmax+6, &X, &Y);
          }
        }
      }
      p[nmax+6].inuse = 0;
      grmes(LIN3, " ");
    }
    Xrange = xmax - xmin; Yrange = ymax - ymin;
    if (Xrange < 1e-12) Xrange = 1e-12;
    if (Yrange < 1e-12) Yrange = 1e-12;
    Xcenter = 0.5*(xmin+xmax); Ycenter = 0.5*(ymin+ymax);
    fx = Xvp_range/Xrange; fy = Yvp_range/Yrange;
    d = (fx < fy ? fx : fy);
    if (!zoomin) d *= 0.85;
    /* Provide some space for new points */
    c1 = Xvp_center - d*Xcenter; c2 = Yvp_center - d*Ycenter;
}

static void
screencoor(int mode, int i, int *pX, int *pY)
{ double xe, ye, ze, xs, ys;
  xe = p[i].xe; ye = p[i].ye; ze = p[i].ze;
  xs = xe/ze;   ys = ye/ze;
  if (xs < xmin) xmin = xs;
  if (xs > xmax) xmax = xs;
  if (ys < ymin) ymin = ys;
  if (ys > ymax) ymax = ys;
  if (mode == 0) return;
  xxx = d*xs+c1; yyy = d*ys+c2;
  if (!zoomin)
  { if (xxx < Xvp_min || xxx > Xvp_max ||
        yyy < Yvp_min || yyy > Yvp_max) inside = 0;
  }
  *pX = IX(xxx); *pY = IY(yyy);
}
```

```
static void show(char c)
{ if (!zoomin)
  { s2[0] = c; textXY(margin + 72, LIN1, s2);
  }
}


static int storepoint(int i, float xw, float yw, float zw)
{ int oldpoint=0;
  double xe, ye, ze;
  if (i < nmax && p[i].inuse)  oldpoint = 1;
  p[i].xw = xw; p[i].yw = yw; p[i].zw = zw;
  if (p[i].inuse == 0) p[i].inuse = 1;
  viewing(xw-xO, yw-yO, zw-zO, &xe, &ye, &ze);
  p[i].xe = xe; p[i].ye = ye; p[i].ze = ze;
  if (xw < xwmin) xwmin = xw;
  if (xw > xwmax) xwmax = xw;
  if (yw < ywmin) ywmin = yw;
  if (yw > ywmax) ywmax = yw;
  if (zw < zwmin) zwmin = zw;
  if (zw > zwmax) zwmax = zw;
  if (ze < zemin) zemin = ze;
  if (ze > zemax) zemax = ze;
  if (i < nmax) object_present = 1;
  return oldpoint;
  /* storepoint normally returns 0;
     it returns 1 if point i already existed */
}


static void textcursor(int col, int line)
{ static char underline[2]="_", dum[2]=" ";
  int j;
  if (char_avail) return;
  do
  { j = 100;
    do textXY(col, line, underline);
      while (--j && !kbhit());
    j = 200;
    do textXY(col, line, dum); while (--j && !kbhit());
  } while (!kbhit());
}


static void transform(void)
{ char ch, str[30];
  int P=-1, Q=-1, R=-1, Pabs=-1, Qabs=-1, Rabs=-1,
      A, B, Aabs, Babs, i, i1, duplicate, refl=0, tmp,
      *pnum, j, j1, n, k, k1, freepos, m, mabs,
      lowest, highest;
  double x, y, z, a, b, c, d, h,
      xP, xQ, xR, yP, yQ, yR, zP, zQ, zR,
      len, fact;
  float alpha=0.0, Sx=1.0, Sy=1.0, Sz=1.0,
      xC, yC, zC, C1, C2, C3,
      xlowest=1.0, xhighest, x1=0.0, y1=0.0, z1=0.0;
  while (nmax > 0 && p[nmax-1].inuse == 0) nmax--;
  duplicate = (query(LIN2, "Move/Copy? (M/C) ") == 'C');
  enquire(LIN2, "Lower bound: ", &xlowest);
```

```
lowest = (int)(xlowest + 0.1);
if (lowest < 1) lowest = 1;
xhighest = nmax - 1;
enquire(LIN3, "Upper bound: ", &xhighest);
highest = (int)(xhighest + 0.1);
if (highest >= nmax) highest = nmax - 1;
if (duplicate)
{ freepos = nmax;
  check_alloc(nmax + highest - lowest);
}
grmes(LIN3, " ");
ch = query(LIN2, "Rotation? (Y/N) ");
if (ch == 'Y')
{ grmes(LIN1, "Rotate about PQ.");
  grmes(LIN2, "Point nrs. P and Q:");
  bufposition = -1;
  if (!rdoldnr(&P) || !rdoldnr(&Q)) return;
  Pabs = abs(P); Qabs = abs(Q);
  x = p[Pabs].xw; y = p[Pabs].yw; z = p[Pabs].zw;
  x1 = p[Qabs].xw; y1 = p[Qabs].yw; z1 = p[Qabs].zw;
  enquire(LIN2, "Angle in degrees:", &alpha);
  alpha = alpha * PIdiv180;
  initrotate(x, y, z, x1 - x, y1 - y, z1 - z, alpha);
  for (i=lowest; i<=highest; i++)
  if (p[i].inuse && (P > 0 || i != Pabs) &&
                    (Q > 0 || i != Qabs))
  { rotate(p[i].xw, p[i].yw, p[i].zw, &x, &y, &z);
    if (duplicate)
    { i1 = freepos++; p[i1].inuse = 1; p[i].inuse = i1;
    } else i1 = i;
    p[i1].xw = x; p[i1].yw = y; p[i1].zw = z;
  }
} else
{ ch = query(LIN2, "Translation? (Y/N) ");
  if (ch == 'Y')
  { grmes(LIN2, " ");
    if (query(LIN1, "Shift vector? (Y/N) ") != 'Y')
    { enquire(LIN1, "delta x = ", &x1);
      enquire(LIN2, "delta y = ", &y1);
      enquire(LIN3, "delta z = ", &z1);
    } else
    { grmes(LIN1, "AB is shift vector");
      grmes(LIN2, "Point nrs. A and B:");
      bufposition = -1;
      if (!rdoldnr(&A) || !rdoldnr(&B)) return;
      Aabs = abs(A); Babs = abs(B);
      x = p[Aabs].xw; y = p[Aabs].yw; z = p[Aabs].zw;
      x1 = p[Babs].xw - x;
      y1 = p[Babs].yw - y;
      z1 = p[Babs].zw - z;
    }
    for (i=lowest; i<=highest; i++)
    if (p[i].inuse &&
        (A > 0 || i != Aabs) && (B > 0 || i != Babs))
    { if (duplicate)
      { i1 = freepos++; p[i1].inuse = 1; p[i].inuse = i1;
      } else i1 = i;
      p[i1].xw = p[i].xw + x1;
      p[i1].yw = p[i].yw + y1;
      p[i1].zw = p[i].zw + z1;
```

```
    }
} else
{ ch = query(LIN2, "Scaling? (Y/N) ");
  if (ch == 'Y')
  { if (query(LIN2, "Uniform? (Y/N) ") == 'Y')
    { enquire(LIN3, "Sx=Sy=Sz= ", &Sx); Sy = Sz = Sx;
    } else
    { grmes(LIN2, " ");
      enquire(LIN1, "Sx = ", &Sx);
      enquire(LIN2, "Sy = ", &Sy);
      enquire(LIN3, "Sz = ", &Sz);
    }
    while (1)
    { grmes(LIN1, "Fixed point:");
      grmes(LIN2, "Center (C), Origin (O)");
      ch = query(LIN3, "or a Vertex (V): ");
      if (ch == 'C')
      { checkall(); xC = xO; yC = yO; zC = zO;
      } else
      if (ch == 'O' || ch == '0')
        xC = yC = zC = 0.0; else
      if (ch == 'V')
      { grmes(LIN2, "Point number: ");
        bufposition = -1;
        if (!rdoldnr(&P)) return;
        Pabs = abs(P);
        xC = p[Pabs].xw;
        yC = p[Pabs].yw;
        zC = p[Pabs].zw;
      } else continue;
      break;
    }
    C1 = xC * (1.0 - Sx);
    C2 = yC * (1.0 - Sy);
    C3 = zC * (1.0 - Sz);
    for (i=lowest; i<=highest; i++)
    if (p[i].inuse && (P > 0 || i != Pabs))
    { if (duplicate)
      { i1 = freepos++;
        p[i1].inuse = 1; p[i].inuse = i1;
      } else i1 = i;
      p[i1].xw = Sx * p[i].xw + C1;
      p[i1].yw = Sy * p[i].yw + C2;
      p[i1].zw = Sz * p[i].zw + C3;
    }
  } else
  { ch = query(LIN2, "Reflection? (Y/N) ");
    if (ch == 'Y')
    { grmes(LIN1, "PQR is plane of refl.");
      grmes(LIN2, "Point nrs. P, Q, R:");
      bufposition = -1; refl = 1;
      if (!rdoldnr(&P) || !rdoldnr(&Q) || !rdoldnr(&R))
        return;
      Pabs = abs(P); Qabs = abs(Q); Rabs = abs(R);
      xP = p[Pabs].xw; yP = p[Pabs].yw; zP = p[Pabs].zw;
      xQ = p[Qabs].xw; yQ = p[Qabs].yw; zQ = p[Qabs].zw;
      xR = p[Rabs].xw; yR = p[Rabs].yw; zR = p[Rabs].zw;
      a = yP*zQ + zP*yR + yQ*zR - yP*zR - zP*yQ - zQ*yR;
      b = xP*zQ + zP*xR + xQ*zR - xP*zR - zP*xQ - zQ*xR;
      c = xP*yQ + yP*xR + xQ*yR - xP*yR - yP*xQ - yQ*xR;
```

```
        len = sqrt(a*a+b*b+c*c);
        if (len == 0.0) len = 1e-15;
        a /= len; b /= len; c /= len;
        d = a*xP + b*yP + c * zP;
        for (i=lowest; i<=highest; i++)
        if (p[i].inuse &&
        (P > 0 || i != Pabs) &&
        (Q > 0 || i != Qabs) &&
        (R > 0 || i != Rabs))
        { if (duplicate)
          { i1 = freepos++;
            p[i1].inuse = 1; p[i].inuse = i1;
          } else i1 = i;
          x = p[i].xw; y = p[i].yw; z = p[i].zw;
          h = a*x +b*y + c*z; fact = 2.0 * (d-h);
          p[i1].xw = x + fact * a;
          p[i1].yw = y + fact * b;
          p[i1].zw = z + fact * c;
        }
      } else {grmes(LIN2, " "); return;}
    }
  }
}
if (duplicate)
{ grmes(LIN1, "Range of new points:");
  sprintf(str, "%d-%d", nmax, freepos-1);
  pressanykey(str);
  nmax = freepos;
}
grmes(LIN3, "Please wait ...");

modified = 1; checkall();
while (nface >0 && pface[nface-1] == NULL) nface--;
if (duplicate)
{ if (2*nface >= MAXFACES)
  { grmes(LIN3, "Too many faces"); getch(); display();
    return;
  }
  freepos = nface;
  for (j=0; j<nface; j++)
  { if (pface[j] == NULL) continue;
    j1 = freepos++;
    pface[j1] = NULL;
    n = pface[j][0];
    if (n<0) ermes("n<0 in transform");
    if ((pface[j1] = (int *)farcalloc(n+1, sizeof(int)))
       == NULL)
      ermes("Not enough memory");
    pface[j1][0] = n;
    for (k=1; k<=n; k++)
    { k1 = (refl ? (n > 3 ? (k < 4 ? 4-k : 4+n-k)
                          : n+1-k)
               : k);
      m = pface[j][k1]; mabs = abs(m);
      if (mabs < lowest || mabs > highest) break;
      pface[j1][k] =
      (mabs == Pabs && P < 0 ||
       mabs == Qabs && Q < 0 ||
       mabs == Rabs && R < 0
       ? m : (m < 0 ? -p[mabs].inuse : p[m].inuse));
```

```
        }
        if (mabs < lowest || mabs > highest)
        { farfree(pface[j1]); freepos--;
        }
    }
    nface = freepos;
  } else
  if (refl)    /* Invert the orientation of all faces: */
  { for (j=0; j<nface; j++)
    { if (pface[j] == NULL) continue;
      n = pface[j][0];
      if (n < 3) continue;
      pnum = pface[j];
      tmp = pnum[1]; pnum[1] = pnum[3]; pnum[3] = tmp;
      k1 = (n - 3)/2;
      for (k=1; k<=k1; k++)
      { tmp = pnum[3+k];
        pnum[3+k] = pnum[n+1-k];
        pnum[n+1-k] = tmp;
      } /* E.g. old: 1 2 3 4 5 6 7 8. */
    }   /*      new: 3 2 1 8 7 6 5 4. */
  }     /* (Any vertex except 2 may be concave. */
  display();
}

static void viewing(float x, float y, float z,
                    double *pxe, double *pye, double *pze)
{ *pxe = v11*x + v21*y;
  *pye = v12*x + v22*y + v32*z;
  *pze = v13*x + v23*y + v33*z + v43;
  if (*pze <= EPS)
    ermes("Please use a greater value of rho");
}

static void wrfile(void)
{ int i, j, n, k;
  char ch;
  FILE *fp;
  grmes(LIN2, "Output file: ");
  if (kbhit()) getch();
  if (*filnam) grmes(LIN3, filnam);
  textcursor(margin + 8*strlen(filnam)+8, LIN3);
  if (ch = mygetch(), ch != '\n' && ch != '\r')
  { ungetch(ch);
    getstr(margin, LIN3, filnam);
  }
  if (*filnam == '\0' || (fp = fopen(filnam, "w")) == NULL)
  { grmes(LIN3, "Can't open file"); return;
  }
  for (i=0; i<nmax; i++)
  if (p[i].inuse)
    fprintf(fp, "%d %f %f %f\n",
                i, p[i].xw, p[i].yw, p[i].zw);
  if (nface > 0)
  { fprintf(fp, "Faces:\n");
    for (j=0; j<nface; j++)
    { if (pface[j] == NULL) continue;
      n = pface[j][0];
      if (n < 0) ermes("n<0 in wrfile");
      for (k=1; k<=n; k++) fprintf(fp, " %d", pface[j][k]);
```

```
        fprintf(fp, ".\n");
    }
}
  grmes(LIN2, " ");
  grmes(LIN3, " ");
  fclose(fp);
  modified = 0; /* File and data structure identical */
}

static void zoom(int code)
/* zoom can be called after initgr */
{ if (code)    /*  1 = large;  0 = small  */
  { Xvp_min = 0.25; Xvp_max = x_max - 0.25;
    Yvp_min = 0.4; Yvp_max = y_max - 0.4;
  } else
  { Xvp_min = 0.25; Xvp_max = 6.3;
    /* To reserve space for commands */
    Yvp_min = 0.4; Yvp_max = 6.7;
        /* zoom(0) will not be called when pridim = 1 */
        /* so we have x_max = 10.0, y_max = 7.0      */
  }
  zoomin = code;
  Xvp_range = Xvp_max - Xvp_min;
  Yvp_range = Yvp_max - Yvp_min;
  Xvp_center = 0.5*(Xvp_min + Xvp_max);
  Yvp_center = 0.5*(Yvp_min + Yvp_max);
}
```

# Appendix B

```c
/* HLPFUN: A function for hidden-line                      */
/* elimination, using device-independent pixels.          */
/* This version includes a provision for curved surfaces */

#include <stdio.h>
#include <math.h>
#include <ctype.h>
#include <alloc.h>
#include <conio.h>
#include <string.h>
#include <process.h>
#include "grpack.h"
#define max(x,y)     ((x)>(y)?(x):(y))
#define min(x,y)     ((x)<(y)?(x):(y))

#define max3(x,y,z)  ((x)>(y)?max(x,z):max(y,z))
#define min3(x,y,z)  ((x)<(y)?min(x,z):min(y,z))
#define xwhole(x)    ((int)(((x)-xmin)/deltaX))
#define ywhole(y)    ((int)(((y)-ymin)/deltaY))
#define xreal(i)     (xmin+((i))*deltaX)

#define M -1000000.0
#define NSCREEN 15
#define BIG 1.e30
int abs(int i);

static void
  check_kbhit(void),
  add_linesegment(int P, int Q),
  viewing(double x, double y, double z,
    double *pxe, double *pye, double *pze),
  linesegment(double xP, double yP, double zP,
              double xQ, double yQ, double zQ, int k);

void
  ermes(char *str), /* See also module D3D */
  coeff(float rho, float theta, float phi),
  init_viewport(void);

static int
```

```
    counter_clock(int i0, int i1, int i2, int code),
    includesvertex(int h, int i, int j),
    sameside(double xj, double yj,
        double xl, double yl,
              double xh, double yh,
              double xi, double yi),
    allocsize(int divfactor, int elsize);

extern int nmax, nface, **pface;
extern float xO, yO, zO, xmin, xmax, ymin, ymax;

static int ipixmin, ipixmax, ipixleft, ipixright,
    ipix, jpix, jtop, jbot, j_old, jI, topcode[3], *POLY,
    npolyalloc, *vertexconvex, ntrsetalloc, npoly,
    isize=sizeof(int), LOWER[NSCREEN], UPPER[NSCREEN],
    LOW[NSCREEN], UP[NSCREEN], ntrset, maxvertex, jface,
    nTRIANGLE, nTRLIST, iTRIANGLE, iTRLIST, inode, itria,
    *trset;



extern double v11, v12, v13, v21, v22, v23, v32, v33, v43,
    PIdiv180;
static double d, c1, c2,
    eps=1e-5, meps=-1e-5, oneplus=1+1.e-5,
    Xrange, Yrange, Xvp_range, Yvp_range,
    deltaX, deltaY, denom, slope,
    Xleft[3], Xright[3], Yleft[3], Yright[3],
    a, b, c, surfl;

struct linsegface
{ int i; double a, b, c; struct linsegface *next;
} *lsegfacenode(void);

struct vertex
{ int inuse;
    float xw, yw, zw;
    double xe, ye, ze;
    struct linsegface *connect;
} *VERTEX, *pvertex;

extern struct vertex *p;

static struct triangle
{ int A, B, C;
    double a, b, c, h;
} *TRIANGLE, *ptriangle;

static struct lseglist
{ double xP, yP, zP, xQ, yQ, zQ;
    int k;
    struct lseglist *next;
} *lsegstart, *auxlseg, *lsegnode(void);


struct trlist { unsigned int ptria; unsigned int next; }
    *TRLIST, *pnode;

struct
{ int tr_cov;
```

```
    float tr_dist;
    unsigned int start;
} SCREEN[NSCREEN][NSCREEN], *pointer;


void hlpfun(float rho, float theta, float phi,
            float surflimit)
{ int P, Q, ii, vertexnr, i, kk, i0, i1, i2, code, count,
  polygonconvex, loopcount, jtr, j, n, k;

  struct linsegface *ptr, *dummy, *dummy0;

  double
    Xvp_min=0, Xvp_max, Yvp_min=0, Yvp_max,
    fx, fy, Xcentre, Ycentre, Xvp_centre, Yvp_centre,
    xP, yP, zP, xQ, yQ, zQ, XP, YP, XQ, YQ,
    Xlft, Xrght, Ylft, Yrght,
    xxP, yyP, zzP, xxQ, yyQ, zzQ;

  textXY(40, 40, "Please wait ...");
  Xvp_max = x_max; Yvp_max = y_max;
  surfl = surflimit;
  npolyalloc=200;
  POLY=(int *)farcalloc((long)npolyalloc, (long)isize);
  vertexconvex=
    (int *)farcalloc((long)npolyalloc, (long)isize);
  if (POLY == NULL || vertexconvex == NULL)
  { ermes("Memory: polygon");
  }

  VERTEX = p;
    /* Now VERTEX points to the same memory area as p does
       in module D3D
    */

  /* Initialize screen matrix */
  for (ipix=0; ipix<NSCREEN; ipix++)
  for (jpix=0; jpix<NSCREEN; jpix++)
  { pointer=&(SCREEN[ipix][jpix]);
    pointer->tr_cov=-1; pointer->tr_dist=BIG;
    pointer->start=-1;
  }

  coeff(rho, theta, phi);

  maxvertex = nmax-1; /* nmax is defined in module D3D */
  dummy = lsegfacenode();
  for (i=1; i<=maxvertex; i++)
    VERTEX[i].connect = (VERTEX[i].inuse ? NULL : dummy);
            /* dummy indicates: not in use            */
            /* NULL  indicates: empty list (but in use) */

  /* Compute screen constants */
  Xrange=xmax-xmin; Yrange=ymax-ymin;
  Xvp_range=Xvp_max-Xvp_min; Yvp_range=Yvp_max-Yvp_min;
  fx=Xvp_range/Xrange; fy=Yvp_range/Yrange;
  d=(fx<fy ? fx : fy);
  Xcentre=0.5*(xmin+xmax); Ycentre=0.5*(ymin+ymax);
  Xvp_centre=0.5*(Xvp_min+Xvp_max);
```

```
Yvp_centre=0.5*(Yvp_min+Yvp_max);
c1=Xvp_centre-d*Xcentre; c2=Yvp_centre-d*Ycentre;
deltaX=oneplus*Xrange/NSCREEN;
deltaY=oneplus*Yrange/NSCREEN;
/* Now we have:  Xrange/deltaX < NSCREEN */

iTRLIST = 0; iTRIANGLE = 0;
nTRLIST = allocsize(4, sizeof(struct trlist));
TRLIST = (struct trlist *)farcalloc((long)nTRLIST,
 (long)sizeof(struct trlist));

nTRIANGLE = allocsize(3, sizeof(struct triangle));
TRIANGLE = (struct triangle *)farcalloc((long)nTRIANGLE,
 (long)sizeof(struct triangle));

if (TRLIST == NULL || TRIANGLE == NULL)
  ermes("Memory: triangles");

for (j=0; j<nface; j++)
{ if (pface[j] == NULL) continue;
  n = pface[j][0];
  if (n < 0) ermes("Internal error: n < 0");
  if (n == 1) ermes("Polygon with only one vertex");
  POLY[0] = pface[j][1]; npoly = 1;
  for (k=2; k<=n; k++)
  { i = pface[j][k];
    if (npoly==npolyalloc)
    { npolyalloc += (npolyalloc>>2);
      POLY = (int *)
        farrealloc(POLY, (long)npolyalloc*isize);
      vertexconvex = (int *)
        farrealloc(vertexconvex, (long)npolyalloc*isize);
      if (POLY == NULL || vertexconvex == NULL)
        ermes("Memory: polygons");
    }
    POLY[npoly++]=i;
  }
  if (npoly==1) ermes("Internal error: npoly = 1");
  if (npoly==2)
  { add_linesegment(POLY[0], POLY[1]); continue;
  }
  jface = j;
  if (!counter_clock(0, 1, 2, 0)) continue;
                                        /* backface */
  for (i=1; i<=npoly; i++)
  { ii=i%npoly; code=POLY[ii]; vertexnr=abs(code);
    if (code<0) POLY[ii]=vertexnr; else
      add_linesegment(POLY[i-1], vertexnr);
  }

  /* Triangulation of a polygon */

  count=1; polygonconvex=0; i1=-1;
  while (npoly>2)
  { if (!polygonconvex)
    { polygonconvex=1;
      for (ii=0; ii<npoly; ii++)
      { i0 = (ii==0 ? npoly-1 : ii-1);
        i2 = (ii==npoly-1 ? 0 : ii+1);
        vertexconvex[ii] = counter_clock(i0, ii, i2, 0);
```

```
            if (!vertexconvex[ii]) polygonconvex=0;
          }
        }
        loopcount=npoly;
        do
        { if (++i1 >= npoly) i1=0;
          i0 = (i1==0 ? npoly-1 : i1-1);
          i2 = (i1==npoly-1 ? 0 : i1+1);
        } while (--loopcount && !polygonconvex &&
           (!vertexconvex[i1] || includesvertex(i0, i1, i2)));
          /* Store triangle: */
        counter_clock(i0, i1, i2, count++);
        npoly--;
        for (ii=i1; ii<npoly; ii++) POLY[ii]=POLY[ii+1];
      }
}
/* Add nearest triangles to screen lists:  */
for (ipix=0; ipix<NSCREEN; ipix++)
for (jpix=0; jpix<NSCREEN; jpix++)
{ pointer=&(SCREEN[ipix][jpix]);
  if (pointer->tr_cov >= 0)
  { pnode = TRLIST + iTRLIST;
    pnode->ptria = pointer->tr_cov;
    pnode->next  = pointer->start;
    pointer->start = iTRLIST;
    if (++iTRLIST == nTRLIST)
       ermes("Memory: Triangle list");
  }
}
farfree(POLY); farfree(vertexconvex);
ntrsetalloc = 1000;
trset = (int *)
   farcalloc(ntrsetalloc, sizeof(unsigned int));
if (trset == NULL) ermes("Memory: set of triangles");
lsegstart = NULL;
clearpage();
init_viewport();

/* Draw all line segments as far as they are visible */
for (P=1; P<=maxvertex; P++)
{ pvertex=VERTEX+P; /* = &VERTEX[P] */
  ptr = pvertex->connect;
  if (ptr == dummy || ptr == NULL) continue;
  xP = pvertex->xe; yP = pvertex->ye; zP = pvertex->ze;
  XP= xP/zP; YP=yP/zP;
  for ( ; ptr != NULL; ptr = ptr->next)
  { Q = ptr->i;
    pvertex=VERTEX+Q; /* = &VERTEX[Q] */
    xQ = pvertex->xe; yQ = pvertex->ye; zQ = pvertex->ze;
    XQ=xQ/zQ; YQ=yQ/zQ;
    /* Using the screen lists, we shall build the  */
    /* set of triangles that may hide points of PQ: */
    if (XP<XQ || (XP==XQ && YP<YQ))
    {Xlft=XP; Ylft=YP; Xrght=XQ; Yrght=YQ; } else
    {Xlft=XQ; Ylft=YQ; Xrght=XP; Yrght=YP; }
    ipixleft=xwhole(Xlft); ipixright=xwhole(Xrght);
    denom=Xrght-Xlft;
    if (ipixleft != ipixright) slope=(Yrght-Ylft)/denom;
    jbot=jtop=ywhole(Ylft);
    for (ipix=ipixleft; ipix<=ipixright; ipix++)
```

```
      { if (ipix==ipixright) jI=ywhole(Yrght); else
              jI=ywhole(Ylft+(xreal(ipix+1)-Xlft)*slope);
        LOWER[ipix]=min(jbot,jI); jbot=jI;
        UPPER[ipix]=max(jtop,jI); jtop=jI;
      }
      ntrset=0;
      for (ipix=ipixleft; ipix<=ipixright; ipix++)
      for (jpix=LOWER[ipix]; jpix<=UPPER[ipix]; jpix++)
      { pointer=&(SCREEN[ipix][jpix]);
        inode= pointer->start;
        while (inode >= 0)
        /* At the end of the list we have inode=-1 */
        { pnode = TRLIST + inode; itria = pnode->ptria;
          /* The triangle will be stored only if it is not
             yet present in array trset (the triangle set).
          */
          if (ntrset==ntrsetalloc)
          { ntrsetalloc += (ntrsetalloc >> 2);
            trset = (int *)
             farrealloc(
             trset, (long)ntrsetalloc*sizeof(unsigned int));
            if (trset == NULL)
              ermes("Memory: triangle set");
          }
          trset[ntrset]=itria; /* sentinel */
          jtr=0;
          while (trset[jtr]!=itria) jtr++;
          if (jtr==ntrset)
          { ntrset++; /* Store triangle */
          }
          inode=pnode->next;
        }
      }
      /* Now trset[0], ..., trset[ntrset-1] is the set of */
      /* triangles that may hide points of PQ.            */
      linesegment(xP, yP, zP, xQ, yQ, zQ, 0);
      while (lsegstart != NULL)
      { xxP=lsegstart->xP;
        yyP=lsegstart->yP;
        zzP=lsegstart->zP;
        xxQ=lsegstart->xQ;
        yyQ=lsegstart->yQ;
        zzQ=lsegstart->zQ;
        kk=lsegstart->k;
        auxlseg = lsegstart; lsegstart = lsegstart->next;
        farfree(auxlseg);
        linesegment(xxP, yyP, zzP, xxQ, yyQ, zzQ, kk);
      }
    }
  }
  farfree(dummy); farfree(trset);
  for (i=1; i<=maxvertex; i++)
  if (VERTEX[i].inuse)
  { dummy = VERTEX[i].connect;
    while (dummy != NULL)
    { dummy0 = dummy;
      dummy = dummy->next;
      farfree(dummy0);
    }
  }
```

```
    farfree(TRLIST);
    farfree(TRIANGLE);
}


void coeff(float rho, float theta, float phi)
{ double th, ph, costh, sinth, cosph, sinph;
  /* Angles in radians: */
  th=theta*PIdiv180; ph=phi*PIdiv180;
  costh=cos(th); sinth=sin(th);
  cosph=cos(ph); sinph=sin(ph);
  /* Elements of viewing matrix V: */
  v11=-sinth; v12=-cosph*costh; v13=-sinph*costh;
  v21=costh;  v22=-cosph*sinth; v23=-sinph*sinth;
              v32=sinph;        v33=-cosph;
                                v43=rho;

}


static void add_linesegment(int P, int Q)
/* This function may insert line segment PQ in the linked
   list starting in VERTEX[P].connect. (If necessary, we
   first exchange the values of P and Q such that P becomes
   the smaller of the two.) If PQ has been stored in the
   list previously, it is not duplicated. If a previously
   stored segment PQ is found, we compare the face to which
   it belongs with the face to which the new one belongs.
   If the normal vectors to these two faces are almost
   parallel (the inner product between their normal vectors
   being greater than 'surflimit'), the old line segment is
   deleted.
*/
{ struct linsegface *ptr, *new, **pp, **pp0;
  int iaux;
  if (P>Q) { iaux=P; P=Q; Q=iaux; }
  /* Now: P < Q */
  pp0 = pp = &(VERTEX[P].connect);
  ptr = *pp;
  while (ptr != NULL && ptr->i != Q)
  { pp = &(ptr->next); ptr = *pp;
  }
  if (ptr == NULL)
  { new = lsegfacenode();
    new->i = Q; new->a = a; new->b = b; new->c = c;
    new->next = *pp0; *pp0 = new;
  } else
  if (a*(ptr->a) + b*(ptr->b) + c*(ptr->c) > surfl)
  { *pp = ptr->next; farfree(ptr);
  }
}


static int counter_clock(int i0, int i1, int i2, int code)
/* code = 0: compute orientation;
   code = 1: compute a, b, c, h; store the first triangle;
   code > 1: check if next triangle is coplanar; store it
*/
{ int A=POLY[i0], B=POLY[i1], C=POLY[i2], i, l;
  double xA, yA, zA, xB, yB, zB, xC, yC, zC, r,
         XA, YA, XB, YB, XC, YC, h0,
```

```
        DA, DB, DC, D, DAB, DAC, DBC, aux, dist,
        xR, yR, dev, tol;
static double h;

if(A<0)A=-A; if(B<0)B=-B; if(C<0)C=-C;

pvertex=VERTEX+A;
xA = pvertex->xe; yA = pvertex->ye; zA = pvertex->ze;

pvertex=VERTEX+B;
xB = pvertex->xe; yB = pvertex->ye; zB = pvertex->ze;

pvertex=VERTEX+C;
xC = pvertex->xe; yC = pvertex->ye; zC = pvertex->ze;

h0 = xA * (yB*zC - yC*zB) -
     xB * (yA*zC - yC*zA) +
     xC * (yA*zB - yB*zA);

if (code==0)
{ if (h0 <= eps) return 0;
    a = yA * (zB-zC) - yB * (zA-zC) + yC * (zA-zB);
    b = -(xA * (zB-zC) - xB * (zA-zC) + xC * (zA-zB));
    c = xA * (yB-yC) - xB * (yA-yC) + xC * (yA-yB);
    r = sqrt(a*a+b*b+c*c); if (r==0.0) r=eps;
    a = a/r; b = b/r; c = c/r; h = h0/r;
    return 1;
}

/* If h0=0, plane ABC passes through E and hides nothing.
   If h0<0, triangle ABC is a backface.
   In both cases iTRIANGLE is not incremented and the
   triangles of the polygon are not stored.
   a, b, c will be used in add_linesegment.
*/
dev = fabs(a*xC+b*yC+c*zC-h); tol = eps+0.001*fabs(h);
if (dev > tol)
{ to_text();
printf("Vertices not in the same plane:\n");
for (i=1; i<=pface[jface][0]; i++)
printf("%d ", pface[jface][i]);
exit(1);
}

ptriangle = TRIANGLE + iTRIANGLE;
ptriangle->A = A; ptriangle->B = B ; ptriangle->C = C;
ptriangle->a = a; ptriangle->b = b ; ptriangle->c = c;
ptriangle->h = h;

/* The triangle will now be stored in the screen lists
   of the associated pixels; first the arrays LOWER,
   UPPER, LOW, UP are defined:
*/
XA=xA/zA; YA=yA/zA;
XB=xB/zB; YB=yB/zB;
XC=xC/zC; YC=yC/zC;
DA=XB*YC-XC*YB; DB=XC*YA-XA*YC; DC=XA*YB-XB*YA;
D=DA+DB+DC;
DAB=DC-M*(XA-XB); DAC=DB-M*(XC-XA); DBC=DA-M*(XB-XC);
topcode[0]=(D*DAB>0); topcode[1]=(D*DAC>0);
```

```
topcode[2]=(D*DBC>0);
Xleft[0]=XA; Yleft[0]=YA; Xright[0]=XB; Yright[0]=YB;
Xleft[1]=XA; Yleft[1]=YA; Xright[1]=XC; Yright[1]=YC;
Xleft[2]=XB; Yleft[2]=YB; Xright[2]=XC; Yright[2]=YC;
for (l=0; l<3; l++)   /* l = triangle-side number */
if (Xleft[l]>Xright[l] ||
    (Xleft[l]==Xright[l] && Yleft[l]>Yright[l]))
{ aux=Xleft[l]; Xleft[l]=Xright[l]; Xright[l]=aux;
  aux=Yleft[l]; Yleft[l]=Yright[l]; Yright[l]=aux;
}
ipixmin=xwhole(min3(XA,XB,XC));
ipixmax=xwhole(max3(XA,XB,XC));
for (ipix=ipixmin; ipix<=ipixmax; ipix++)
{ LOWER[ipix]=UP[ipix]=10000;
  UPPER[ipix]=LOW[ipix]=-10000;
}

for (l=0; l<3; l++)
{ ipixleft=xwhole(Xleft[l]); ipixright=xwhole(Xright[l]);
  denom=Xright[l]-Xleft[l];
  if (ipixleft != ipixright)
  slope=(Yright[l]-Yleft[l])/denom;
  j_old=ywhole(Yleft[l]);
  for (ipix=ipixleft; ipix<=ipixright; ipix++)
  { if (ipix==ipixright) jI=ywhole(Yright[l]); else
      jI=ywhole(Yleft[l]+(xreal(ipix+1)-Xleft[l])*slope);
    if (topcode[l])
    { UPPER[ipix]=max3(j_old,jI,UPPER[ipix]);
      UP[ipix]=min3(j_old,jI,UP[ipix]);
    } else
    { LOWER[ipix]=min3(j_old,jI,LOWER[ipix]);
      LOW[ipix]=max3(j_old,jI,LOW[ipix]);
    }
    j_old=jI;
  }
}

/* For screen column ipix, the triangle is associated
   only with pixels in the rows
   LOWER[ipix],...,UPPER[ipix].
   The subrange LOW[ipix]+1,...,UP[ipix]-1 of these rows
   denote pixels that lie completely within the triangle.
*/
for (ipix=ipixmin; ipix<=ipixmax; ipix++)
for (jpix=LOWER[ipix]; jpix<=UPPER[ipix]; jpix++)
{ pointer=&(SCREEN[ipix][jpix]);
  if (jpix>LOW[ipix] && jpix<UP[ipix])
  { xR=xmin+(ipix+0.5)*deltaX;
    yR=ymin+(jpix+0.5)*deltaY;
    denom=a*xR+b*yR+c*d;
    dist =
    fabs(denom)>eps ? h*sqrt(xR*xR+yR*yR+1.)/denom : BIG;
  /* The line from viewpoint E to pixel point (xR, yR, 1)
     intersects plane ABC at a distance dist from E.
  */
    if (dist < pointer->tr_dist)
    { pointer->tr_cov=iTRIANGLE; pointer->tr_dist=dist;
    }
  } else /* Add triangle to screen list: */
  { pnode = TRLIST + iTRLIST;
```

```
      pnode->ptria = iTRIANGLE;
      pnode->next = pointer->start;
      pointer->start = iTRLIST;
      if (++iTRLIST == nTRLIST)
        ermes("Memory: Triangle list");
    }
  }
  if (++iTRIANGLE == nTRIANGLE) ermes("Memory: Triangles");
  return 1;
}


static void viewing(double x, double y, double z,
                    double *pxe, double *pye, double *pze)
{ *pxe = v11*x + v21*y;
  *pye = v12*x + v22*y + v32*z;
  *pze = v13*x + v23*y + v33*z + v43;
}


static void linesegment(double xP, double yP, double zP,
                    double xQ, double yQ, double zQ, int k)
{ /* Line segment PQ is to be drawn, as far as it is not
     hidden by the triangles trset[k] to trset[ntrset-1].
  */
  int A, B, C, i, Pbeyond, Qbeyond,
    outside, Poutside, Qoutside, eA, eB, eC, sum;
  double a, b, c, h, hP, hQ, r1, r2, r3,
    xA, yA, zA, xB, yB, zB, xC, yC, zC,
    dA, dB, dC, labmin, labmax, lab, mu,
    xmin, ymin, zmin, xmax, ymax, zmax,
    C1, C2, C3, K1, K2, K3, denom1, denom2,
    Cpos, Ppos, Qpos, aux, eps1;
  struct triangle *ptriangle;


  while (k<ntrset)
  { itria=trset[k]; ptriangle=TRIANGLE+itria;
    a=ptriangle->a; b=ptriangle->b; c=ptriangle->c;
    h=ptriangle->h;

    /* Test 1: */
    hP=a*xP+b*yP+c*zP; hQ=a*xQ+b*yQ+c*zQ;
    eps1=eps+eps*h;
    if (hP-h<=eps1 && hQ-h<=eps1) {k++; continue;}
                                    /* PQ not behind ABC */
    /* Test 2: */
    K1=yP*zQ-yQ*zP; K2=zP*xQ-zQ*xP; K3=xP*yQ-xQ*yP;
    A=ptriangle->A; B=ptriangle->B; C=ptriangle->C;
    pvertex=VERTEX+A;
    xA = pvertex->xe; yA = pvertex->ye; zA = pvertex->ze;
    pvertex=VERTEX+B;
    xB = pvertex->xe; yB = pvertex->ye; zB = pvertex->ze;
    pvertex=VERTEX+C;
    xC = pvertex->xe; yC = pvertex->ye; zC = pvertex->ze;
    dA=K1*xA+K2*yA+K3*zA;
    dB=K1*xB+K2*yB+K3*zB;
    dC=K1*xC+K2*yC+K3*zC;
    /* If dA, dB, dC have the same sign, the vertices */
    /* A, B, C lie at the same side of plane EPQ. */
```

```
eA= dA>eps ? 1 : dA<meps ? -1 : 0;
eB= dB>eps ? 1 : dB<meps ? -1 : 0;
eC= dC>eps ? 1 : dC<meps ? -1 : 0;
sum = eA+eB+eC;
if (abs(sum)>=2) { k++; continue; }
/* If this test succeeds, the (infinite) line PQ   */
/* lies outside pyramid EABC (or the line and the  */
/* pyramid have at most one point in common.       */
/* If the test fails, there is a point             */
/* of intersection.                                */

/* Test 3: */
Poutside=Qoutside=0; labmin=1.; labmax=0.;
for (i=0; i<3; i++)
{ C1=yA*zB-yB*zA; C2=zA*xB-zB*xA; C3=xA*yB-xB*yA;
  /* C1 x + C2 y + C3 z = 0  is plane EAB */
  Cpos=C1*xC+C2*yC+C3*zC;
  Ppos=C1*xP+C2*yP+C3*zP;
  Qpos=C1*xQ+C2*yQ+C3*zQ;
  denom1=Qpos-Ppos;
  if (Cpos>eps)
  { Pbeyond= Ppos<meps; Qbeyond= Qpos<meps;
    outside= Pbeyond && Qpos<=eps ||
             Qbeyond && Ppos<=eps;
  } else if (Cpos<meps)
  { Pbeyond= Ppos>eps; Qbeyond= Qpos>eps;
    outside= Pbeyond && Qpos>=meps ||
             Qbeyond && Ppos>=meps;
  } else outside=1;
  if (outside) break;
  lab= fabs(denom1)<=eps ? 1.e7 : -Ppos/denom1;
  /* lab indicates where PQ meets plane EAB */
  Poutside |= Pbeyond;
  Qoutside |= Qbeyond;
  denom2=dB-dA;
  mu= fabs(denom2)<=eps ? 1.e7 : -dA/denom2;
  /* mu tells where AB meets plane EPQ */
  if (mu>=meps && mu<=oneplus &&
      lab>=meps && lab<=oneplus)
  { if (lab<labmin) labmin=lab;
    if (lab>labmax) labmax=lab;
  }
  aux=xA; xA=xB; xB=xC; xC=aux;
  aux=yA; yA=yB; yB=yC; yC=aux;
  aux=zA; zA=zB; zB=zC; zC=aux;
  aux=dA; dA=dB; dB=dC; dC=aux;
}
if (outside) {k++; continue;}

/* Test 4: */
if (!(Poutside || Qoutside)) return; /* PQ invisible */

/* Test 5: */
r1=xQ-xP; r2=yQ-yP; r3=zQ-zP;
xmin=xP+labmin*r1; ymin=yP+labmin*r2;
zmin=zP+labmin*r3;
if (a*xmin+b*ymin+c*zmin-h<-eps1) { k++; continue; }
xmax=xP+labmax*r1; ymax=yP+labmax*r2;
zmax=zP+labmax*r3;
if (a*xmax+b*ymax+c*zmax-h<-eps1) { k++; continue; }
```

```
     /* If this test succeeds, an intersection of PQ
        and the pyramid lies in front of plane ABC.        */

     /* Test 6: */
     if (Poutside || hP<h-eps1)
     { auxlseg=lsegstart;
       lsegstart = lsegnode();
       lsegstart->xP = xP; lsegstart->yP = yP;
       lsegstart->zP = zP;
       lsegstart->xQ = xmin; lsegstart->yQ = ymin;
       lsegstart->zQ = zmin;
       lsegstart->k = k+1; lsegstart->next = auxlseg;
     }
     if (Qoutside || hQ<h-eps1)
     { auxlseg=lsegstart;
       lsegstart = lsegnode();
       lsegstart->xP = xmax; lsegstart->yP = ymax;
       lsegstart->zP = zmax;
       lsegstart->xQ = xQ; lsegstart->yQ = yQ;
       lsegstart->zQ = zQ;
       lsegstart->k = k+1; lsegstart->next = auxlseg;
     }
     return;
   }

  move(d*xP/zP+c1, d*yP/zP+c2);
  draw(d*xQ/zQ+c1, d*yQ/zQ+c2);
}


void init_viewport(void)
{ float len=0.3, len1=0.2;
  move(0.0, len); draw(0.0, 0.0); draw(len, 0.0);
  move(x_max-len, 0.0); draw(x_max, 0.0); draw(x_max, len);
  move(x_max, y_max-len1); draw(x_max, y_max);
  draw(x_max-len1, y_max);
  move(len1, y_max); draw(0.0, y_max);
  draw(0.0, y_max-len1);
  /* The distinction between len and len1 enables us to
     tell the top from the bottom.
  */
}


static int includesvertex(int h, int i, int j)
/* Does triangle hij include another vertex? */
{ int l;
  double zh, zi, zj, zl, XH, YH, XI, YI, XJ, YJ, XL, YL;

  pvertex = VERTEX + POLY[h]; zh = pvertex->ze;
  XH = pvertex->xe / zh; YH = pvertex->ye / zh;

  pvertex = VERTEX + POLY[i]; zi = pvertex->ze;
  XI = pvertex->xe / zi; YI = pvertex->ye / zi;

  pvertex = VERTEX + POLY[j]; zj = pvertex->ze;
  XJ = pvertex->xe / zj; YJ = pvertex->ye / zj;

  for (l=0; l<npoly; l++)
```

```
  { if (!vertexconvex[l] && l != h && l != i && l !=j)
    { pvertex = VERTEX + POLY[l];  zl = pvertex->ze;
      XL = pvertex->xe / zl;
      YL = pvertex->ye / zl;

      if (sameside(XH, YH, XL, YL, XI, YI, XJ, YJ) &&
          sameside(XI, YI, XL, YL, XJ, YJ, XH, YH) &&
          sameside(XJ, YJ, XL, YL, XH, YH, XI, YI))
        return 1;
    }
  }
  return 0;
}


static int sameside(double xj, double yj,
                    double xl, double yl,
                    double xh, double yh,
                    double xi, double yi)
/* Do points j and l lie on the same side of line hi? */
{ double a, b, c;
  a=yh-yi; b=xi-xh; c=xh*yi-yh*xi;
  return (a*xj+b*yj+c)*(a*xl+b*yl+c)>0.0;
}


struct lseglist *lsegnode(void)
{ struct lseglist *p;
  p = (struct lseglist *)
      farmalloc((long)sizeof(struct lseglist));
  if (p == NULL) ermes("Memory: line segment PQ");
  return p;
}


struct linsegface *lsegfacenode(void)
{ struct linsegface *p;
  p = (struct linsegface *)
      farmalloc((long)sizeof(struct linsegface));
  if (p == NULL) ermes("Memory: edges");
  return p;
}


static int allocsize(int divfactor, int elsize)
{ long lll;
  lll = (farcoreleft()/divfactor)/elsize;
  return (lll < 32767 ? (int)lll : 32767);
}
```

# Bibliography

Ammeraal, L. (1986). *Programming Principles in Computer Graphics*, Chichester: John Wiley.

Ammeraal, L. (1986). *C for Programmers*, Chichester: John Wiley.

Ammeraal, L. (1987). *Computer Graphics for the IBM PC*, Chichester: John Wiley.

Ammeraal, L. (1987). *Programs and Data Structures in C*, Chichester: John Wiley.

Borland International (1987). *Turbo C User's Guide*, *Turbo C Reference Manual*, *Turbo C Version 1.5 Additions and Enhancements*.

Coxeter, H. S. M. (1961). *Introduction to Geometry*, New York: John Wiley.

Earle, J. H. (1987). *Engineering Design Graphics*, Reading, Mass.: Addison-Wesley.

Escher, M. C., *et al.* (1972). *The World of M. C. Escher*, New York: Harry N. Abrams.

Foley, J. D., and A. van Dam (1982). *Fundamentals of Interactive Computer Graphics*, Reading, Mass.: Addison- Wesley.

Hearn, D., and M. P. Baker (1986). *Computer Graphics*, Englewood Cliffs, NJ: Prentice-Hall.

Kernighan, B. W., and D. M. Ritchie (1978). *The C Programming Language*, Englewood Cliffs, NJ: Prentice-Hall.

Knuth, D. H. (1968). *The Art of Computer Programming*, *Vol. I*, Reading, Mass.: Addison-Wesley.

Newman, W. M., and R. F. Sproull (1979). *Principles of Interactive Computer Graphics*. New York: McGraw-Hill.

Norton, P. (1985). *Programmer's Guide to the IBM PC*, Washington: Microsoft Press.

Pal, I. (1974). *Raumgeometrie in der Technischen Praxis*, Budapest: Akademiai Kiado.

# Index

Adapter, 166
ANSI C, 84
Aspect ratio, 22, 166
Auxiliary lines, 21
Axes, 13, 21

B-spline curve, 65, 123
B-spline surface, 134
Backface, 19, 33, 194
Blending function, 125
Bold lines, 21
Bounding prism, 161

C language, 62
Cable, 69, 127
Central object point, 5
Central projection, 5
CGA, 164
Classic C style, 84
*Clear*, 16
Clear screen, 166
Clockwise, 19
Concave, 19, 33
Cone, 58, 92
Contour, 192
Convex, 19, 33
Coordinate axes, 13
*Copy*, 40
Counter-clockwise, 19, 194
Cube, 17, 51
Cursor, 15, 166
Curve, 123
Curved surface, 26, 192
Cutaway view, 63
Cylinder, 26, 56, 90, 144

D3D, 205
Default, 22
Default viewpoint, 12
*Delete*, 13
Disk, 3, 8
Dodecahedron, 26, 101

Dot-matrix printer, 22
Driver file, 180

Editor, 71
EGA, 164
Engineering drawing, 12
Entire screen, 21, 22
Error messages, 88
Escher, M.C., 75
Executable code, 3
Exploded view, 80
Eye coordinates, 160

Faces, 18, 32
Fixed point, 44, 46
Font, 189
Front view, 12
Function prototype, 85

Golden section, 103
Graphics adapter, 166
Graphics mode, 165
GRPACK, 168
GRPACK1, 180

Helix, 151
Hexahedron, 97, 99
HGA, 164
*Hidden*, 36
Hidden lines, 23, 189
HLPFUN, 237
Hole, 33
HP plotter, 23, 26
Huge memory model, 167

Icosahedron, 108
Image size, 6
*initgr*, 187
*initgraph*, 187
*Insert*, 13
Integrated environment, 88

*Jump*, 16

Knot, 70

Line of intersection, 26
Line of sight, 5
Line segment, 33
Line thickness, 12, 30
Linear list, 194
Linking, 118
*List*, 20
Loose line segment, 26
Low-level graphics, 163
Lower bound, 14, 40

Matrix printer, 22
Memory model, 167
Message area, 9
Minus sign, 35
Mirror, 48
*Mode*, 20, 22
Modern C style, 84
*Move*, 40

Object file, 23, 30, 32
Octahedron, 97, 100
Orientation, 42
Output file, 23

Parallel projection, 6, 8, 12
Pentagon, 101
Period, 20, 33
Perspective image, 12
Perspective transformation, 160
Pitch, 76
Pixel, 22
Pixel coordinates, 164
Plane, 19
Plane of reflection, 48
Platonic solid, 97
Plotfile, 23, 195
PLOTHP, 199
Plotter, 23, 195
Point numbers, 13, 15, 21, 31
Polygon, 19
Polyhedron, 97
Positioning, 5
*Print*, 22
Prism, 51, 90
Project file, 118
Prototype, 85
Pyramid, 58, 92

*Quit*, 12

Ragged lines, 23
Range, 40
*Read*, 9
Reef knot, 75
Reflection, 48

Regular polyhedron, 97
Right-handed, 3
Rotation, 42, 117
RS232, 198

Scaling, 5, 46, 197
Screen, 9
Screen coordinates, 160
Screw thread, 76, 149
Sector, 65
Serial communications, 198
Shift vector, 45
Side view, 12
Size of image, 6
Smooth curve, 65
Software disk, 8
Solid model, 16, 18, 23
Solid of revolution, 62
Sphere, 58, 94, 112
Spherical coordinates, 3
Spring, 66
Square screw thread, 76
Standard component, 56
*static*, 179

Table, 51
Tee-joint, 144
Tetrahedron, 97, 98
Text editor, 71
Text mode, 165
Thickness, 12
Thread, 69
Threshold angle, 30, 192
Top view, 12
TRAFO, 119
*Transform*, 43
Transformation, 40
Translation, 45
Translation matrix, 120
True length, 12
Turbo C, 84
Turbo C Version 1.5, 179

Uniform scaling, 4
Unit of length, 5
Upper bound, 14, 40

View, 12
Viewing direction, 5
Viewing distance, 5
Viewing surface, 5
Viewing transformation, 160
Viewpoint, 5, 8, 12
Viewport, 165
*void*, 86, 87

Wire-frame model, 16, 23
World coordinates, 160
*Write*, 31